EXPLORING THE WORK OF
DONALD MELTZER

Donald Meltzer

EXPLORING THE WORK OF
DONALD MELTZER

A Festschrift

edited by

Margaret Cohen & Alberto Hahn

London & New York
KARNAC BOOKS

First published in 2000 by
H. Karnac (Books) Ltd., 58 Gloucester Road, London SW7 4QY

A subsidiary of Other Press LLC, New York

British Library Cataloguing in Publication Data

A C.I.P for this book is available from the British Library

ISBN 1 85575 240 9

10 9 8 7 6 5 4 3 2 1

Edited, designed, and produced by Communication Crafts
Printed in Great Britain by Polestar Wheatons Ltd, Exeter

www.karnacbooks.com

CONTENTS

ACKNOWLEDGEMENTS

The Editors would like to thank the other members of the organizing committee of the conference who gathered together the papers
for this Festschrift—Jonathan Bradley, Ricky Emanuel, Margaret
Rustin, and Gianna Williams—as well as Michael Rustin, whose
inspirational force launched this initiative. We are grateful to the
many colleagues who helped with their invaluable time in reading
the papers, to Daniel Hahn for his assistance with the editing, and
to Cesare Sacerdoti of Karnac Books for encouraging and supporting this publication.

CONTRIBUTORS

Jean Bégoin is a psychiatrist and psychoanalyst in Paris, trained in the Freudian/Kleinian tradition. He has written, since 1964, various clinical papers for the *Revue Française de Psychanalyse* and the Belgian *Bulletin de Psychologie Clinique*. Together with James Gammill and Genevieve Haag and other colleagues, he created in 1974 the GERPEN, a study group that worked in France with Donald Meltzer, Martha Harris, and Frances Tustin. He also translated Meltzer's *The Psycho-Analytical Process* and *Sexual States of Mind* into French and wrote the Preface to the French translation of *The Claustrum*.

Roberto Bertolini works privately as a child psychotherapist in Rome, and he teaches and supervises extensively on the Tavistock Model Courses, both Observational and Clinical, in Italy. He is a visiting teacher for the programme "Working with Disruptive Adolescents" at the Tavistock Clinic in London. Originally educated as a doctor and neurologist in the medical school of the Catholic University in Rome, he later qualified as a child psychotherapist at the Tavistock Clinic. He has published on neuro-psychology, on personality development in borderline psychotic children and adolescents, and on drug misuse. His current interests are mainly focused on the emotional development of premature babies and on intersubjective communication in borderline patients.

Paolo Carignani holds an M.A. in psychoanalytic observational studies from the University of East London and trained as a child psychotherapist at the Centro di Studi Martha Harris in Florence. He is a teacher on the Tavistock Model Observational and Clinical Courses in Venice and on Observational Courses in Rome and is the author of several papers on psychoanalytic observation and child psychotherapy. He is on the teaching staff of the Tavistock/ UEL PG-Dip M.A. in Psychoanalytic Observational Studies.

Margaret Cohen is a child and adult psychotherapist in private practice in London. She works in the Neo-Natal Intensive Care Unit and the Paediatric Oncology Unit at the Whittington Hospital, London, and has written about prematurity, among other subjects. She teaches at the Tavistock Clinic in London and in Italy.

James Fisher is in full-time private practice in London as a psychoanalytic psychotherapist. He is the author of *The Uninvited Guest: Emerging from Narcissism towards Marriage*, and he co-edited and contributed to *Intrusiveness and Intimacy in the Couple*.

Alberto Hahn is a member of the British Psycho-Analytical Society and works in private practice in London, teaches psychoanalysis at the Tavistock Clinic, and lectures abroad. He is the translator into English of the *Introduction to the Work of Bion* and the editor of *Sincerity and Other Works: Collected Papers of Donald Meltzer*. He has written a number of clinical and theoretical papers, among them "Observation and Intuition in the Psychoanalytic Situation", "On Complaining", "The Nature of the 'Object' in the Claustrum", and "Ways of Thinking about Adolescent Psychopathology".

Didier Houzel is professor of child and adolescent psychiatry at the University of Caen in France. He is a member of the Association Psychanalytique de France. He had monthly supervisions with Dr Meltzer from 1981 to 1985 and is interested in psychoanalytic treatment of autistic and psychotic children. He has published a number of papers, including "Precipitation Anxiety and the Dawn of Aesthetic Feelings" (*Journal of Child Psychotherapy*) and "Bisexual Aspects of the Countertransference in the Therapy of Psychotic Children" (in *Countertransference in Psychoanalytic Psychotherapy with Children and Adolescents*).

Shirley Hoxter is a child psychotherapist trained at the Tavistock Clinic, where she was a student and later a staff member from 1949 to 1986. She became Senior Tutor responsible for organizing the Child Psychotherapy Training Programmes. She has contributed to *Explorations in Autism*, *The Child Psychotherapist*, and *Psychotherapy with Severely Deprived Children*.

Suzanne Maiello is a child psychotherapist in private practice in Rome. She is a founder member and former president of the Italian Association of Psychoanalytic Child Psychotherapy (A.I.P.P.I.). She has published work on prenatal auditory experience and memory, in *The Sound-Object*, and on the prenatal roots of autism, in *Prenatal Trauma and Autism*. She received the Frances Tustin Memorial Prize in 1997.

Donald Meltzer was educated at Yale and New York University College of Medicine. He trained in adult and child psychiatry at Washington University in St Louis and came to England in 1954 to complete his psychoanalytic training with Melanie Klein. He has worked in close collaboration with Wilfred Bion, Roger Money-Kyrle, and Esther Bick and taught at the Tavistock Clinic and at the British Psycho-Analytical Society where he was a Training Analyst. He also lectures extensively in, among other countries, Italy, Spain, France, Norway, and Argentina and has his private practice in Oxford. His books *The Psycho-Analytical Process*, *Sexual States of Mind*, *Studies in Extended Metapsychology*, *Explorations in Autism*, *Dream Life*, *The Kleinian Development*, *The Apprehension of*

Beauty, and *The Claustrum* and his collected papers (*Sincerity and Other Works*) have been widely translated.

Clara Nemas is a Training Analyst of the Buenos Aires Psychoanalytic Association. She qualified in medicine at the University of Buenos Aires and trained at the Maudsley Hospital as clinical assistant from 1973 to 1975. She is committed full-time to private psychoanalytic practice and is at present the Vice-President of the Buenos Aires Psychoanalytic Association. She is involved in teaching Kleinian and neo-Kleinian theory in various psychoanalytic societies in Argentina and is the author of numerous papers on adolescents and psychoanalytic theory, technique, and ethics.

Psychoanalytic Group of Barcelona consists of psychoanalysts with a background in psychiatry and psychology who are committed to teaching activities and work in institutions of mental health and private practice: Aurora Angulo Carrasco, Claudio Bermann, Miriam Botbol Acreche, Rosa Castellà Berini, Dolors Cid Guimerà, Nouhad Dow, Perla Ducach-Moneta, Lluís Farré Grau, Lucy Jachevasky, Carmen Largo Adell, Yolanda LaTorre Guevara, Monserrat Martínez del Pozo, Jesús Sánchez de Vega, and Carlos Tabbia Leoni.

Margaret Rustin is a consultant child psychotherapist, organizing tutor of the Child Psychotherapy Training, and Dean of Postgraduate Studies at the Tavistock Clinic. She has co-authored *Narratives of Love and Loss* and *Psychotic States of Children* and co-edited *Closely Observed Infants.*

Michael Rustin is professor of sociology of the University of East London and also teaches at the Tavistock Clinic. His books include *For a Pluralist Socialism, The Good Society and the Inner World,* and, with Margaret Rustin, *Narratives of Love and Loss.*

Carlos Tabbia Leoni has a degree in philosophy and psychology from Argentina and is a doctor of psychology from the University of Barcelona. A founder member of the Psychoanalytic Group of Barcelona and a training psychotherapist for the A.E.P.P. and E.F.P.P., he works in private practice and in the public health

service (community assistance to psychotic patients). He is a con-
tributor to *Clínica Psicoanalítica con Niños y Adultos* and co-editor
of *Adolescentes*.

Gianna Williams is a consultant child and adolescent psychotherapist at the Tavistock Clinic Adolescent Department. She is
a course tutor for the Tavistock/UEL PG-Dip. M.A. in Psychoanalytic Observational Studies. She is the author of *Internal Landscapes
and Foreign Bodies: Eating Disorders and Other Pathologies* and of
a large number of book chapters and clinical papers. She is also a
co-author of *The Emotional Experience of Learning and Teaching*.

Meg Harris Williams is a writer and artist with a particular interest in the relationship between psychoanalysis and aesthetic
appreciation. She has worked closely with Donald Meltzer and has
written about Bion as well as about Milton, Keats, Emily Brontë,
and other poets. Recent books include *Five Tales from Shakespeare*
and a novel, *A Trial of Faith: Horatio's Story*, based on *Hamlet*.

INTRODUCTION

When in November 1996 a group of child psychotherapists and psychoanalysts met to plan how to celebrate
Donald Meltzer's 75th birthday, it was clear that each
person felt an attachment marked by affection and gratitude towards him as a person, a clinician, a teacher, and a thinker and
wanted this to be expressed in an exploration of his work. A conference was therefore planned, and it was hoped that the contributions would show something of the work in progress inspired
by Meltzer's work all over the world. The response we received in
the form of scientific contributions and enrolment was quite outstanding.

A selection of the papers presented at the conference, which
was held at the Tavistock Clinic in January 1998, appears in this
Festschrift. In the process of rereading most of the presentations,
there was one question that seemed repeatedly to crop up: what
are the qualities that make Meltzer's work so attractive to clinicians—and what part of ourselves do his theories on the internal
workings of the mind address—to make these theories so inspiring? While not attempting to answer this complex question, we

might offer a few tentative observations that could bring us closer to understanding the creative virtuosity of Meltzer's thinking.

His early psychoanalytic experience in England, with Melanie Klein as his analyst and teacher and with the first generation of senior Kleinian analysts, forged in him a deep commitment to the understanding of psychic reality—a position he has consistently maintained throughout his professional life. This, together with his love of psychoanalysis, is clearly conveyed in his writings, as a teacher and as a practising analyst.

The 1950s and 1960s provided a hothouse of productivity in which major theoretical and clinical issues were aired. Subjects such as the vicissitudes of projective identification in neurosis and psychosis, the status of the death instinct and envy, and the pathology of the paranoid–schizoid position were explored and discussed in an eager atmosphere of mutual respect and enthusiasm, and it was from this atmosphere that Meltzer's first writings emerged. Always firmly rooted in Melanie Klein's developing ideas, we discover from early on in his dialogue with Adrian Stokes, *Painting and the Inner World* (1963), a way of thinking about the mind and primitive object-relations that is distinctive, deep, and original, a view later corroborated in *The Psycho-Analytical Process* (1967) and all the writings that followed. These capacities make his observations and interpretations into a vehicle that clearly conveys how the thinker thinks and how the author feels *vis-à-vis* the clinical situations he encounters.

Nourished among other things by his teaching experience during his association with the Tavistock Clinic Child Psychotherapy Training, by Wilfred Bion's work, and by Mattie Harris' stimulating companionship, he produced a series of books full of new ideas and theories that provided a refreshing departure in the area of autism and dimensionality, dream and symbolization, the aesthetic conflict, the pathology of the claustrum, and the clinical applications of Bion's ideas. The list of his contributions is too long to spell out here but will be familiar to those colleagues who have been exposed to his teachings and indeed have been irrevocably influenced by them. Together with his books, his travels have allowed his work to become known in various countries, and it was this that made the birthday conference such a successful international event.

We would have liked all of the papers read at the conference to have been included in this Festschrift, but to our regret we were limited to the length our publishers considered viable. The difficult selection procedure we had to go through took its toll on the timing of this publication, which has been unavoidably delayed.

The complete list of papers read at the conference is as follows (in alphabetical order):

Jean Bégoin (France):
  "Love and Destructivity: From the Aesthetic Conflict to a Revision of the Concept of Destructivity in the Psyche"
Roberto Bertolini (Italy):
  "The Light Meter, the Thermostat, the Tuner: The Compositional Aspects of Communication with Very Disturbed Adolescents"
Jonathan Bradley (U.K.):
  "Emotional Experiences: Route to Thinking or Mindlessness"
Paolo Carignani (Italy):
  "Clinical Notes on the Organizing Function of Time during Puberty"
Elisabeth Eckardt (Germany):
  "A Clear View and a Confused Mind"
Ricky Emanuel (U.K.):
  "The Claustrum, Psychic Retreats, and the Buddha"
James Fisher (U.K.):
  "Reading Donald Meltzer: Identification and Intercourse as Modes of Reading and Relating"
Debbie Hindle (U.K.):
  "'I'm Not Smiling, I'm Frowning Upside-Down'"
Didier Houzel (France):
  "The Beauty and the Violence of Love"
Shirley Hoxter (U.K.):
  "Experiences of Learning with Donald Meltzer"
Bianca Lechevalier (France):
  "Working Through the Aesthetic Conflict in the Analysis of a Former Autistic Adolescent Girl"

Sheila Navarro de Lopez (Argentina):
"Clinical Elements in Some Forms of Perversion of Thought"

Suzanne Maiello (Italy):
"'Song-and-Dance' and Its Developments:
The Function of Rhythm in the Learning Process of Oral and
Written Language"

Donald Meltzer (U.K.):
"A Review of My Writings"

Romana Negri (Italy):
"Donald Meltzer's Contribution to a Preliminary Study on
Foetal Life (the Connection between Foetal Life and the First
Two Years of Life of Five Couples of Non-Identical Twins)"

Clara Nemas (Argentina):
"Development Is Beauty, Growth Is Ethics"

Psychoanalytic Group of Barcelona (Spain):
"A Learning Experience in Psychoanalysis"

Margaret Rustin and Michael Rustin (U.K.):
"Beckett: Dramas of Psychic Catastrophe"

Kenneth Sanders (U.K.):
"Up at the Breasts and Down at the Genitals—
Epistemological and Geographical Metapsychology"

Angelika Staehle (Germany):
"'I Collect Words from You'. From 'Mindlessness' to Words
with Meaning in the Analysis of a Female Patient"

Carlos Tabbia Leoni (Spain):
"Living in Intrusive Identification"

Gianna Williams (U.K.):
"Reflections on 'Aesthetic Reciprocity'"

Meg Harris Williams (U.K.):
"Keats's 'Ode to Psyche'"

Meg Harris Williams (U.K.):
"The Aesthetic Perspective in the Work of Donald Meltzer"

Victoria Zolotnicki (Argentina):
"The Truth of Lies in Dreams"

Although we were sorry not to be able to include all these papers, we did in the end manage to settle for a selection from different countries and which also covers different themes from Meltzer's work.

In the opening chapter, Donald Meltzer touches on some nodal issues in the development of his thinking. In reviewing his work he emphasizes the importance of dismantling the "preformed" transference, in particular in adult patients, in order to allow the establishment of the analytic situation. He also suggests that geographical confusions can lead to impasse and to claustrum phenomena, and he promotes the notion of a negative grid to replace the "death instinct" as a working hypothesis. This would allow us to distinguish between behaviour, thinking, and emotions and to move away from a judgemental view of an instinct of viciousness. He also explores his personal experience in the shift from "enjoyment of being an analyst" to "pleasure in the experience of the relationship of patient and analyst".

Shirley Hoxter (U.K.) focuses on her personal experience at the time that Meltzer began to be associated with the Tavistock Course in Psychoanalytic Psychotherapy of children and young people and his teaching activities as supervisor and seminar leader between the mid-1950s and mid-1970s. She talks about his role in the psychoanalytic education of early generations of child psychotherapists, her own experience of supervision with Meltzer, her participation in the work group on autism which came to fruition with the publication of *Explorations in Autism* in 1975, and the series of lectures on Freud, Melanie Klein, and Bion that became the subject of his trilogy of books on the Kleinian development.

Clara Nemas (Argentina), in her epistemological investigation of "values" in the work of Freud, Klein, and Bion, focuses on the transformation of ethics in Meltzer's theory of mental development. Nemas's *tour de force* reviews Meltzer's ideas on the subject and, after discussing the aesthetic conflict, proposes a new addition to our understanding of the place of ethics in the psychoanalytic conception of the growth of the personality.

Didier Houzel (France) also takes the aesthetic conflict as his point of departure in linking beauty and violence. The attractiveness of the aesthetic object is linked to the "death instinct", and he underlines the danger posed by the aesthetic object to the self. It is suggested that as a result of this violence, the presence of "precipitation anxiety" requires the creation of "psychic shapes" to provide levels of stability. An example of these would be the maternal and paternal containing capabilities that will make a contribution to the bisexuality of the container and act as a mediator in the (oedipal) relation to the other parent.

Meg Harris Williams (U.K.) analyses the dynamics of poetic creation and the literary and symbolic content of Keats's "Ode to Psyche", thought of here as a "hymn to inspiration". Psyche and Cupid are described as Gods (internal objects) that mediate in infusing their qualities into the poet's mind—an elaboration on the idea of the inspirational source of the internal object in introjective identification.

The next three chapters by our Italian colleagues also deal in a clinical context with the internal characteristics of objects and their importance in the introjective process. Suzanne Maiello describes how rhythm, as an internalized characteristic after prenatal and early postnatal experience, allows symbols to be formed and how the development of language can be seen as a transformation of oral experiences of rhythmicity.

Paolo Carignani discusses, through a series of acute observations, his ideas on the development of the perception of time during puberty and how it can be used as a means of communication between patient and therapist. This clinical enquiry, carried out through a case discussion of a 10-year-old girl, examines those mental functions that enable the perception of passing time in the organization of mental processes.

Roberto Bertolini presents three clinical illustrations with adolescents in which he shows that each patient needs to experience, through the analytic interaction, a well-defined "compositional dimension", which is rooted in the sensorial perception of primitive communications that is so active in the early mother–child relationship. He refers here in particular to the modulating, moderating, and organizing characteristics of the object.

Thoughts about the qualities of the internal object continue with Jean Bégoin's paper (France). He explores the difference between enigma and mystery in the aesthetic object. The reciprocity between the baby and the mother, contained by the father, confirms the baby's ability to develop, and also to love and feel loved. When this specificity is not present, we have horror, psychic pain, and despair. Bégoin thinks that this pain is essentially depressive pain at being unable to develop, with the meaning of psychic death.

The experience of an object as infinitely precious and beautiful and the primacy of the attendant depressive feelings is emphasized by Gianna Williams (U.K.). Meltzer has described poignantly the meeting of mother and baby at birth—a dazzling moment—with a beauty and pain from which the baby may then recoil. Gianna Williams illustrates this with clinical material.

The three previous papers talk about psychic horror, and this topic is elaborated in Margaret and Michael Rustin's (U.K.) discussion of Samuel Beckett's plays *Waiting for Godot* and *Happy Days*. These plays are seen as evoking a loss of contact with good objects, with the ensuing experience of horror. In *Happy Days*, the catastrophe seems to originate with the baby's response to too brilliant a vision.

Carlos Tabbia Leoni (Spain) describes the desolation of being inside an object—living in intrusive identification—illustrating his thoughts with Beckett's *Endgame* and with clinical material of a borderline patient who might appear successful in the external world but, in fact, lived an internal existence stripped of intimacy.

It is with Wittgenstein's remarks about the mystery of communication that James Fisher (U.K.) begins, the experience of how strange the other is. He distinguishes between unconscious identification and unconscious intercourse. He emphasizes the potentially catastrophic change that the impact of great art or psychoanalysis can have on us. Being open to such an impact requires a letting go—that is, giving one's object freedom and so allowing introjection. Fisher thinks that this state of mind, akin to unconscious intercourse, will allow a true meeting, whereas identification can be a defensive manoeuvre to protect ourselves against the threat of catastrophic change.

Our final chapter is written by the Psychoanalytic Group of Barcelona (Spain) who give an account of setting up a training experience for themselves with Meltzer. They describe in a very personal way the vicissitudes of such a project, the turmoil and the joy, and they draw conclusions about the nature of teaching and learning psychoanalysis.

This thought brings us back to our original meetings to plan the conference, and even at that stage we were thinking about a publication that might record it. There was considerable discussion about the purpose of this enterprise: if this was to be a birthday present, a gift, was it one that Donald Meltzer would receive with pleasure? Would such a conference be antithetical to what he stood for and taught? These were questions we kept coming back to, without being able to come up with a definitive answer. But our wish to say thank you has remained an overriding consideration, and this book is an embodiment of that.

Margaret Cohen & Alberto Hahn
January 2000

EXPLORING THE WORK OF
DONALD MELTZER

CHAPTER ONE

A review of my writings

Donald Meltzer

It's been absolutely lovely seeing so many people I know. It links immediately with the consulting-room, where you get one person after another that you know. And so different from wandering around airports with thousands of people you don't know, and being reminded of how many people there are in the world. No, it's lovely to know so many people; and, as I said yesterday, if women still wore lipstick that came off, my face would have looked like a barn door!

I am going to indulge myself in an attempt to review my experience of the past forty years. It won't be a gallop, it won't even be a canter—it will be an amble through these forty years, for myself to notice what has changed, because the changes are usually so slow and so different from patient to patient that one never bothered to pull them together, but I'll try to do that for you. I don't know how accurate it will be—the changes probably won't fit any one patient, but a sort of aggregate of experience.

The first thing that comes to my mind is, of course, that when in 1965 I wrote *The Psycho-Analytical Process* (1967) it was written primarily with my experience with children in mind, and the idea of the gathering of the transference seemed absolutely correct; but as my practice moved more and more into work with adults, it's fairly clear that nothing so effortless takes place with adult patients. It becomes clear that instead of this effortless attracting to the analytic setting all of the transference processes of the patient's life, it seems necessary to dismantle something that I've come to think of as the "preformed transference" of the adult patient; the preformed transference, based on greater or lesser knowledge of or fantasies about the analytic method and the analytic experience, has to be taken down like an old shed at the bottom of the garden before anything new can be constructed. It can occur very quickly, in a few weeks, or it can take months or years to dismantle this preformed transference, a component of which is sometimes the erotic transference whose dismantling both analyst and patient tend to resist. As with Keats's "pleasant pain", it requires a certain ruthlessness to get rid of, and to establish the analytic situation, as Mrs Klein called it, which is the situation into which the transferences of a person's life are sucked, rather like a vacuum-cleaner; it can be called "the gathering of the transference", although it does seem to involve a much more active process with adults than with children.

The second thing that is very different from the book written in 1965 is the recognition that the geographical confusions are often a terrific impasse—where either part or all of the personality is in a state of projective identification that leads to seeing the world in that peculiar way characteristic of projective identification, which I finally wrote about in The Claustrum (1992a). The whole problem of releasing the personality, or more usually part of the personality, that is living in projective identification is a very difficult one, and in many ways not an analytic task. I do not know how to define it. I tried to indicate how I think one can go about it, mainly descriptively—by describing the kind of world that the person or part of the personality is living in, and to distinguish it from the outside world as seen from the outside, which very often it greatly resembles (in one aspect or another, particularly its hierarchical organization, its bureaucratic management, its emphasis on survival, the joylessness of it, and so on)—but it is often very difficult to show a patient in any convincing way that it isn't exactly the way the world is. And, of course, I gradually discovered that as this descriptive picture is built up from the patient's material and becomes more and more convincing, what then tends to fall away is the identificatory aspect of the projective identification— almost always, in one form or another, the grandiose aspect of projective identification. Of course, it doesn't always seem to be very grandiose, because there can be projective identification with a very dishevelled, dilapidated figure; it doesn't look very grandiose until you hear that they are the *most* miserable person in the world, or the *most* criminal, or despicable, and so on, and you get this picture of the grandiosity of depression that Freud himself was very keen to spot. "The most—the mostest . . ." And as this grandiosity gets eroded, what then begins to appear is the claustrophobia, the sense of being imprisoned in a state of mind without knowing how to get out of it.

What I discovered gradually, as I became more successful at helping patients escape from that state of mind, was the realization that while patients are living in projective identification you do not know them. Not only is the world that they are living in different from the world that you, as a sane person, are living in, but the personality of such patients is different, is adapted to that grotesque world of projective identification, and when they emerge from that state of mind, they emerge as from a chrysalis of some sort, and they throw off what Bion calls their "exoskeleton". Like Keats's description of Psyche, they start to flutter their wings and you begin to see something colourful and lively and attractive; and of course with borderline patients, whose almost entire personality is submerged in projective identification, this is a very long process that requires a lot of endurance on the part of both analyst and patient. It's not so surprising that analysts can endure it, when they have some idea of the nature of the problem they are working with; what's more surprising is that the patients endure it, because the analytic experience, from the analyst's point of view, seems for the patient to be completely unsatisfactory. They are constantly aware of the inadequacies, the failures, which, in the constant state of the patient's keen perceptions and voyeurism, make the analytic work a misery for the patient. Nor is it terribly interesting for the analyst; as I say, it doesn't really involve analytic work, it doesn't involve very much in the way of exploring the workings of the mind—it mostly involves describing the consequences of this particular state of mind induced by projective identification, and ultimately that isn't really very interesting. When it's new to you it's quite interesting, but it's like seeing the same C-grade movie over and over again; it loses its punch in spite of the beauty of the actors and actresses and scenery and so on. The work in this phase of analysis, of the geographic confusion, is never a delight. But the patient emerges from that like Theseus emerging from the labyrinth thanks to the web of Ariadne: it enabled him to follow out the route that had led him in, and that was the route for getting out. This is what patients who are trapped in projective identification have to do—to discover the route by which they got into this state. And, of course, that varies from patient to patient, as there is no single web of Ariadne that the analyst can assume from patient to patient—he has to discover with each patient just what was the route that led in. He can say, in a general way, that it was probably infantile masturbatory, intrusive, and so on, but that doesn't really tell you very much; it's like knowing the latitude without knowing the longitude—it doesn't navigate you very much. But once the patient does begin to emerge—although patients oscillate and run back in as soon as they can, because what they meet when they come out is rather terrible depression and a sense of wasted time in their lives, and "it's too late for this" and "too late for that", and so forth—things do settle down into an analysis that is really, by and large, a pleasure, because the patient becomes able to cooperate and becomes interested in the analytic work, and then it becomes cooperative work—and *that* is really where the pleasure lies, in the sense of cooperation.

I have noticed that my pleasure in the analytic work has changed from the early days, when of course there was great pleasure in doing what my teachers taught me to do, and finding out that they were right, that things went in such-and-such a way. But then, of course, there comes a time when you cast off from the pier and into the open sea and are on your own, and you know then that you don't know how to navigate—you just hope for the best and try to remain a feeling and thinking individual and rely on your patients' cooperation. Then things get exciting, and the quality of the pleasure in the analytic work is rather egocentric, as it does not actually embrace the patient very much and tends to remain a one-sided enthusiasm.

Patients, of course, always complain that you don't care about them, you just care about the work—and you realize that at that point in your development it's true. You don't love your patients, you love the work, or at least the work seems to excite and stir you, and you feel that you have to write about everything that comes along. Then you discover that you don't write very well, and you get discouraged but are amazed that people read your books, and that keeps you going from book to book—until you finally become convinced that you hate writing, and then you discover another method, which is to just talk and let other people write about what you talk about; that's very easy, and the last ten years have been really a sort of semi-retirement from the work of writing, leaving it to other people to tape it and write about it and so on.

The various groups that Catharine Mack Smith and I go to who have undertaken to shoulder this burden started with the Barcelona group, which I inherited from Dr Grinberg; this group functioned with an amazingly cohesive bunch of friends who learnt at a break-neck pace and wanted to produce a book—a book about my work. I managed to convince them to produce a book that was really a book about their work and not about my "marvellous" supervision. Then this spread to other groups, which took this backpack off my back, this obligation to do the writing.

So there was also that change from slogging away out of obedience to my teachers, to being on my own and beginning to discover things from my own way of working, which was full of enthusiasm and full of a kind of joyousness that didn't include my patients but rather exploited them; and I began to produce papers and finally books. Of course, the exploitation of the patients sometimes hit rocks like the patients resenting being written about, and I had some tiffs about that—but on the whole . . . I myself was written about by Mrs Klein and felt it a great honour and expected my patients to feel honoured, but not all of them did. I think they should have. . . . It was in the tradition—I couldn't see any good reason for giving a patient a veto on my writing about him or her, because I was really quite clear that I wasn't writing about the patient at all: I was writing about my imaginative construction of the patient and of the analytic process which had, at best, a kind of "shadows on the wall" resemblance to the person and the person's life—I think that is true of analysis. What you can write about, what is analytical material, is really just a particular shadow of the total personality. You'd have to be a really great artist to write about a person; I'm often amazed, when I read literature, at the liveliness with which characters jump out of the page—in Dostoevsky, or this recent book that I read called *The God of Small Things* (Roy, 1997), where a host of people absolutely jump out and wiggle about in a most lively fashion—such marvellous writing. Of course, in writing psychoanalytic material, if we stick to the patient's dreams, we have a possibility of bringing things to life; the moment we get away from the patient's dream material things go very flat and prosaic and unimaginative, which takes us back to the question of why the patient should feel honoured: because that creative aspect of his capacity for dreaming is being given a publishable form—it is the patient who creates the really lively part of any paper I've ever written. And I notice that when people refer to a paper—"You know, the one about the woman who dreamt so-and-so and so-and-so", "Oh, yes"—the dreams that form the landmarks of the analysis also form the dramatic aspect of a patient that can find publication; in a sense, writing analytic papers is a kind of plagiarism.

These realizations about the analytic work came to me gradually, very much as a result of the experience of discovering that patients could be helped to emerge from projective identification; when they did so, a quite totally unknown person emerged, almost always much more likeable, almost always much more ready to cooperate and enjoy working with you; but of course it did also extend the period of analysis. I went through a period of great optimism in which I was very pleased that analyses were only taking two and a half to four years—till I gradually discovered that these patients were coming back five years later wanting and needing more analysis. I am now not surprised to discover suddenly, "Oh, you've been here seven years. That's nice—getting to know one another."

The whole shift in my experience of the analytic process is, of course, the shift from the pseudo-science of my early days, having grown up through medicine and through a romance with neurology and neurophysiology. I can't imagine what in the world made me fall in love with Melanie Klein's work, because by the time I came to the United Kingdom—by which time I had become "the Kleinian in St Louis"—I realized I didn't know a thing about it. As soon as I started working analytically and having supervisions in London, I very quickly realized that though I had read all her books I hadn't really understood a word of them—and that was really very exciting. And of course having analysis with her—talk about a gallop—was a breath-taking process. Poor "Richard" (Klein, 1961) had only three months, as she galloped through his mind; but she worked at that pace almost all the time. She had a Japanese print of a galloping horse at the foot of her couch, which I dreamt about the first night of my analysis with her—that I was on that horse, without a bridle and without a saddle, and he was going. ... And whether it was terrifying or exciting I couldn't tell—it finally contributed to the chapter, years later, in *The Apprehension of Beauty* (Meltzer & Harris Williams, 1988a) concerning the love and fear of horses.

So this change that I'm describing to you was a change from enjoying being an analyst and having patients, to a pleasure in the experience of the relationship of patient and analyst, the extreme intimacy of it. By that time I had already discovered that you ended up in analyses that really went the distance, as it were, when you ended up loving your patient and they loving you—and that the ending of an analysis of that sort was very much like a beloved child going out into the world, and your feeling very uncertain of the patient's equipment to deal with his or her generation of dangers, because the patient's generation of dangers wasn't the same as the dangers that you yourself had navigated. So not only did I discover that the analyses were lasting longer, they were also lasting longer because I was holding on and thinking—it's not ready, not ready—then thinking I had better just leave it up to the patient to decide, since I really had very little in the way of equipment for deciding questions about the patient's readiness. Wittgenstein's phrase "now I can go on" is his way of describing that moment in learning when you are able to extrapolate what you have learnt into analogous circumstances, to extend it, as it were. "Now I can go on"—and I discovered that there was no way that I as the analyst could know "now you can go on". "You can go on" means "get out"—and it's not really suitable.

As far as *Sexual States of Mind* (1973) is concerned, I don't think very much has changed in my feeling or my understandings about the role of sexuality, except that I think it has become a much less important factor in my interest with my patients, particularly being a male analyst; the heterosexuality of female patients which tends to blossom very early in this preformed transference tends also to go away fairly quickly and leave space for the real analytic work. But I can see that in terms of a "model of the mind", and the ways in which my thinking developed, sexuality has become just one aspect of the attempts to comprehend life's experiences, and, of course, Bion's work—particularly his Grid—rescued me from utter confusion. When I left the United States Air Force in this country and said goodbye to my nice salary, I didn't yet have a work permit, and I went through some rather lean days before Hanna Segal helped me to get my citizenship here. During those days I tried to cook up some sort of research project that I could get funds for, and one of them was an attempt to form a grid, a periodic table, of mental development, which had nothing in it of the genius with which Bion constructed his. It was just an attempt at a notational system for what we already knew about development, and it was utterly uninteresting and never reached any development at all—and was gladly chucked as soon as I got my citizenship and could begin to receive patients and to earn a living. So when Bion's Grid came along I gobbled it up; it struck me as a marvellous stroke of genius, the way that he had constructed it, not of what we already knew but of what we didn't know, which was fundamentally the way Mendeleev's grid in chemistry was constructed. The important things in it were the empty spaces.

That sort of switch-over into Bion's interest in mental functions was a slow but very great move in my way of working; my work had very largely had a Kleinian preoccupation with structure, with the distribution of parts of the self and objects and so on, which was very much in keeping with my natural bent of thinking very concretely and structurally. Bion's way of thinking in terms of factors and functions seemed much more imaginative and much more abstract, but it didn't come so easily to me, and I had to find my way into it by way of language. My new interest in language started in the mid-1970s (with a fairly intensive study of linguistics), and I began to badger my patients about words and the use of words. I like Jean Bégoin's contribution (chapter nine), which distinguishes between the qualities of the "ambiguous" object and the qualities of the "mysterious object". Those sorts of differentiations, linguistic differentiations, eventually crept into my way of working, till I became a sort of nag—"What do you mean? Why do you use that particular word instead of this word or that word?", and so on. I don't know how much this involved a departure from psychoanalysis or the psychoanalytic method, but it certainly mated with another aspect of my work which took me further and further away from colleagues in London, and that is my clinging to the concept of "part-objects"; likewise, my seeing Bion's preoccupations with factors and functions and the Grid, and ideas of thought disorder, in combination with the functions of part-objects, which was very Kleinian but wasn't very obviously Bionic. But it is how my imagination worked—there's no arguing about it—it wasn't a question of theory, it was a question of my imagination being so absolutely fixed on dreams as being the fundamental information that allows you to construe what is going on in somebody else's head. It was that belief that dreams tell the truth that stuck me to part-objects and their functions, and to seeing not that dreams were necessarily full of symbols but that many dreams were full of part-objects. That the house "*was* the mother*", not "was a representation or a symbolic representation of the mother"—for this patient it *was* the mother. That the aeroplane really *was* daddy's penis—it didn't just represent it. So the differentiation between symbols and part-objects seemed to me to be revealed by dreams and showed the concreteness that infused all of these processes of thought and feeling and prevented them from finding any sort of resolution. This led so easily to their being transformed into patterns of acting-out; the acting-out of a dream that was very concrete, rather than symbolic, in its references, was the easiest thing in the world, and the most natural thing, too—to go from representation to action, when the representation itself was so concrete that just walking into your home transformed your mental state, or that getting on board an aeroplane immediately presented you with claustrophobia. So I began to see that the concept of acting-out, which was related to the transformation of mental imagery into action in the outside world, was very closely connected with the concreteness of part-objects, and that a lot of attention had to be paid to them, that these objects could not just be treated as symbols available for "thinking" but were only representations available for "action". In a sense, Bion's Grid didn't quite get it right because on the horizontal axis the last item is action rather than communication, and this was misleading—though I think he corrected all that in *A Memoir of the Future* (1975) with its marvellous, endless debate in the third book. I'm sure it was clearly meant to be *endless* debate. And that is built into the Grid—the possibility of endless debate, because, as he says, every thought that in its process of digestion reaches the point of being a concept can be fed back into the Grid as a preconception and worked through again at a still higher level—and this is where I think Bion realized that his vertical axis was not quite correct, that it needed not to develop to these mathematical levels but to emotional levels such as the aesthetic level and eventually the spiritual level.

Of course, I felt a little high-handed hijacking the Grid, as it were, and altering it to suit my own bias or purposes—and to think that I was improving on it. That's just the way it was, that's what I discovered was happening in my use of it, in my use of these linguistic experiences. The implication of there being a negative grid for the creation of lies and propaganda, as against a method for digesting thoughts into processes of thinking, made it unnecessary to think of destructiveness as anything other than a way of describing behaviour, and that one didn't need something like a death instinct or "*Homo homini lupus*", that "nothing is as vile as man" and things of that sort—that one did not need this kind of pessimism, that distinguishing between behaviour, thinking, and emotions was good enough to differentiate between thinking and lies, confabulations, propaganda, statistics, and so on. Thinking of this differentiation as the basis of behaviour, one could derive from it all of the vicious actions and genocide that you wanted to account for. One didn't have to posit an instinct of viciousness. I don't suppose I was ever very convinced about the death instinct anyhow, having never had to kill anybody. Although I did feel inwardly prepared to do so under various kinds of necessity, I never really felt it as a necessary piece of my equipment for surviving in the world, so I was very happy to find a way of letting it go as a concept, and it greatly facilitated the abandoning of being judgemental and of needing to construct moral grounds for feeling superior to other people. That letting go of the theory of the death instinct was a great relief, and, of course, it plays a very great part in analysing your patient and recognizing the problems of a patient's dreams.

When a concept like the combined object begins to find representations in patients' dreams, it is often very difficult to recognize. A patient who was approaching the end of her analysis dreamed that *she was in her university classroom and noticed that one of her tutors, of whom she is very fond and for whom she has a lot of admiration, was in drag, and this didn't seem in any way surprising to her. It didn't seem out of place that he should be sitting there dressed as a woman—he had on a rust-coloured wig, wasn't particularly attractive, but it seemed to suit the function of his being there.* Now that sort of representation of the combined object takes you aback for a minute—"Is that alright?" It's a bit like Keats's "pale-mouth'd prophet"—"Now wait a second", one has to think about that: "Is that alright, for a prophet to be 'pale-mouth'd'?"

Well, as I said, it's been a kind of amble through what has—I think—insidiously changed in my way of working, in my way of understanding things, the kind of pleasures and pains of psychoanalytic work. I can't really consider the years as a psychiatrist and as a psychoanalytic student in the United States as really psychoanalytic work—it was in such a different, rigidly hierarchic context, where obedience seemed to be the major requirement, like for a priest; I think I did feel "obedient" to my teachers, but I didn't feel that it was expected or demanded here, when I came to Mrs Klein and the British Psycho-Analytical Society—though I think that gradually that institution did become less tolerant, more authoritarian, and less interesting during the years that I was there, leading up to my finally withdrawing from it.

CHAPTER TWO

Experiences of learning with Donald Meltzer

Shirley Hoxter

In this chapter, I hope to convey to you the very substantial contributions that Donald Meltzer made to the development of the Tavistock Clinic's training course concerning the psycho-analytic therapy of children and young people. I shall concentrate mainly upon Meltzer's direct teaching activities, as supervisor and seminar leader in the period between the late 1950s and the mid-1970s. My accounts of these learning events are based largely on my own memories of encountering the mind of such a highly intelligent, original thinker and my personal emotional struggle of slowly learning how to learn from him.

I hope that this may throw some light upon what brought Meltzer and the Tavistock child psychotherapists together and what has continued to hold us together over such a long period. Surviving painful times, this relationship has been maintained even when we have been "absent objects" to one another for long periods.

This conference may be regarded as an affirmation of our relationship and our wishes to maintain it as a living experience. Using the language of Bion's concepts, I consider that the "container–contained" aspects of our relationship could often be categorized as "symbiotic", following Bion's definition as quoted by Meltzer (1978a, Part III): "Symbiotic—the thought and the thinker correspond and modify each other through the correspondence. The thought proliferates and the thinker develops" (p. 111). This seems an apt description of the reciprocal nature of the relationship between Meltzer and ourselves when functioning at its best. By "ourselves" I mean not only the psychoanalytic therapists of children here at the Tavistock, and elsewhere in Britain, but also the many from other lands who have formed a learning relationship with him.

Before we can understand the nature of the relationship between Meltzer and the child psychotherapists and the Tavistock culture that harboured them—and to which they in turn contributed—it will probably be helpful to review a little about each party prior to the time they got together. Indeed, it is hardly possible to appreciate Meltzer's contributions to our training without knowing what we were like before our experiences of learning from him and with him.

Who is Donald Meltzer?

He first arrived here in disguise. His identity was hidden by the uniform of a psychiatrist attached to the armed services of the United States, which had a large presence here in the 1950s. I met him once in this guise, but it was not until some years later that I learnt that he had already trained in the United States as a psychoanalyst and was experienced in psychoanalytic work with both children and adults. Presumably he could have continued to have a profitable career there, but he came here seeking to have all this disrupted and enriched by further analysis from Melanie Klein and further supervision from other Kleinian analysts. He seems to have been determined to find some device to come here and learn from Klein's work by experience, not just from books.

My only other knowledge concerning Meltzer's early career in this country comes from chapters included in the collection of papers to be found in *Sincerity and Other Works* (1994), edited by

Alberto Hahn. The first two chapters are informative concerning Meltzer at this period. In 1955 he wrote a paper entitled "Towards a Structural Concept of Anxiety". This paper is exceedingly abstract but has the merit of showing Meltzer struggling to bring together the influences stemming from his previous training and those he is beginning to encounter from Kleinians. It also shows him boldly determined to think for himself, somewhat jolted by Hanna Segal who drew his attention to the death instinct.

The next paper, written in 1959, is entitled "A Transient Inhibition of Chewing". This paper is of an entirely different nature. In the 1955 paper, Meltzer was making intellectual variations to the structural model of the mind without much trace of emotional conviction. Now, a bare four years later, he is functioning as a highly gifted psychoanalyst, deeply interested in his work and rejoicing in it. Clearly a burst of creativity has been released (perhaps by his own analysis?). Once let loose to obtain clinical experience, Meltzer writes as a songbird might sing when freed from its cage. The paper focuses almost entirely upon clinical material, but it also reveals that he has a masterly understanding of a whole range of Kleinian concepts and can use these with confident ease, both to extend the depth and precision of his insights concerning the patient and to communicate these to the reader.

Thereafter, nearly all Meltzer's writings are characterized by the feature of interrelating theory and clinical experience. Scattered through his writings are a number of explicit references concerning the importance that he attaches to this integration.

This is the Meltzer whom Esther Bick recommended to the child psychotherapists as a supervisor and who later contributed group teaching events to our training.

The early years of the Tavistock training for child psychotherapists

Our training programme was initiated by John Bowlby. He gave us a wonderful gift: the opportunity to obtain clinical experience of child analysis. Within the Health Services this was unique. Bowlby, together with other members of the multidisciplinary

Tavistock staff, trained us to become able to function as members of a multidisciplinary child guidance team, thus enabling us to become acceptable for employment in the public services.

However, for the understanding of psychoanalysis, the all-important component of our training, we relied upon Esther Bick, whom Bowlby had arranged to become our first Senior Tutor (an action that he later came to regret as their ways increasingly diverged). Her fiery espousal of Kleinian insights and her passionate dedication to child analysis were inspirational and set us on our way to pursue lifelong learning. Although a poor writer, she was a brilliant educator in her face-to-face contacts with her students, revealing to us an awareness of the child's inner world and the recognition of unconscious phantasies and their power to influence personality development. Her methods of infant observation were first developed for our training and influenced all our later work.

Bick enlisted a number of eminent child analysts to contribute to our course, both as individual supervisors of our training cases and for clinical and theoretical seminars. But the seminars were either one-offs or for a series of about four. The extraordinary advantage of having our training enriched by such distinguished people was accompanied by the disadvantages of a lack of cohesion and continuity, especially marked in theoretical seminars.

However, we began to suspect that most of them had ceased to work with children. We sensed that only Bick and Meltzer were currently psychoanalysing children and that only they were enthusiastically committed to extending this as an ongoing experience, for themselves, for the children, and for us, the aspiring learners. (This was largely confirmed in a paper by Esther Bick, 1961, deploring "the grave neglect of child analysis".) The passionate commitment to child analysis shown by Bick and Meltzer, the interest, enjoyment, and conviction that that they brought to it, were among the most valuable and influential contributions to our learning experiences.

We were probably a puzzling group for most of our visiting teachers. Bion makes a distinction between learning about psychoanalysis and learning to become psychoanalysts. His implication seems to be that most people entering training have learnt something *about* psychoanalysis but it takes a lifetime of experience

to learn to *become* a psychoanalyst. Thanks to our personal experiences as analysands, to our vivid exposures to the impact of
children in analysis, and to the singular way in which Esther
Bick taught us, I think that we may have been making our way
towards the first steps of becoming analysts of children, whilst
remaining woefully ignorant "about psychoanalysis".

Meltzer mentioned to me his amazement that we seemed to
know so little about the theories of psychoanalysis. Later on, he
wrote about Melanie Klein's apparent lack of concern regarding
theory (Meltzer, 1978a, Part II): "One can hardly ascribe naïveté to
such an astute woman; one must assume that the philosophy of
science did not really interest her" (p. 1). If this might be true of
Klein, there can be little doubt that it was still more true of Bick's
naïveté and lack of concern regarding Freudian theory. It was not
until his series of lecture discussions in the 1970s that Meltzer had
the opportunity to remedy our ignorance of the development of
psychoanalytic theory; I shall return to this later on.

At this point, I wish mainly to emphasize his outstanding gifts
for combining in his teaching a lively depth of interest in the ongoing experiences of child analysis, accompanied by continuous
conceptualization.

Meltzer's early group teaching activities

From the individual supervisions of a number of recently qualified child psychotherapists, Meltzer became familiar with our
strengths and weaknesses. In the group teaching events, which
continued for most of the 1960s, he set about remedying some of
our weaknesses. He also used these occasions to mobilize his own
formulations, many of which were highly original developments
based on Kleinian understandings and increasingly influenced
by Bion. Furthermore, through his teaching work, he greatly expanded his familiarity with a wide range of children in analysis.
He drew upon his experiences of these times in many of his later
publications.

The first of these, dated 1960, has only recently been published
as a paper, in the *Sincerity* collection of papers (Meltzer, 1994),
entitled "Lectures and Seminars in Kleinian Child Psychiatry".

This paper's main concern relates to assessment. It commences with a brilliant but highly compacted exposition of Kleinian concepts.

In this series of lecture-cum-clinical seminars, the illustrative examples of clinical material from sessions with children were contributed by child psychotherapists, most of whom had received individual supervision from Meltzer. For the presentation of such evidence, Meltzer developed an innovative method. A single session was presented in two columns. The first contained a condensed account of the child's communications, in words, play, or behaviour, accompanied by a summary of the therapists' interpretative interventions. Alongside this, a parallel column noted Meltzer's comments on the diagnostic significance of the material; this was frequently accompanied by a critical assessment of the therapist's intervention (or lack of intervention) and its effect upon the subsequent material of the patient. His attention throughout is on the sequence of transference interactions. Not until the end of the clinical discussions does one find a few brief sentences summarizing the child's history.

This approach was revolutionary for those of us who had become well accustomed to the assessment procedures then followed at the Tavistock. Our weekly interdisciplinary case conferences were among our major training events. Assessments took the form of gathering a mass of background information collected by a multidisciplinary team from parents, teachers, and many other sources. Direct observation of the child played a relatively small part, and the child's feelings and phantasies about the referral and those whom he or she met became almost invisible.

In the discussions that followed the complex of assessment material, the emphasis was nearly always upon the causative explanations of the child's presenting symptoms. These were usually related to external causation, such as detrimental life experiences or difficulties in family relationships. Discussion would then ensue between staff members and the more intrepid students. Suddenly, Esther Bick would intervene with an explosive burst of incisive insight, setting us all to rights. A drama of controversy would ensue. The excitement of these weekly tournaments was thrilling until, in time, becoming somewhat dulled by being foreseeable and lacking in outcome.

The trouble lay in the overelaborate complexity of the information accrued and the contrasting oversimplicity of attributing the symptomatology to external causes, whilst paying little attention to the child's contribution or to the inner workings of the child's mind. I once dared to ask what had been going on in this child's mind for all these years, to transform these early causes into the present effects. To answer such questioning, both Bick and Meltzer cut through the clutter of information and focused upon what the child could tell us. Bick tended mainly to attend to the child's unconscious phantasies and the nature of internal objects. Meltzer, on the other hand, also paid close attention to the to and fro of the child's mental functioning as it unfolded in the session, especially concerning the child's projective and introjective processes and the extent and nature of anxieties and splitting, the hopes, fears, and defences, as shown in the transference emerging in a single, closely observed session.

The categories of assessment were probably not intended to be inclusive and seem likely to have been determined by the nature of the cases he was currently supervising. However, the lecture component of these events ranged more widely and were marked by the subtlety and exactitude that he brought to the applications of the diagnostic categories.

Meltzer continued with these lectures-cum-group supervisions to explore and develop with us insights concerning the sorting of geographical confusions and zonal confusions. He expands his thoughts about these in chapters of *The Psycho-Analytical Process* (1967). Attending these seminars as a listener, I was frequently out of my depth and probably not alone in this situation. He required a precision of interpretation which was beyond most of us at that time. For instance, an interpretation was not good enough if it merely distinguished between the "toilet-breast" and the nurturing breast. Frequently it should also distinguish between the nipple and the breast and the related phantasies concerning this part-object, experienced as "divorced" or combined.

He could also be exacting concerning the timing of interpretations; on some occasions, if the interpretation came ten minutes late, it might be deemed to have "rescued" the session, but it was also likely to be considered as no longer appropriate. We students muttered between ourselves about his excessive fussiness.

Later on, it appeared that Meltzer learnt from our difficulties in finding his corrections constructive and adapted his teaching methods. In the chapter entitled "The Cycle of the Process in the Individual Session", he gives a careful exposition of the technique that he developed for the presentation of material in seminars. In the example he then presents, concerning a single session with a child, he has modified the use of the two parallel columns. The material of the session no longer includes the content of the inter-pretations, for, as Meltzer puts it, he has noted that "anxiety and modesty" often persuade students to limit their interpretations. In place of the therapist's interpretations, and Meltzer's comments, the second column now supplies a summary of the groups' formu-lations which followed prolonged discussion.

In *The Psycho-Analytical Process*, Meltzer makes references to Bion's work. So far as I have detected he does not use the term "absent object", but the major theme concerning "the cycle" of the psychoanalytical process seems to have been influenced by this concept, following in detail the vicissitudes of the object when absence is apprehended, defended against in many different ways, briefly re-discovered as a present, good object, and eventually acknowledged and valued even when absent and established as an internal dependable object. This provides a narrative rhythm which may be followed on a daily, weekly, termly, or annual basis. Separateness and separation are closely studied, together with the gradual relinquishment of the more harmful defences used to guard against such universal experiences of emotional pain.

This provided a new dimension to our thinking about separa-tion anxieties, and it probably contributed a vital enablement for our later work with severely deprived children (Boston & Szur, 1983).

Personal experiences
of supervisions with Meltzer

Following the conclusion of my training course, I continued for several years to have supervisions with Esther Bick and only com-menced supervisions with Meltzer after I had attended his group-teaching events. With many qualms, I anticipated a formidably exacting supervisor, the creator of brilliant new thinking, likely to be beyond my comprehension. But what I really wanted was further supportive guidance through the hazards of each session. We had different hidden agenda.

The first case I brought to supervision concerned "Roger", a 7-year-old. Reporting on the commencement of the first session, I mentioned that I hung his coat on the hook, which was too high for him to reach. Meltzer reproached me for a breach of technique and for inappropriately equipping my room. I was accustomed to Bick's strictness concerning technique, but nevertheless I smarted at what I felt was a strong reprimand for a petty detail. A little later, Roger took a tiny toy figure of a boy and showed him holding an elephant by a rope of plasticine attached to his trunk. Meltzer interpreted this as the boy's response to my error of hanging up his coat, myself being the elephant led by the nose. If only I had been able to ignore the scolding and to listen properly! It took me some years of further work before I was able to realize that Meltzer had been immediately onto an important feature of this boy's psychopathology. Whenever Roger received a helping hand, he tended to denigrate the helper with contempt and attribute the achievement to the manipulative skills of the omnipotent part of his personality. This contributed to Roger's learning difficulties and impaired his ability to internalize good and helpful objects. It was, of course, also an example of the way that my own learning ability was impaired by my projections and fear of being found inadequate.

At the end of the first supervision, Meltzer said that he considered the boy to be seriously ill and likely to be a very difficult patient. I was therefore astonished when the following week, after hearing some more material, he said that he could not think why I was bringing this case to supervision—it was quite ordinary and I could very well manage it on my own. Flattering though this was, I knew it to be untrue. I did not dare voice my doubts or point out the discrepancy with the assessment he had made the previous week. On this occasion, I think we were both mistaken: Meltzer in thinking that the case was ordinary enough to be within the ordinariness of my capabilities, and myself for having been too intimidated to speak up.

Following this, I brought three other cases, each presented for a few weeks and then considered to be unsuitable for the supervisions. Then I had a new patient, referred to me by a psychiatrist who had diagnosed him as mentally defective. This was an intriguing 3-year-old, who, under the name of "Piffie", later made his contribution to Meltzer's book on autism (Meltzer, Bremner, Hoxter, Weddell, & Wittenberg, 1975). A shared interest in Piffie enabled Meltzer and me to settle down to work together to discover what we could learn from him.

Nevertheless, I continued to have difficulties in making the best use of my supervisions. One persisting matter was that I never became able to present my material adequately. Piffie attended four times weekly, but I rarely got through an account of much more than half of one session, as Piffie stimulated Meltzer to enter into long disquisitions concerning the autistic condition and the nature of obsessionality[1] which led me into arguments. A further major difficulty was that I could never really accept that Piffie was autistic at the time that I was seeing him.

I wondered whether Meltzer, as supervisor, sought cases (or selected aspects of cases) that provided him with the food for thought required to nurture the gestation of his own brain-children. Now I can say "no matter", for Meltzer certainly also provided his students with plenty of food for thoughts and developments, but at the time this suspicion did matter to me. However, despite my inner complainings, we had enough in common: the sharing of great interest in this fascinating little boy, his eager use of the psychoanalytic experience of the transference, and the thrilling ways in which his capacities for thinking and development unfolded. This shed light on the learning processes of normal infants as well as revealing the impediments of the residual autistic condition.

---

[1] See A *Dictionary of Kleinian Thought* (Hinshelwood, 1991), which reveals that Kleinian thinking concerning obsessional states underwent several revisions and had largely fallen out of use at this time. Meltzer's views struck an original note. Hinshelwood's entry under "Autism" gives a somewhat misleading account of Meltzer's and Tustin's views.

The work group concerning autism

Eventually Meltzer called a halt to my supervisions and enlisted me as a member of a group of those who had already received long periods of individual supervisions with him concerning autistic patients. The other lasting members of the group included John Bremner, Doreen Weddell, and Isca Wittenberg. Together we managed to persevere with some three years of strenuous effort—painful, but eventually enlightening.

Meltzer firmly presided over this process. He required each of us, in turn, to review our past notes and to contribute these for discussion. The reviewing process was an arduous experience. I dreaded re-reading my own inadequate material. However, I found much to be learnt from the experiences of the other members of the group, each of whom had a case far more severely autistic, demanding great patience, sensitivity, and sheer courage.

Apart from the task of reviewing the case material and apart from a notion that a book might arise from the work, for a long time we had little idea of what we were doing. The plan for a book on autism sounded wildly ambitious. Meltzer seemed to be hatching out some thoughts, but not all of these were ready for telling.

Eventually Meltzer brought this phase of our meetings to an end. Each of us was requested to write up our case material and directed to focus on a particular aspect of the autistic condition as illustrated by the child with whom we had worked. It was by then beginning to dawn on me that our disparate cases might be viewed as representing different stages of a continuum of autistic features: but this idea was still somewhat hazy.

To my relief, Piffie was now referred to as a child illustrating "residual autism". I was dismayed, however, that my allotted task was to focus on his obsessionality and his processes of "dismantling".

Piffie, now aged about 12, was well into his second period of therapy. He was tenaciously clinging to what proved to be a long state of protracted latency, with very pronounced obsessional features. During this period, Meltzer sent me a few pages of typescript outlining his concepts concerning "dismantling" or "segmentation".

These new terms were central to Meltzer's understanding of early infantile autism at that time. They differentiated the processes observed in our autistic patients from the splitting functions used in normal development and from the more fragmented splitting and projective identifications found in more pathological states. They refer to modes of experiencing an object with the attention of only one sense at a time; for example, an object that may be seen might not simultaneously be heard, touched, or sucked. In severe states of autism, the coordination of the senses directed towards a single object continues to be fragile. In states of stress—or lack of attention—there is a passive falling apart of the sensory apparatus and of the related object. This may be seen in the states of collapse and the lack of "common sense" (Bion) which are features of most autistic children.

Piffie used this process in a less drastic way than the other children studied. He frequently segmented his objects but did so less upon patterns of sensory experience and sometimes for more defensive purposes. The lack of sadism enables the less autistic child to re-assemble an unharmed, non-persecutory object. In autism, each piece may be sensuously possessed, obsessionally controlled, and selected pieces may be repetitively re-assembled in endless permutations—a predominant feature of my case. Meltzer's notes to me were only a rough draft but were made with such clarity of thought and care that, at last, I could grasp the ideas and implement them in my current and future sessions with Piffie. The previous years of study became usable and valued.

When we met again as a group and heard one another's contributions, I think that we were all astonished to find that the work was beginning to take shape, with some coherent and continuous threads of thinking running through it. From our apparently disparate cases, some significant points in the spectrum of autism became visible.

I was much relieved that the title of the book was to be *Explorations in Autism* (1975). Psychoanalytic explorations of this nature, into autism, psychosis, or other areas hitherto considered to be inaccessible for the psychoanalytic approach, tend, initially, to be disappointingly meagre in terms of therapeutic results. They also fail to produce a complete new theory "explaining" it all. They do, however, reveal fresh insights, tracking a way to enable future psychoanalytic explorers to proceed on relatively familiar territory, perhaps sometimes wondering why their predecessors found the way to be so laborious and fraught with difficulty. (Likewise, within my own lifetime, the mountaineers Edmund Hilary and Sherpa Tsensing achieved reaching the summit of Mount Everest, hitherto deemed impossible, but now within the reach of many, although it continues to demand persistent endeavour, team work, and skills.)

The completed book contains much more than the clinical findings of our four cases. It includes Meltzer's sections on theory and implications of the findings, together with material from his own patients and applications of Bick's work concerning adhesive identifications.

This long period of study was a formative experience for me. In addition to aiding me in future work with patients showing autistic features, I learnt more about how to learn from the patient, from the supervisor, and from sharing experiences in a group and how, later on, by myself, to think about it all and to re-assemble these strata of experience—almost to integrate them.

The growing-up period of the Tavistock Child Psychotherapy Training Programme

During this time of work concerning autism, Meltzer continued to supervise an increasing number of other child psychotherapists.

Meanwhile, our training programmes had greatly expanded. This was largely due to the inspiring influence and the exceptional abilities of Mattie Harris,[2] both in leadership and in her educational empowerments. These enabled her gradually to become our Senior Organizing Tutor after the departure of Esther Bick. The course expanded in terms of duration, the number of students attending (which increased vastly), and also the number, range,

---

[2] For further information concerning the influences of Mattie Harris, see *The Collected Papers of Martha Harris and Esther Bick* (Harris & Bick, 1987), especially the Introduction, "Mattie as an Educator", by Margaret Rustin.

and quality of the teaching events. It became obvious that we could no longer depend upon the goodwill and expertise of the external Kleinian psychoanalysts for supervision and other training events. With increasing experience and maturation, it became more clearly appropriate, as well as evidently imperative, that we ourselves should undertake most of the training and individual supervision of the new generations of students. Those whom Mattie Harris required to supervise training cases were those who had also received further supervision following qualification; such supervision had almost always come from Meltzer. Thus he contributed greatly and highly influentially to the survival and further development of our training programmes.

The question arises, was he over-influential? A charismatic, highly intelligent, independent, and powerful thinker is fated to become a target for projections, and there will always be many who are prepared to idolize or demonize. Students in supervision, like analysands in analysis, seek someone who may be depended upon while they also fight against dependency, aware of the need to preserve the ability to think their own thoughts, feel their own feelings, and follow their own aims. Sorting all this out, usually in the area of projective and introjective identification, is central to the work of analysis, perhaps especially to a so-called training analysis.

The internal work of self-analysis requires one not only to survive the termination of contact with the external analyst, but also to develop beyond the domination of the analyst as an internal object. Supervision and self-supervision follow a similar but less emphatically influential path.

Meltzer has thought deeply about this problem. In his book *Sexual States of Mind* (1973), he discusses this in his chapter "The Genesis of the Super-Ego Ideal" and returns to it again in the chapter concerning "Work, Play and Sublimation". Both chapters use the language and imagery of some dream material. Meltzer stresses the differentiation between "following-in-daddy's footsteps" for the purpose of reaching a "goal" to gaining approval from the parental object and the more mature state of "working under the aegis" of an internalized object who can offer methods and principles for pursuing a freely chosen aim. I think that is what he hoped would eventually arise from our learning experience with him. This concerns the change from "learning to growth" (Bion, 1965).

Freud, Klein, and Bion:
The Kleinian Development

Meltzer had not forgotten his amazement that we child psychotherapists understood so little about psychoanalytic theory. Throughout most of the 1970s he set about remedying this lack and entered into an arduous long-term commitment with several "generations" of students. His introduction to *The Kleinian Development* (Meltzer, 1978a, Part I) reveals how this work was intimately related to his own personal development, as well as being guided by his awareness of our needs and his recognition that our main interests concerned Klein's work and clinical experience.

Concerning the influences of Freud, Klein, and Bion he writes: "my development has been dominated by transference to, and identification with, these three extraordinary people" (p. 2). He continues: "the study and lecturing . . . were intended to discover and define the continuity or discontinuity in my psychoanalytical development in terms of success or failure to develop a combined psycho-analytical object 'under whose aegis' I might hope to work creatively and courageously some day".

These lecture seminars were therefore inspired by his commitment to the internal work of personal integration, and this enlivened the subject matter. But the students were certainly also required to do their own work of reading the texts and attempting their own efforts to digest these. The series of lectures provided a model for the development of the Training Course's five-year programme of reading seminars, to which many other people have later made heroic, long-lasting contributions. They have added a backbone of rigour and disciplined thinking to our training.

We must all be glad that Donald Meltzer came to this country for his further psychoanalytic education and, in doing so, contributed so generously and inspiringly to *our* education.

CHAPTER THREE

Development is beauty, growth is ethics

Clara Nemas

When I received the invitation to participate in this celebration of Donald Meltzer's work, I thought it would be a good idea to make it into an invitation to explore. The penumbra of associations surrounding the word "exploration" seemed to me to involve romantic ideas of unknown, wild, and virgin lands, a compass in my hand, a survival kit. I imagined myself as part of a team with all my colleagues throughout the world with whom, though I may not have actually met them, I would be sharing this project of exploration. I am not sure whether this made me feel more accompanied, but it did give me a measure of courage, not only for the task at hand, but also for overcoming my shyness in this regard, which instead of easing only increased when I tried to "go beyond the prelude".

In the process of trying to find the North on my compass, a starting point from which to orient myself, the subject of ethics came into view. The subject of values—their detailed scrutiny, their development in the psychoanalytic process, the challenge they represent—is one that constantly interests and concerns me in my work as a psychoanalyst. In my personal and professional history, I have had analysts, supervisors, and teachers whose close contact with Meltzer's ideas has had an impact on me, and these ideas, in turn, extend and enrich the theories of Klein and Bion. Their presence in my training, the reading of Meltzer's work, and personal contact with him in recent years have been important factors contributing to my way of thinking about an ethical position in psychoanalysis. All this has influenced my choice of the contents of this chapter; however, beyond any possible explanation, once I had thought of this subject it ensconced itself in me, insisted, and gained its place in the expedition party, with the result that ethics is to be the name of our journey through a territory whose boundaries are not very well defined.

Point of departure

In "Return to the Imperative" (1965), Meltzer writes: "The work of Melanie Klein has, like it or not, introduced, with the concepts of paranoid–schizoid and depressive position, the element of *value* into the psychoanalytic system of thought—that is, into its previously relatively barren area of mental *economics*" (p. 149). I shall start with this statement in order to try to follow the underlying pattern of the subject of values in Meltzer's work.

In the introduction to Part I of *The Kleinian Development* (1978a), in the presentation of his critical, non-reverential reading of his teachers—Freud, Klein, and Bion—Meltzer defines the models of the mind explicit and implicit in each of them—the neurophysiological model in Freud, the mythological or theological model in Klein, and the philosophical model in Bion—which are related to each other as the root is to the trunk and the branches, only to flower and bear fruit in clinical work in the office, with the assistance of faith.

Is Freud's neurophysiological, economic model free of values? Obviously, values do not come into play in relation to energies and economic principles but, rather, in relation to other human beings; therefore, it is probable that only a theory taking into account the object relation would include the subject of values in an explicit way. However, psychoanalysis under the guidance of its creator, and beyond the ethics it shares with science in general, "virtually inaugurated a new era of human ethics" (Racker, 1961). This is evident in Freud's struggle against the hypocrisy that preaching that what should not exist in people because of "moral" precepts simply did not exist and was denied one way or another. We have a description of his position, written by someone who was very close to him in the early years:

> ... from the psychoanalytic point of view there were no sharp divisions between sick and healthy, that in the healthy person also the unconscious may dominate though he is unwilling to admit it, for to do so would hamper his actions. He therefore attempts to rationalize, and employs all possible stratagems to prove that his thinking and decisions follow the line of pure reason and are therefore of high quality. Although Freud certainly did not underestimate the neurotic in his patients, he attempted always to support and strengthen the kernel of health, separated from the chaff of neurosis. [quoted in Gardiner, 1972, p. 156]

Some of you may have recognized these words, written by the Wolf Man in his recollections of Sigmund Freud. Referring to invitations to explore, the Wolf Man says:

> I can only say that in my analysis with Freud I felt myself less as a patient than as a co-worker, the younger comrade of an experienced explorer setting out to study a new, recently discovered land. [p. 158]

These examples speak of Freud's ethical position as a person; however, in his works, we do not find any social or ethical theory, but rather a concern for the origins of morality, religion, social institutions, and authority.

People's discontent in culture is determined by the repression of instinctive satisfaction, whether in its erotic or its thanatic current. Freud says that if civilization demands a massive instinctual sacrifice, what it offers in return is not so much security of pleasure as the absence of suffering. But if we compare this conception offered in *Civilization and its Discontents* as a counterpoint to the ideas proposed by Meltzer as early as 1968 in his work on tyranny, we find a hypothesis that I shall take as a point of departure to examine the problem of values in the Kleinian development.

The key to this topic involves the extension of two metapsychological concepts. One is the geographical dimension, describing an internal world as a living space—a generative theatre of meaning—where we live in a way that is just as real as in the external world. The other is the structural dimension, portraying the relationship between the self and the objects that constitute family life, and differentiated from narcissistic organization. Both concepts have made our ideas on the most primitive and the most highly developed aspects of humankind broader and more complex.

Freud did not describe the internal world as a generator of meanings in our relation with the external world, and he visualized the relationship between human beings and culture as a submissive one. He had similarly described the servitudes of the ego at a time when he had not yet totally grasped the complexity of an un-unified human mind. In the Kleinian perspective, psychic reality is externalized, and it tinges our relationship with the external world. According to this view, it is possible to discern how the mind's destructive aspect is put into action in all areas of social debate: ecology, abortion, education, pollution, and so forth. It is here that we can understand the discontent of humankind with civilization, in the framework of a conflict between the life and the death instincts, which Bion redefines as taking place between the activity of symbol formation and the non-thinking aspect of human behaviour that attacks human relationships.

Symbol formation and ethical values— the family and the community

It is no coincidence that the previous section ended with a reference to Bion. The struggle surrounding the philosophical problem of meaning and intention that Meltzer has addressed in his article "Tyranny" (1968) acquires new meaning with Bion's contribution in dividing mental life into *proto-mental*—that is, learned social adaptive behaviour or group mentality—and *mental*—that is, meaningful manifestations of the thinking personality or individual mentality. The boundary between the two lies in the process of symbol formation: the capacity for representing our emotional experience, if we are able to tolerate these affects.

Bion speaks of the proto-mental level of function in his book *Experiences in Groups* (1961), proposing not only a level of function where physical and psychological events are not differentiated, but yet another level where primitive mentality is mainly concerned with group membership. At the same time, the individual can be thought of as a group, represented as a dramatization between his ego, his internal objects, and his thoughts without a thinker.

Bion described two modes of group relations: the work group and the basic assumptions group in its three categories: *dependence, fight–flight, and pairing.* The work group "meets to 'do' something; in this activity, according to the capacities of the individuals, they cooperate" (Bion, 1961, p. 143). The characteristics of the group organized around basic assumptions are exactly the opposite of those described for the work group. Bion makes two important additions. He explains that "time plays no part in basic-assumption mentality" and that the activities that "require an awareness of time tend to arouse persecution". Related to this attitude towards time is "the absence of any process of development", since any stimulus for development meets with a hostile response. From the perspective of the child's vision of the world, this group classification corresponds to two childhood conceptions of the parental couple: if they are seen as being occupied with the children's upbringing, they are a work group. If they are considered only from the point of view of the combined object, occupied with sensual exchange to the exclusion of the babies, they are a basic assumptions group.

But we shall see how this subject relates to the problem of values. Let us return for a moment to the time when *Sexual States of Mind* (Meltzer, 1973) was published. Adult sexuality was described as reflecting the qualities—and as being under the aegis—of the internal parents. They are the origin of our system of values, and we constitute our ethical aspirations through identifications with them. They influence our way of life in that our choices in the world must take into account the well-being of the object. This means that we must shift the centre of our concerns from anxieties regarding the self to the examination of our motivations as a way of life.

Family life thus described is an epic-romantic narrative: in the nuptial chambers, the woman in distress, need, and danger is res- cued by the man who is her servant, her benefactor. The adult aspect, modest and humble, preserves the creativity of the internal gods, puts the children to sleep, and sustains the hope of being touched by the god's grace. The work ethic implies that a good man is one who does what he must do in cooperation with others in the pursuit of a valid, non-delusional task, carried out with passion.

At this point, we can relate Meltzer's family model to Bion's ideas about groups. We can consider the family as a work group with inactive, primitive forms of basic assumption organization. At times of stress, the family can lose its sophistication and be- come more primitive and tribal. In terms of each member of the family group, the action of these primitive aspects takes place through intrusive projective identification inside the internal ob- jects, configuring a mental state that Meltzer called "the claus- trum". This internal configuration provokes effects on the outside, since it is externalized in the family, generating atmospheres rang- ing from indolence and passiveness, excitement and delinquency, to states of terror, sado-masochistic relationships, and fatal pun- ishments.

But if the family is the seat of the "mental", whence does the proto-mental threaten? Within the bounds of the individual, the proto-mental is in the character organization, as opposed to per- sonality: "It is the exterior armouring of social character, acquired mindlessly by primitive modes of identification, training, mim- icry, conditioning, etc." (Meltzer et al., 1986, p. 27). In the external world, the proto-mental is expressed by the tribal mentality oper- ating in civilized forms of organization—that is, the community. We simultaneously live in several worlds—the world of intimate relations, the claustrophobic world of the inside of objects, con- tractual relations, institutions—and with luck we manage to keep the no-where of the delusional world at arm's length. Perhaps the most important—and, as usual, what is important is also what is difficult—is not to confuse the meanings, values, and operational modes of each of these worlds.

Simone's experiences: between the family and the crèche

We might imagine that the expression of the model of the mind we have just described would require a crystallized character and a complex political organization. Meltzer says that we would be deceiving ourselves if we thought it possible to carry on an activity with others without participating in the communal aspect, for "... there is always a community. And since there is a community, there are problems of organization and communication where the borderland between friendly and hostile, communication and action, governing and ruling, opposing and sabotaging becomes obscure" (Meltzer, 1992a, p. 153).

The horticultural concept of the mind proposed by Melanie Klein, in which, if all goes well, development is seen as stemming from the roots towards the trunk, the branches, and the fruits, may seem a bit naive in relation to the conflicts that individuals have to face in today's world. Bion has depicted the complex interaction, as well as the failures of interaction, between the different structures comprising the mind of modern humans, and he has done so in a strange and ingenious way, in *A Memoir of the Future* (1975, Book One). But with her background in Kleinian development, Esther Bick (1964) has used the method of observation of babies with their families in order to give us common mortals access to the possibility of discovering these complex mental phenomena in the everyday life of the nursery, which we later reencounter in the psychoanalyst's office.

Freud had already taught us that sexuality is not missing from the nursery, and so we had to accept infantile sexuality. Then we learned from Melanie Klein that aggression is equally present there, and we had to tolerate the existence of criminal phantasies in normal children. Now we shall see how the tribal mentality, with its basic assumptions, also finds a place in the world of children.

Meltzer's commentaries, in chapter 13 of *Studies in Extended Metapsychology* (Meltzer et al., 1986), on the observation in Rome by Maura Gelati of a little boy going to day-nursery are so illuminating, and Gelati's report on the observations so evocative and suggestive, that I think they would provide the best background for the ideas I wish to convey.

Let's start with the story. Simone, a little boy not quite 1 year old, is sent to a crèche so that his mother may resume her work as a teacher. His parents, loving and sensitive, have been agonizing about whether to put the child into day-care or to leave him at home in the care of grandparents. Finally, they decided on the first option, in the belief that this would be the best solution for the baby himself. The observations at the crèche cover nearly five months of Simone's life, from the time he enters day-care at 10 months, 20 days, until he is 15 months old; they are so vivid and detailed that we feel we are there during the observations.

As soon as he enters, on the first day, Simone is confronted with Myriam, a girl 12 months old, who systematically and very skilfully takes away any toys that Simone attempts to play with. Simone begins to look vexed, pulls Myriam's hair angrily, and tries to console himself in different ways, such as sucking his thumb. His mother is quite perplexed, confused in regard to her values, and gives him conflicting instructions. She is concerned that Simone should meet adult expectations and not hurt other children. She soon realizes that the problem is how Simone is to meet the other children's aggression.

Only a few days later, we see a significant change in Simone's behaviour. The moment he sees a little girl crying, he throws his toy away and immediately grabs her by the hair. He behaves the same way towards a 6-month-old baby. In this action, Meltzer sees evidence of the boy's adaptation to the culture of the crèche, the hair-pulling being a severe disciplinary measure applied to crying babies.

A few months later, we see how Simone attempts to resist being taken to the crèche, and how he is pressured to "be good" and not to cry at being "sent away from his nice home". All this time, the adults treat Simone gently and affectionately, trying to make him see the advantages of adapting and being "like that child over there, the one who never cries". There is no need to treat him roughly; propaganda is a sufficiently persuasive method of social pressure for the purposes of adaptation.

After this outbreak of rebellion, we see Simone growing away from the "pains of babyhood" and becoming "one of the boys", and our heart sinks as we see him, in the light of Meltzer's understanding, adapt so well and become, in the nurse's words, a "well-balanced child, both with the other children and with adults".

Simone is now 1 year, 12 days old. We find he has become a little man who says goodbye to his daddy at the door of the crèche with a great show of how easy it is for him to do it, and how well he has now learned to "pretend" he is crying. We learn that he has been forbidden to go into the kitchen because he had gone into the pantry and left the mark of his four front teeth on the entire top layer of the tray of apples. By now, no distress is so terrible that it cannot be overcome by a biscuit. "Simone is easily bought off by a biscuit."

Suddenly, the images transport us to a rapid-action scene in a movie. Simone is walking around the room confidently, oblivious of the dangers involved, and we feel as if he were risking suicide by crossing a busy street without traffic lights: "the older children . . . are riding up and down on their tricycles at some speed, avoiding those on foot only at the last moment". The observer is anxious, but neither the children nor the nurse seem to worry. A little girl smaller than Simone who is eating a bread stick walks by, and he grabs half of it quite matter of factly, but drops a little piece of bread that he had found on the floor when the nurse warns him that it's garbage. When another child, a little older, demands the observer's attention, Simone attempts to get it back again by showing her the skill he has acquired on the slide.

Meltzer has assigned a poetic name to this narration of the child's adaptation and the dilemma of his parents. He calls it a "parable of our confusing times", an era when parents feel the conflict between the desire to bring their children up gently in an atmosphere of affection and trust on the one hand, and the fear of not equipping them properly for self-defence in a hostile world on the other. That this hostile world, both political and brutal, is part of the organization of the nursery is confirmed by the observation of Simone and by our daily observations, even though we, like the nurse, may dismiss it as simply another ingredient to "what all children do".

In Simone's adaptation, Meltzer sees an incipient dissociation between the family area's intimate relationships, and the sphere of social relations.

> A sense of hierarchy, identification with authority, sanctimonious punitiveness, arrogant exhibitionism and male chauvinism are all suggested, at the expense of tenderness, gentleness and sensitivity of which he is clearly capable. Simone is certainly not unarmed nor long perplexed by the structure of the crèche and its social order. . . . No, he gives promise of being a good organization-man, and that is what we are determined to be worried about. [Meltzer et al., 1986, p. 148]

In the final observation, when we sorrowfully take leave of Simone, he is already 15 months old. Our hopes revive, guided by Meltzer's understanding. The atmosphere of love and trust in which Simone was raised seems to have been a container for his good internal resources. We see Simone recovering from his flirtation with group culture, and the result is "a forward thrust in his strength, imaginativeness, urge to language formation and respect for the space of others" (p. 153). His parents also seem to have recovered from their anxiety that he should be well-adjusted.

Some ideas on integration and reparation: their ethical implications

I would now like to invite you to return to the point of departure of this chapter, which was Meltzer's statement that Melanie Klein introduced the subject of values to psychoanalysis and developed a model of the mind that he termed theological. A large part of the neo-Kleinian contribution to the subject of values turns upon the evolution of the concept of the superego. This agency was conceived by Freud as a patriarchal figure of the Old Testament, an authority to be feared and obeyed without question. Money-Kyrle (1978) called this emotional configuration "the morality of fear", and he thought that there must be another aspect of morality based not on fear but on love, this being Melanie Klein's contribution: her description of the persecutory and the depressive anxieties. Elaborating on these ideas, Meltzer says:

> ... judgment about the world, and about ourselves and our fellow men, is adversely affected by our hostility. The wish to find fault, as an expression of envy in particular, but driven also by submission to our persecutors, blinds us to the virtues of our enemies and the faults of our allies ... envy and hatred induce the projection of hated parts of the self out into the world, obscuring our capacity for observation of the external world and depriving us of the conflict which drives our inquiry into the internal world. ... Only ... piecemeal revelations of the truth can liberate men from the more primitive models which affect their judgments and guide their actions ... but the rectification of this model of the world involves men in a *transformation of their values*, for while the truth may liberate them from persecutory anxieties, it imposes upon them love for the worlds, both inner and outer, and consequent guilt for the damage caused by their greed and destructive envy. [1978a, p. xi]

For Klein, this transformation of values depends on the relation between the self and the internal objects (Meltzer's superego-ideal), which concretely inhabit the mind and exercise a maternal function by promoting development. If we consider, as I propose in this chapter, a " combined" development of the ideas of Bion and Meltzer, then the superego-ideal can be seen not just as a monitor of the development of the self, but also as the creative aspect of the mind: this mystic bit of the mind, ensconced in the internal objects, receives new ideas and makes them available to the self, even in the form of ethical ways of living.

For Meltzer, the clarifiying distinction that mental pain may be persecutory or depressive has definitely left the question of free will in good standing. This concept derives from the idea of responsibility for psychic reality, since from the psychoanalytic viewpoint ethical principles are not limited to behaviour with the external objects but also involve the internal ones. Furthermore, although Klein never spoke in philosophical terms, she thought that the emotional meaning of the external world depended on the relation between the self and the internal objects. It is not strange that Meltzer considers Klein's model of the mind evocative of theology, since we can easily imagine the Kleinian position as localizing divine grace in the internal objects and assigning the narcissistic and childish aspects of the self the power of free will to obstruct or accept the gift of grace, if you allow me a somewhat free version of Saint Thomas Aquinas.

I would now like to discuss the ways in which the creative power of the internal objects may be obstructed or enhanced by the ways in which we exercise our ethical and personal responsibility for our "eternal fate". In my opinion, the Kleinian ideas have contributed greatly to the elucidation of this question of ethics, with the concept of integration illuminated by the aesthetic conflict proposed by Meltzer.

Meltzer considers that one of Melanie Klein's most surprising discoveries, from the ethical point of view, is that the differentiation between good and bad, which begins with splitting and idealization, gradually improves its balance between benevolences and malevolence as integration proceeds. The idea of integration is the key to Kleinian theory. Although it comes up early in her work, she develops it in greater depth and breadth in her paper, "Envy and Gratitude" (1957). I am aware that there are many ways to define integration, but I propose that we consider it as the *development of the capacity for containing one's own emotional experience*. The capacity for integration means withdrawal of the bad aspects of the self that had been projected into the internal objects. This withdrawal implies a rehabilitation of the internal parents and can be considered, in my opinion, as a form of possible reparation undertaken by the infantile self. In other words, this is a modest contribution by the infantile self to the possibility that the internal parents—no longer infiltrated by bad parts of the self—repair each other.

The link between ethics and aesthetics

I think that the aesthetic conflict implies a change of paradigm in the sense that conflict in relation to the present object is prior in significance to anxieties with regard to the absent object. In

Meltzer's vision of developmental processes, Klein's conception of the depressive position

> ... stands human values on its head, looking back at the relin-quished object instead of forward to development and the pos-sibility of an enriched object which the very relinquishment makes attainable. It has, as it were, a linear structure of posses-sion and loss, rather than a complex image capable of gather-ing both past and future into the immediacy of the present experience. [Meltzer, 1988, p. 27]

He goes on to say that

> Bion has seen it more correctly in his little formula $Ps \leftrightarrow D$ as the repeated oscillation in integration and values that must be traversed with every "catastrophic change" throughout life. [p. 27]

Another consequence of the change of paradigm implicit in the idea of aesthetic conflict is that the epicenter of mental pain is no longer situated in the absence of the gratifying object: it shifts towards a new focus—the incipient disappearance of the object of admiration and awe, or of reverence and awe in Bion's words. The accent is now placed on the fleetingness of the emotional moment when the symbol is born, open to the new and the unknown, constantly questioning. Meltzer says that it was only in "Envy and Gratitude" (1957) that Melanie Klein broke with the assertion that mental pain was related to frustration, and that even then this break was not complete. According to Meltzer (1988, p. 19), it was Bion who solved this ambiguity in Learning from Experience (1962), ". . . when he described emotions as 'links' (L, H and K) and threw over the traditional dualities of love and hate in favour of a more complex and philosophically far more penetrating confrontation". This confrontation is now conceived of as a struggle between emotionality—love, hate, and the desire to know—and anti-emo-tionality—hypocrisy, passivity, and philistinism. From this per-spective, the good and the gratifying as well as the bad and the frustrating have been unknotted. In this model, the good is what enables one to go on thinking.

I would now like to make a connection between the concept of integration linked to reparation, as discussed in the previous section, and the ideas on aesthetic conflict. A point that they undoubtedly share is the concept of interiority. The main element in the aesthetic experience is the enigmatic quality of the inside of the object, since its central experience of pain resides in uncertainty verging on suspicion. I think that the aesthetic conflict, with its spatial view of the mind, introduces the idea of concern for the integrity and privacy of the interior of the object, for what we could call the object's private self. I consider that this concern checks the peremptoriness and violence of the trespassing of the boundaries of the object's privacy by means of projective identification, and it is also a thrust towards integration in the direction of taking back into one's own mind those aspects of the self that have been intruders inside the object. The acceptance of the opacity of others' minds, and even of one's own mind, strongly affects both the way we relate to our objects and the way we conceive of our task as psychoanalysts.

The ethics of technique—the working atmosphere

Also in relation to our task as psychoanalysts, I would like to include a final point in this presentation: the ethics of technique in Meltzer. He thinks that the psychoanalytic method has—and acquires for some of his patients—an aesthetic quality. He also tells us that each analyst's model of the mind influences the atmosphere in his or her office; it is this emotional working climate that I wish to discuss now.

In her article "Personification in the Play of Children" (1929), Melanie Klein said ". . . that the analyst must simply be a medium in relation to whom the different imagos can be activated and the phantasies lived through, in order to be analyzed" (p. 209). This is quite a modest position with respect to the analyst's role in the transference, to which Meltzer adds a dimension: he proposes that the transference object is not the analyst himself or herself, but rather the analyst's internal objects, which the analyst shares with his or her patients. The analyst's relation with his or her own internal objects is the origin of intuition for understanding the patient; in this sense, something about the atmosphere in the office is very similar to the upbringing of children in family life.

The container–contained model that Bion contributes is useful for Meltzer when he describes the analytic situation. Sometimes, with some patients, the entire analysis must be contained for a time in the analyst's mind, but in a developing psychoanalytic process the container is formed by the analyst's attentive receptiveness and the patient's cooperativeness. This shared responsibility for the analytic task transforms the relationship between analyst and patient into a work group of two, operating in a non-authoritarian atmosphere in which each does his or her job according to his or her capabilities. The function of understanding, divested of the expectation of knowing, allows for greater freedom to speculate and to make imaginative conjectures.

The atmosphere created by an analyst who opens up his or her mind, showing and sharing how he or she thinks, encourages the patient's development. The analyst's aspiration is not to increase knowledge, but to resolve confusions in development, to clarify forms of dependence on the good objects, and to explore the way the narcissistic aspects of the personality try to sequester the infantile aspects. If this objective is accomplished, while at the same time shifting the basis of value judgement from moral to developmental criteria, it is possible to stimulate the curiosity to explore both motivations and consequences and to sustain interest throughout the emotional storms.

This benevolent attitude towards infantile structures whose bent is mistaken, and even towards the narcissistic aspects rivalling with the internal parents, excludes any compromise with the perverse areas of the personality that would drain the vitality from object relations. The technical tool for detecting these areas of the mind in the paradoxes of thought is provided by Bion's contribution on the L, H, and K links, and the formulation of the negative grid of attack on emotionality and truth. From this perspective, the end of an analysis requires previous investigation of the extent to which the patient's life situation reflects compromises that fall short of ethical requirements originating in the parental objects. Analysis thus conceived leads necessarily to an ethical position that involves reviewing the patient's way of life and treatment of others, the way sexuality is tinged with perversion, the relationship with money, and so forth.

The journey's end

I consider that Meltzer's work, a post-Kleinian development, always evidences concern for the subject of mental development. Just as Meltzer explicitly proposes an aesthetic perspective from which to consider development—that *development is beauty*—in this chapter, I have tried to convey what I have detected as a more implicit ethical point of view in his psychoanalytic conception of mental growth: in parallel, I would say that *growth is ethics*.

I hope that the end of this journey has brought us to a new point of departure, one enabling us to set out on new explorations. The idea of development—both of persons and of ideas—puts us in touch with the past, the present, and the future, not as linear development, but rather as a space impregnated with discovery and rediscoveries, invariance and transformation. Development viewed in a linear and causalistic way not only flattens our expectations for the future, but also deprives us of a meaningful anchor to our history. This is why I think that our next journey might perhaps begin once more with the origins of psychoanalysis, and that a new Wolf Man might return and tell us how it was in those pioneering times when they embarked on the exploration of a recently discovered territory, where much terrain is still awaiting discovery.

CHAPTER FOUR

The beauty and the violence of love

Didier Houzel

M elanie Klein was fundamentally original in the way, for example, she so quickly adopted the second theory of the instincts as proposed by Freud in 1920 in *Beyond the Pleasure Principle*, in spite of the fact that, at the same time, it was rejected by most psychoanalysts. Klein's support for the theory of the death instinct constituted one of the sources of her remarkable gift for exploring the world of psychosis and the more primitive levels of psychic development. That said, she never really succeeded in integrating the concept of the death instinct with her own metapsychological model; she endeavoured to assign to all mental suffering and to every defence mechanism some degree of fantasy content based on a libidinal or aggressive cathexis either of the individual's own body or of the object. She did this, for instance, in her earlier writings where, following Karl Abraham, she described the aggressive impulses of infancy in terms of oral, anal, urethral, and muscular attacks, this sadistic phase reaching a climax at the end of the first year of life. Once she had adopted

---

Translated from the original French by David Alcorn.

the theory of life and death instincts, she was able not only to investigate the deepest layers of the unconscious even more thoroughly, but also to draw up such an outstandingly coherent map of the mind and its development that, even today, its riches are far from exhausted. Nonetheless, Klein did to some extent fail in her attempt to formulate a concrete description of mental and psychopathological processes, in so far as her sole reference was to zones and functions of the body; it was only at a much later date, when she introduced the concept of envy (1957), that she went some way to remedying this situation. But even then her description remained incomplete, given that she still felt obliged, in her account of its pathogenic and non-pathogenic effects, to claim that envy was constitutional in origin; in so doing, she moved away from the field of investigation specific to psychoanalysis, something that never fails to generate serious epistemological, theoretical, and even technical difficulties.

It was left to Bion to take the decisive step that returned the concept of primary envy to the metapsychological fold, thanks to his model of an object whose role is to contain projections directed at it and transform them into thinkable elements. Thereafter, it became possible to conceive of envy and its vicissitudes in terms of deficiencies in the containing and transforming functions of the object. Bion used the concept of reversed alpha function and the negative grid to describe the processes involved when such fundamental deficiencies occur; it was no longer necessary to refer to a domain extraneous to metapsychology, as Klein had done with constitutional factors. It must, however, be admitted that Bion's descriptions remain general and abstract; their bare bones lack the kind of flesh that would bring them fully to life and make them suitable not only for a retrospective understanding of session material or therapeutic processes, but also for getting to grips with the here and now of a session, thereby encouraging the analyst in his or her work of creating metaphors with which to formulate interpretations that lead to change.

It fell to Donald Meltzer to breathe life into what had remained too much of an abstraction in Klein's and Bion's theories. Giving life in this way means not only showing how processes are implemented in mental space according to recognizable criteria, but also supplying them with imaginative substance and emotional content. In formulating his ideas on projective identification into the internal object, the geography of the mind, and the aesthetic conflict, Meltzer did precisely this. In this chapter, I concentrate on this third innovation, which, to my way of thinking, has changed the very bedrock of metapsychology (Meltzer & Harris Williams, 1988a).

The theory of the aesthetic conflict gives us a new understanding of the issues Freud raised in 1920 when he introduced the idea of the death instinct. The impact of the aesthetic object on the nascent Self lies at the heart of primary destructiveness. Mental growth can be considered as a means of escaping from this destructiveness and resolving the problem it causes for the Self. I see this as a dynamic feature that can be expressed as follows: the loved object possesses so much attraction that the Self is threatened with annihilation. In my view, a dynamic perspective on the theory of the aesthetic object calls for a kind of hypothesis similar to that of the black hole in astrophysics. The Self is threatened with destruction in the same way that all matter and energy caught up in the gravitational field of a black hole is doomed to disintegration. It is the aesthetic object's seductive force, its very attractiveness, that is at the root of that primary destructiveness Freud called the death instinct. Thus beauty—in Meltzer's sense— and violence are intrinsically related. If it is to escape the effects of this destructiveness, the mind must develop psychic shapes to serve as levels of stability in the gradient that the caesura of birth creates between Self and object.

In previous papers (Houzel, 1989, 1995), I suggested the term "precipitation anxiety" to describe the primitive anxieties related to gradient dynamics. My first insight into this phenomenon occurred during the supervision of a child analysis I was fortunate to have with Donald Meltzer. My patient, a young psychotic boy, used to thrust little doll-figures into lumps of plasticine until they disappeared from sight. Donald Meltzer suggested that the boy was representing a very primitive version of his sexual drives, experienced as an irresistible force capable of thrusting him into an amorphous magma that could completely swallow him up. I have since identified another type of precipitation anxiety, this time in autistic children. In the analytic treatment of the autistic child, there is always a phase reminiscent of a catastrophic kind of birth that apparently threatens to drag him down into a bottom-less pit in which he will disintegrate. The autistic child often rep-resents this fantasy in a very direct and evocative way: for example, sitting on a chair, he will throw himself backwards and slide down towards the floor, head-first like a baby at birth. There is an expression of sheer terror on his face throughout all this, as though he were trying to tell us that, if a baby cannot feel wel-comed and contained by his parents' care and attention, emer-gence from the womb into the external world threatens him, in fantasy, with a destructive fall. In my view, this kind of anxiety is typical of many psychopathological structures that feature what Frances Tustin called "autistic enclaves". I shall give a clinical illustration of this in an adult neurotic patient.

I must, however, endeavour first to define the kind of stabil-ity I am referring to when I say that it is necessary to construct stable psychic forms in order to overcome precipitation anxiety. The scientific literature identifies three types: Hamiltonian stabil-ity, simple stability, and structural stability. I shall not discuss in detail the first of these. *Hamiltonian stability*, named after the Brit-ish mathematician who defined it, refers to the stability of move-ment in space with respect to a referential frame—for example, the uniform movement of a body in an absolute vacuum, with no acceleration or deceleration, as posited by the Newtonian laws of physics. The second type, *simple stability*, corresponds to the com-mon-sense idea of something that is stable—that is, a body re-mains in the same place over time for as long as there is no sufficiently strong external force to displace it. In a dynamic sys-tem such as gravity, a stable object in the sense of simple stability consumes at least some of the energy available to the system. If we imagine a spatial representation of energy strata, the body in question would be at the bottom of a valley, surrounded by higher levels of energy; if the field of forces is too weak to lift it up over the summit or crest of the mountains and into a neighbouring valley, the body will tend to return to its original position.

Structural stability, however, is dynamic, in that it is the dy-namics of the given system that generate the observed stable states, not the initial position of the body. Here, as before, stability refers to the fact that a phenomenon returns to its original state as long as its control parameters vary only within certain defined limits; this is not, however, a static position but a dynamically oriented state of the given event. In other words, even if the body moves from one position to another or is subjected to acceleration and deceleration, its state or shape remains constant. An intuitive representation of this type of stability is given by the at present well-documented fact that a dynamic system can generate states featuring such structural stability. The forms an object may adopt are no longer to be looked upon as preconceived or predetermined independently of the forces to which it is subjected, but as the actual consequences of those forces, the only constants in a system subjected to continual change. It is this kind of stability that I find helpful for understanding mental growth and symbol formation.

In *Beyond the Pleasure Principle*, Freud (1920g) refers explicitly to notions of stability in his new formulation of the theory of the instincts, particularly in the passage in which he introduces the concept of the principle of constancy:

> The facts which have caused us to believe in the dominance of the pleasure principle in mental life also find expression in the hypothesis that the mental apparatus endeavours to keep the quantity of excitation present in it as low as possible or at least to keep it constant. This latter hypothesis is only another way of stating the pleasure principle; for if the work of the mental apparatus is directed towards keeping the quantity of excitation low, then anything that is calculated to increase that quantity is bound to be felt as adverse to the functioning of the apparatus, that is as unpleasurable. The pleasure principle follows from the principle of constancy: actually the latter principle was inferred from the facts which forced us to adopt the pleasure principle. Moreover, a more detailed discussion will show that the tendency which we thus attribute to the mental apparatus is subsumed as a special case under Fechner's principle of the "tendency towards stability", to which he has brought the feelings of pleasure and unpleasure into relation. [p. 9]

The French psychoanalyst Michèle Porte (1990) points out that Freud is here making a somewhat debatable use of Fechner's principle, given that the concept to which he explicitly refers can be interpreted in the sense of structural stability; Freud, however, is obviously reading it to mean simple stability—that is, the return to a minimal energy level in the dynamic system that is for him the mental apparatus. The quotation from Fechner that Freud uses as a basis for his hypothesis runs as follows:

> In so far as conscious impulses always have some relation to pleasure or unpleasure, pleasure and unpleasure too can be regarded as having a psycho-physical relation to conditions of stability and instability. This provides a basis for a hypothesis into which I propose to enter in greater detail elsewhere. According to this hypothesis, every psycho-physical motion rising above the threshold of consciousness is attended by pleasure in proportion as, beyond a certain limit, it approximates to complete stability, and is attended by unpleasure in proportion as, beyond a certain limit, it deviates from complete stability; while between the two limits, which may be described as qualitative thresholds of pleasure and unpleasure, there is a certain margin of aesthetic indifference. . . . [Fechner, 1873, quoted in Freud, 1920g, pp. 8–9]

Fechner is also well known for defining psycho-physical laws according to which variations in sensory experience depend not on the intensity of the stimulus but on the logarithm of the ratio between two consecutive stimuli. If 1 gram is added to a 100-gram weight in a subject's hand, the person will feel no difference in sensation, whereas if 1 gram is added to a 10-gram weight, the person will feel a difference. The new sensation is proportional to the logarithm of 1 divided by 100 in the first case—an insignificant quantity—and of 1 divided by 10 in the second, a measure which is no longer insignificant. This argument contains the premises for what would later be called structural stability. Looked at from the point of view of simple stability, in both cases the applied force is the same; hence, the result—variation or non-variation of the corresponding sensation—should also be the same. However, from the point of view of structural stability, the two situations are not identical. In the first case, the perceptual field remains structurally stable—it lies within Fechner's "margin of aesthetic indifference"—whereas in the second, in spite of the fact that the absolute variation in the applied force is the same, the perceptual field is no longer structurally stable and the perceived sensation changes.

Fortunately for us, our perceptual apparatus does possess structural stability, otherwise the slightest dynamic tremor—which happens all the time—would completely disrupt our sensations, change the shape of objects in our environment, and prevent us recognizing them as similar from one moment to the next, in much the same way as occurs in nightmares. What Freud was really trying to find out perhaps was whether our mental apparatus does possess structural stability, but his failure to distinguish between simple and structural stability gave rise to a certain abstruse or even contradictory quality that, understandably enough, perplexed many of his contemporaries.

To my mind, another aspect of the same problem lies in the fact that *Beyond the Pleasure Principle* confuses two types of dynamic. In the one, which I propose to call gradient dynamics, a given event develops between two opposing poles—for example, a waterfall between two levels of altitude or electrical energy between two poles in a circuit; in the other, which I propose to call conflict dynamics, the event is subjected to two forces pulling in opposite directions. In his second theory of the instincts, Freud refers to a gradient of energy between two poles, one of which is situated at the most complex and organized extremity and the other at the least complex and least organized. Yet he is still attempting to force his theory into a mould appropriate to conflict dynamics, as he had done for his original theory, which involved two opposing forces derived from different sources: the self-preservative instincts as opposed to the sexual ones. This is no doubt what led him to give somewhat paradoxical descriptions: he writes, for example, that the pleasure principle both governs the life instinct, heir to the sexual drives, and supports the death instinct in its attempt to reduce tension and bring the mental apparatus back to a minimal level of energy.

In my view, the two types of dynamic I describe cannot be reduced one to the other; each is indispensable for mental development and functioning. In the absence of conflict dynamics, there can be no object relation. In order for there to be a relationship with an external object, there must be a gradient between Self and object, by means of which each attracts the other; however, the gradient thus created is so intense that it would precipitate the

Self into downfall and destruction if conflict dynamics were not also there to apply pressure and alleviate the downward plunge. The destructive attraction that the object represents for the Self is one of the aspects of what Meltzer calls the aesthetic conflict. In this downward plunge, the Self, attracted by the beauty of the object and under the spell of the intensity of its surface qualities, needs to encounter helpful resistant forms in order not to be swept away into destructive precipitation. Thus the Self is involved also in conflict dynamics, which I would describe as a struggle not between self-preservative and sexual instincts, but between the tendency to penetrate or even break into the object and the latter's capacity to show some resistance in the face of attempts to break into it, a capacity that is linked to the bisexual qualities of the object. I shall come back to this point after a clinical illustration of the hypotheses I am developing here.

A clinical illustration

My patient is a young woman who, when she began analysis, complained of mood swings and irritability. Shortly after beginning treatment, she told me of a recurrent dream that provoked a great deal of anxiety in her:

She could see an enormous tortoise emerging from the depths of a lake; the tortoise was bleeding from its wounds.

I took this dream to represent an autistic enclave, the emergence from which in the course of the analysis might prove extremely painful and terrifying.

The analysis began with four sessions per week. After three years, we had to reduce the frequency temporarily from four to three because of the patient's pregnancy. At the beginning of the fifth year, we went back to four sessions per week. Shortly after the resumption of our original rhythm, the patient reported the following two dreams:

In the first dream, she finds herself in a house surrounded by several children, all babies; a rat climbs on to her hand and rubs its anus against her palm, with a to-and-fro movement that she feels particularly repugnant.

In the second dream, *she is again in a house with many children. A lorry full of marvellous toys arrives; they are a gift from one of the fathers. She thinks this is wonderful, an extraordinary mark of love, but at no point does she actually see the donor.*

She associated this second dream to the analysis, where she receives so many good things. The following day, she reported another dream:

She sees one of her former student friends from the drama school that she attended as an adolescent. He has become quite famous and is beginning to make a name for himself, having directed quite a complicated production. He is accompanied by a woman and a child, and he is pulling at some backdrops placed on a kind of lorry. Suddenly, the cabin of this lorry breaks loose, changes into a plane, and flies skywards—but the sky is sort of theatrical.

In the session, the patient added that, the previous day, she had not told me the whole truth about her dreams. She had been able to tell me the dream about the generous father because she had heard me breathing gently and had assumed that I had fallen asleep and was therefore not listening to her, as though she could talk about the good things she received from the analysis and the positive aspects of the transference only if she felt that I was not paying attention to her. She went on to tell me about a telephone conversation she had had with her father; it had been an enjoyable conversation, since she had had only nice things to say to him and therefore things had gone well. She had been thinking about her life and the analysis; she wondered what else she had to work out in her analysis, since things were fine with her or at least seemed to be. She might be running the risk of raising new problems more than anything else.

I made the following interpretation: she seemed to be talking about a problem of proximity—the rat rubbing its anus against the palm of her hand, the father who brings lots of good things as long as he is not actually present (in the dream, she cannot see him), the analyst represented as offering good things as long as he is asleep and supposed not to be listening, the successful friend who flies away into a theatrical sky. I added that all this seemed to have to do with proximity to masculine figures.

She then went on to speak of how difficult it was for her to recognize her own sexual needs, and of how she tended not mention the subject in her analysis, even though she could quite easily recognize such needs in other people, particularly in her work as a psychotherapist. She then associated to a memory of her adolescence when she was attending drama school: she was having lessons from a young director who had been a pupil of Grotowski, who used to do a lot of work with the body. This young instructor also made his students do long physical exertions. One day, my patient had been unable to do the given exercise, which consisted in adopting a position as though preparing for a somersault and holding it for some considerable length of time. She had begun to cry and had had to stop. She told me that the position had brought into her mind a picture of birth. After this, she told me how anxious she felt at being an object of desire; this reminded her of an incident during her childhood when, at about 7 or 8 years of age, she had been sexually interfered with by an older boy, her cousin. This made her terrified of being desired.

A few sessions later, she reported the following dream: *She seems to be feeding children. She is preparing little tubs and putting some coloured cream dessert into them, a different colour for each child. Together, they make up all the colours that exist.*

She associated to the difficulties she experienced with her male patients. She told me of a young man she had seen again recently, who had changed completely: when she first began treating him, he was very shy and reserved. This time he was wearing a bright orange salopette, his hair was all over the place, and he had rings just about everywhere—in his ears, his nostrils. ... She had managed to establish good contact with him only after experiencing maternal feelings towards him; that had happened once she had noticed that the logo on his salopette was that of a manufacturer of children's clothing. She went on to talk about the transference and about how difficult it was for her to make transference interpretations. She then began to criticize the very idea of transference interpretations, saying that it could be a way of avoiding responsibility for what transpired between patient and therapist: "He's transferring that onto me, but it's really his problem, nothing to do with me really!!" For instance, with respect to her male patients, she could tell herself that it was nothing to do with her, it was just their transference. But in fact she did wonder what part she played in their difficulties. She then went on to speak of her own analysis, saying that I too could claim that she would have the same kind of relationship with any other analyst, so really it was nothing to do with me.

I returned to her dream material, emphasizing the coloured aspect of the food she was preparing for the children and her associations to the young man in the bright orange salopette, as an illustration of the erotic excitement she might feel in our relationship. I added that she might be afraid I would not care about this, like a mother who did not care what her child had to face up to. I referred to the maternal feelings she had experienced towards her patient and which helped her to communicate with him, and I referred also to the fact that, in the dream, the colours incorporated in the baby food were given a maternal slant, so to speak. She needed to feel that I would care for her in a maternal way and protect her from the overexcitement involved in the eroticized aspect of the transference. I linked this to the sexual interference she had been subjected to as a child, saying that she had perhaps wanted to blame her parents, in particular her mother, for not protecting her.

She told me that her parents had been aware of what was going on but had done nothing to protect her; but what she really reproached her parents with was their failure to protect her from her uncle's indelicate remarks: when she was still a young adolescent, he would say that he wanted to be her first lover. Her parents were there when he made that remark. Had they been afraid of annoying her uncle? She had never known how to defend herself; her younger sister would have handled that kind of thing much better—whenever anyone insulted *her*, she just sent them packing.

Conclusion

The material in the case study above seems to me to be a good illustration of the close links that exist between primitive anxiety related to a catastrophic birth experience, as expressed in the drama-school physical exercise, and the sexual anxiety involved in the oedipal situation, reactivated through an eroticized transference. In my view, it also highlights how important it is, for symbol formation, for psychic bisexuality to be integrated and for each parental object to mediate the other. It is on this latter topic that I would like to conclude this chapter.

As I mentioned before, in my understanding of Meltzer's theory of the aesthetic object, the caesura of birth creates a gradient of psychic energy between the Self and the object. The object thus becomes a powerful attraction for the Self, which, caught up in the surrounding gravitational field, may feel threatened with annihilation. The "black hole" model of astrophysics is particularly apposite here: all matter and all energy that fall into the magnetic pull of the black hole lose their own structure and are irretrievably engulfed. How can such a catastrophe be avoided? I suggest that symbol formation—the manner in which the mother's capacity for reverie gives shape to psychic events—generates layers of stability in the precipice into which the Self is in danger of falling. Thanks to this function, the object is no longer engulfing; it becomes, in the poet Verlaine's words, "a chosen landscape" (1869). Reverie, however, should not be seen as exclusive to the mother, for *paternal* reverie also exists: this more global view of reverie implies a mother in identification with both of her own parents, and it associates the child's father in a two-fold manner—indirectly, through the importance he has in the mother's eyes, and directly, through his own cathexis in his infant.

My basic hypothesis is that integration of psychic bisexuality is necessary for slowing down gradient dynamics in the way I have mentioned—that is, by means of the dynamics of conflict. Opposing forces confront each other, and out of these confrontations new areas of equilibrium and new layers of stability can arise. The rawness of the infant's drives and of the mother's attractiveness has to face the challenge of the paternal elements, integrated firstly as the containing object, then as the combined object, and finally as the primal scene. The dynamics of conflict can generate stable psychic shapes, endowed with a stability that is *structural* rather than merely *simple*. These stable forms are what, following Freud, we call "representations".

That is how I conceive of the necessary mediation by the paternal object of the infant's relationship to the maternal object. It operates, of course, in the oedipal situation with the prohibition of incest, but it is present before this, for instance in what Melanie Klein defined as the process of "reparation", and earlier still in what I have proposed to call the bisexuality of the psychic envelope or container (Houzel, 1997). The containing object must possess maternal/feminine aspects and paternal/masculine ones combined in correct proportions if it is to have the requisite qualities that enable it to be receptive without laying itself open to breaking and entering; in this way, the container can gather together the various projections it receives and allow them to begin to combine amongst themselves.

In return, the relationship to the paternal object must be mediated by the maternal one, otherwise the former is experienced as a destructive object trespassing brutally on the space of the Self and generating an exciting kind of attraction that cannot be worked through. This was the way the rat appeared to my patient when she dreamt of how it rubbed its anus against the palm of her hand, at the point in her analysis in which the increase in the number of sessions reawakened an eroticized paternal transference; she was able to link this to her abusive cousin, while the good idealized aspects of the paternal figure were projected into the generous but invisible donor-father of the second dream or the brilliantly successful friend from drama school who flies off into the sky. To the boy in the oedipal situation, a paternal object unmediated by the maternal one would resemble the statue of the Commander in *Don Juan*, tearing him away from the delights of a purely feminine world and precipitating him into hell.

CHAPTER FIVE

Keats's "Ode to Psyche"

Meg Harris Williams

K eats's "Ode to Psyche" is one of the most beautiful and original poems in the English language, though rarely recognized as such. More usually it is taken as his slightly stumbling first effort at a personal ode form before the better-known Great Odes: more straightforward in its emotional tone, and less susceptible to convenient forms of cynical modernist interpretation. The poem is a joyous hymn to inspiration. It has its doubts and its questions, but they are answered immediately by the poet himself—leaving nothing for the critical intellect to do. Indeed, nobody *could* answer them but the poet, since they are questions of vision, not of value or interpretation—asking, what is he seeing? not, what does it mean? What can a well-qualified critic do with a poem in which he is so evidently regarded as superfluous? There are, of course, cynical solutions which can help the reader evade the impact of the poem. It has been taken as voyeuristic self-indulgence; it has been taken as a political or social allegory of literary pedigree—the lower-middle-class young poet claiming that it is time for him to supersede those jaded old Olympians (Shakespeare, Milton, Byron, etc.). "Quite the little poet!" as one of Keats's acquaintances described him (to his humorous disgust) during his lifetime (letter in Gittings, 1987, p. 212.).

Recognizing that there is a problem in trying to confront the poem head-on (a problem of the "dazzle of the sunrise" type), I would like here to approach it "sidelong" (to borrow a word of Keats's), by offering a brief sketch of its psychological and artistic background—Keats's personal struggle. Luckily we have an enormous amount of information for this, owing to his uniquely intimate journal-letter of February–May 1819, which was written to his brother George and his wife. George had married hastily and emigrated to America the previous summer, leaving Keats to nurse their youngest brother Tom, who then died of tuberculosis in December 1818. The journal culminates in the "Ode to Psyche", which was written at the end of April 1819, and marks Keats's spectacular recovery from the depression and writing-block that beset him after Tom's death. The journal records in prose and poetry the fascinating process of his battling with and gradual emergence from that depression. By 19 March, Keats can say: "Ask yourself whether I have not that in me which will well bear the buffets of the world", adding that a recent sonnet that he is about to transcribe "was written with no Agony but that of ignorance; with no thirst of anything but knowledge when pushed to the point" (in Gittings, 1987, p. 230). The agony at Tom's death is in the process of being transmuted into an agony of ignorance, and his saviour will be "knowledge". At the same time, also pushing Keats to the point during that period, are enigmatic hints of his growing involvement with Fanny Brawne. Both these propellants allow for recognition of his "violent temperament", which, he says, has always been "smothered", repressed; now it can become fuel to his recovery (p. 230). The characteristic language of the journal during the weeks before writing the "Ode" recalls earlier descriptions in which he sees his poetic course as a journey through vast tracts of air and space, for which he needs to be "fledg'd" (p. 92). Keats now envisages himself as "straining at particles of light in the midst of a great darkness—without knowing the bearing of any one assertion of any one opinion. Yet may I not in this be free from sin?" (p. 230). Lack of knowledge is not a "sin" when the context is one of striving towards it: "Do you not think I strive—to know myself?" Gradually aspects of potential knowledge—glimmerings of light, the brushing of fledgling wings—make themselves felt in the space, in the darkness, "pressing on his identity" (a characteristic phrase of Keats's). They are, in the literal (and Bionic) sense, "feelings", registered by the actively unconscious mind. These impressions begin to make shapes and sensuous patterns. Such patterns cannot occur in mid-air, disembodied, but only in conjunction with the mind that receives them. They correspond in fact to what Keats is soon to describe as the "provings and alterations and perfectionings" that make an "intelligence" into a "soul" with its own individual identity (p. 251). That is how he puts it in his famous description of the "Vale of Soul-making", written just before the "Ode to Psyche" and intimately twinned with that poem, in the roles of aesthetic theory and aesthetic practice.

Keats's "system of salvation" (as he calls it) is often spoken about as if it were another neo-Christian justification of the value of suffering—in its most degraded form, none other than the British stiff upper-lip. But suffering in itself has no virtue for Keats—unless in the older equivalence of "passion" and "suffering". There is a sense in which every feeling, every impression, disturbs the developing soul. The heart must "feel and suffer in a thousand diverse ways" if it is to act as medium between the world and the soul. Keats summarizes his "system" in the following words:

> I began by seeing how man was formed by circumstances— and what are circumstances?—but touchstones of his heart?— and what are touchstones?—but provings of his heart?—and what are provings of his heart but fortifiers and alterers of his nature?—and what is his altered nature but his soul?—and what was his soul before it came into the world and had these provings and alterations and perfectionings?—An intelligence—without Identity—and how is this Identity to be made? Through the medium of the Heart? And how is the heart to become this Medium but in a world of Circumstances? [p. 251]

It is through the heart—the seat of emotion—that the mind "sucks its identity". It requires "circumstances" in order to function, to have something to digest. Such "touchstones" set the process in motion. For identity, unlike intelligence, is not a quality or attribute but a structure; by nature, it has to grow, to take shape. In

Keats's view, this is what differentiates the souls of adults from those of children: children are born with "sparks of God's own essence" and return directly to God, whereas the "salvation" of adults takes place according to their individual identity. And for Keats, "salvation" is synonymous with soul-making.

Almost everything in the February–May journal-letter records some minute "touchstone" by means of which Keats reshapes his soul at that period, working towards the revelation of the "Ode to Psyche". Here I shall just describe two of the landmarks that are particularly relevant to an appreciation of how the material of the "Ode" finds its form. The first is an account of a dream, which Keats associates with his reading of the story of Paolo and Francesca in Dante, and which also echoes Apuleius' description of the myth of Psyche (the source for the "Ode"):

> I had passed many days in rather a low state of mind and in the midst of them I dreamt of being in that region of Hell. The dream was one of the most delightful enjoyments I ever had in my life—I floated about the whirling atmosphere as it is described with a beautiful figure to whose lips mine were joined as it seemed for an age—and in the midst of all this cold and darkness I was warm—even flowery tree tops sprung up and we rested on them sometimes with the lightness of a cloud till the wind blew us away again ... [p. 239]

Keats then wrote a sonnet on the dream—but this, he said, had "nothing of what I felt in it". (And, indeed, the poem cannot be written after the dream—the dream must occur during the writing of the poem itself.) Yet in Keats's letter, there is another side to this dream of warmth and delight. Immediately before, he refers to a matter that had greatly tormented and infuriated him— namely, a series of faked love letters that an acquaintance had written to his brother Tom before his death, and which Tom had taken as genuine, causing much distress. Keats had recently been looking over this tawdry correspondence, and it had taken on a peculiar significance for him, of a death-dealing false art. It was as if Tom's life, and the soul of poetry, had had insufficient "violence of temperament" to ward off this grotesque caricature of the Muse who brings love and poetry. Returning to the delightful dream, we can see that this, also, has acquired something of the claustrophobia that exists in the original Dante—the windblown warmth without structural anchorage. It has something of the "smothering" quality that Keats described as repressing his healthy "violence". "He is a rat", says Keats of the letter-faker; "I will harm him all I possibly can" (p. 239). But, as yet, Keats the poet is not "fledg'd"; he is still being blown up or blown about by his emotions. However, he is gathering the fuel necessary for poetic flight, structural soul-making.

The next phase (a week later) is the stunning transformation of the rat-Muse into "La Belle Dame Sans Merci". In this well-known ballad, written on 21 April, Keats brings together the two faces of the Muse (delight and death) in the genuine sense of aesthetic conflict. This time the number of protagonists has increased to three (which, as the ancient Greeks knew, is the maximum number required for infinite dramatic potential): a knight, a lady, and a listener or questioner who asks the knight to relate his story. It is the questioner who has *the dream of the poem*; the knight, who falls in love with the lady—sits her on his pacing steed, listens to her fairy's song, eats her fairy food—has *a dream within the poem*:

> She took me to her elfin grot
> > And there she wept and sigh'd full sore
> And there I shut her wild wild eyes
> > With kisses four.
>
> And there she lulled me asleep
> > And there I dream'd—Ah woe betide!
> The latest dream I ever dreamt
> > On the cold hill side.
>
> I saw pale kings and princes too
> > Pale warriors, death-pale were they all
> They cried, La belle dame sans merci
> > Thee hath in thrall.
>
> I saw their starv'd lips in the gloam
> > With horrid warning gaped wide
> And I awoke and found me here
> > On the cold hill's side.

The infant-like knight, who mistakenly believed that it was his own "pacing steed" that set the rhythm of love and nourishment (reinforced by the onward inevitability of the ballad movement), awakes to find himself—not abandoned—but one of many, a chorus of fledgling birds with starved lips gaping wide, on their mother's "cold hill side" (repeated). Like the Greek chorus, these pale warriors affirm the unwiseness of straying beyond the bounds of convention in search of experience. Does poetry have sufficient riches to sustain them? Is the food death, or dearth? The Muse giveth and she taketh away. Such is the knight's story:

> And this is why I sojourn here
>   Alone and palely loitering;
> Though the sedge is wither'd from the lake
>   And no birds sing.

In the poetic winter, "no birds sing" (another repeated phrase). The common-sense solution to periods of dearth, as the questioner points out at the beginning of the poem, is to store your larder ready for winter like a squirrel:

> The squirrel's granary is full
>   And the harvest's done.

This is the granary of worldly and emotional securities. The ambiguity of the ballad lies ultimately with the questioner: he is no ordinary squirrel, or he would not have been straying late by the lakeside, inviting this encounter with the knight of poetry. The end of the poem appears to return to the beginning: on the edge of the lake, the knight "loiters" (an evocative word—like an adolescent on a street corner), and the questioner looks on. But now, he has listened; the knight's dream rings in his ears, though no birds sing. And his own story has yet to be told. Will he tamely follow the squirrels back to their cosy nests, or will he even now be tempted to follow the knight, in search of fairy food and flowers, despite the "horrid warning" of his dream? Even as we phrase this choice we realize that the choice has been superseded by the very existence of the poem. The ballad form is always a march of fate, but in this case the march halts at the feet of the third actor. The questioner is in a position to know more than either the squirrels or the starving fledglings; the dimensions of the experience expand; another dream is taking place.

It is Keats's joke to say, after transcribing the poem, "we must temper the Imagination as the Critics say with Judgment" (p. 244).

The joke is that the aged academic dichotomy between imagination and judgement (sense and sensibility, etc.) has now itself been superseded. Now the questioner becomes the poet of the "Ode to Psyche", written at some point within the next ten days. Meanwhile Keats has been experimenting with ways of expanding and loosening the sonnet form ("freeing the Muse's garlands", softening its "pouncing rhymes"), and his ode form is irregularly based on extended, interlinked sonnets, but eschewing the aggressiveness of the couplet, and instead pivoting the sections on short lines drawn from the ballad form; thus, echoes of the ballad's onward movement reinforce the ode's unfolding pageantry. It is, says Keats, the first time he has taken "even moderate pains" with his writing, and "I think it reads the more richly for it" (p. 253). This more capacious and fluid form is capable of responding to the type of mental search that the poet needs to conduct within it. It transcends the trickiness of the sonnet, the shapelessness of the "floating" dream, and the fatefulness of the ballad. The pace is variable and allows for question, pause, revelation, and affirmation. The diction also varies, between Keats's characteristic sensuous word-clusters ("cool-rooted flowers, fragrant-eyed") and emphatic simplicity ("Holy the air, the water and the fire"). Above all, the focus is both outward- and inward-looking—preserving the space or caesura between the goddess Psyche and the individual poet's own soul. Her story and his coexist. There is an active and a passive component to his dream.

The opening lines of the "Ode" are indelibly printed with echoes of Milton's *Lycidas*, the poem in which Milton comes to terms with his grief over his mother's death:

O Goddess! Hear these tuneless numbers, wrung
    By sweet enforcement and remembrance dear . . .

The lines are a type of poetic shorthand, whose emotional content can probably hardly be understood unless one hears Milton behind them, saying:

I come to pluck your berries harsh and crude,
And with forced fingers rude
Shatter your leaves before the mellowing year.
Bitter constraint, and sad occasion dear,
Compels me to disturb your season due . . . [lines 2–6]

The opening lines of *Lycidas* are, like "Psyche", a revised sonnet, in fact a sonnet that is broken by the force of the emotion it contains—hence force, shatter, pluck, compel, disturb, and so forth. The "leaves" (laurels) of poetry are shattered by the violence of grief. And, in muted form, the entire impact of *Lycidas* is compressed into those two lines of "Psyche". Keats, in his tentative approach to the Muse of his poem, says that his language is "tuneless"—"wrung" from his inner urgency. He knows from Milton that the Muse will hear the poet's appeal even—or especially—if it is dull or dissonant, and that "violence" of temperament is no disqualification. This is not only his grief over Tom, but in a more abstract way (as in *Lycidas*, where Milton expresses the same thing) his rage over poetry-killing forces in the art world and in the world in general—the "rat" who wrote fake love-letters and killed Tom. Indeed, the idea of "Tom" which we deduce behind Keats's work at this point no longer represents merely his brother, but a personification of vulnerable nature; it also seems to lie behind the remarks on the salvation of children—whose souls have not had the chance to be "made".

And although "Psyche" is a poem of happiness, not of suffering in the ordinary sense, it is none the less essential that this muted violence should be present in it, and part of, its motivation, for this is what makes it a poem of soul-making—a poem in which the desire for knowledge is real. Immediately there is a distinction drawn between a dream such as the Paolo and Francesca one, and this poem-dream:

> Surely I dreamt to-day, or did I see
>   The winged Psyche with awakened eyes?

This is a dream with "awakened eyes": the poet's inner state is responding to Psyche's own recent awakening—from sleep and from neglect. ("I am more orthodox than to let a hethen goddess be so neglected", wrote Keats: p. 253.) Psyche, the Soul, moves from a state of abstraction, to embodiment as a goddess: a movement co-extensive with the opening of the poem itself. This process of entering-in to the poem reflects Keats's idea in the "Soul-making" letter that "Mediators" such as those of heathen mythology greatly simplify the "system" of soul-making (p. 251). His description suggests that indeed these "mediating" figures make the bridge between the infant consciousness and the growing personality to which "identity" has begun to accrue.

The first stanza of the poem, depicting the embrace of Cupid and Psyche in their forest bower, is a reformation of Keats's Paolo and Francesca dream. The bower replaces the dream's restless floating; the figure of Cupid replaces the poet as lover; and, unlike the dream, "their lips touched not"—the moment is of arrested time, before and after a continually renewed lovemaking, "ready still past kisses to outnumber". Thus there is no voyeuristic quality; the moment responds to the dreamer, and, as he enumerates its features, gives him the opportunity for leisurely recognition:

> The winged boy I knew;
> But who wast thou, O happy, happy dove?
> His Psyche true!
> O latest born and loveliest vision far
> Of all Olympus' faded hierarchy!

The emotional route to recognition is via Cupid, who—as love—is already known to the poet; it is the connection between love and the soul which comes as a revelation to him. "His Psyche true" echoes in rhyme and rhythm the Belle Dame's words to the knight, "I love thee true". She had spoken in her "language strange" which he had first assumed he understood, and later doubted when she abandoned him. Here there is no such ambiguity, since the poet is not swept up in the same close identification. He is not part of it; he does not possess it; he cannot be abandoned by it. Instead, the "love" shines on him mediately, reflected from the vision of the Mediator.

At the beginning the poet had spoken of his "tuneless numbers", and indeed the ode's sensuousness has been primarily visual, but from this point the ode is infused with music:

> Fairer than Phoebe's sapphire-regioned star,
>   Or Vesper, amorous glow-worm of the sky;
> Fairer than these, though temple thou hast none,
>   Nor altar heaped with flowers:
> Nor virgin-choir to make delicious moan
>   Upon the midnight hours — . . .

At the beginning the poet had been unsure whether he was dreaming or seeing—whether his eyes were "awakened". His tuneless numbers were the only way he could approach the goddess. But now, as he enumerates the attributes of worship that Psyche—as a new goddess—would appear to lack, he finds that paradoxically, they do in fact seem to accrue to her, but in a way generated by her own internal qualities rather than by religious custom (those days of "happy pieties"). The voice, the lute, the pipe, come to be emanations of Psyche herself, like her own "lucent fans,/Fluttering among the faint Olympians". And now the poet can make the confident and emphatic statement:

I see, and sing, by my own eyes inspired.

This line is the hinge of the poem: when the poet commits himself to the reality of his vision and the worship of the new goddess. His previous gods of poetry fall back into the shadows, like Milton's pagan gods before the brightness of "Christ's Nativity" (in his ode of that name—the other major influence on "Ode to Psyche"). Yet, as with Milton's, their colour and music is transferred onto the next generation. Immediately Keats repeats the lines, almost word for word, with an aura of ritual transfer and confirmation—their music is now *his*.

And this is peculiarly the poet's function. Inspired by internal qualities of the Muse, he now sees that his job is to echo and reflect them, re-using the sensuous materials of his art: "So let me be thy choir . . . thy voice, thy lute, thy pipe . . ." etc. With repetition comes intensification and, also, the establishment of a teaching relationship. The poet is learning to play his part, faithfully tracing poetry's sensuous qualities—going "the same steps as the Author", as Keats wrote some time back in the journal (p. 93). This is the firm basis on which he now comes to that "untrodden region" of his own mind, to make the glorious affirmation of the final stanza:

Yes, I will be thy priest, and build a fane
    In some untrodden region of my mind,
Where branched thoughts, new grown with pleasant pain,
    Instead of pines shall murmur in the wind:
Far, far around shall those dark-clustered trees
    Fledge the wild-ridged mountains steep by steep;
And there by zephyrs, streams, and birds, and bees,
    The moss-lain Dryads shall be lulled to sleep;

And in the midst of this wide quietness
A rosy sanctuary will I dress
With the wreathed trellis of a working brain,
    With buds, and bells, and stars without a name,
With all the gardener Fancy e'er could feign,
    Who breeding flowers will never breed the same:
And there shall be for thee all soft delight
    That shadowy thought can win,
A bright torch, and a casement ope at night,
    To let the warm Love in!

And now we can see the identity between poetry-making and soul-making, the sensuous and the supra-sensuous. "To let the warm Love in"—the short (three-foot) ballad-style line that triumphantly concludes the poem—is a joyous revision of "La Belle Dame's" reiteration of being left "On the cold hill's side". The difference derives from the fact that, at last, the poet has discovered his active role—has discovered how to work on his materials without possessing either Love or the Muse; has discovered the conditions in which his mind and thoughts may grow; has discovered, in short, that Psyche's bower is the ideal source (in the sense of Platonic pattern) of the Vale of Soul-making. The poet will build a shrine in some untrodden region of his mind—a construction of welcome and receptivity, not of capture or ownership. This new knight is not a rider, a drifter, or a colonizer; he has discovered that he is in fact a builder. This is the nature of his "priesthood"; he must build his mental salvation. By implication, even when the shrine appears unoccupied, the poet is not abandoned—his role tending the small garden amongst the lofty pine-thoughts still carries on. "Pleasant pain" is a condition of "new growth". While poetic Fancy breeds flowers for him, responding to his handiwork, the high branches wave and imperceptibly multiply, murmuring amongst themselves, without his direct intervention.

Far, far around shall those dark-clustered trees
    Fledge the wild-ridged mountains steep by steep . . .

Steep by steep, step by step, the mental landscape unfolds, "fledging" the brain by following its terraced contours—establishing "clusters" of meaning, felt on the pulses. In the cinematic vision of this stanza, the wild and distant vision ("far, far around"—"dark" "wild" and "steep"), with its aura of mystery and inaccessibility, gradually focuses down to the "wreathed trellis" image of the wrinkled brain-folds. But now, we note, the "wild wild eyes" of the Belle Dame have lost their terror. The descending movement echoes, but revises, the floating from treetop to treetop of the Paolo and Francesca dream, and the myth in which Psyche was carried to earth by gentle winds. (It also echoes the descent of Peace in Milton's "Nativity Ode".) But it is no aimless floating; it is, rather, a "fledging": it delineates a structure. The focus moves to the garden within nature's wildness, the intimate area of cultivation, with its bee-sounds (zephyrs–streams–birds–bees–moss–Dryads–sleep-midst-quietness)—like Yeats's "bee-loud glade"—and ultimately, to the "window ope at night".

Now Cupid's nightly visits to the realms of "shadowy thought" can be made without interference (what Milton calls the "nightly visitation unimplored": *Paradise Lost*, IX.22); for one type of work goes on in the day, another type at night. Reversing the myth in which Cupid is burnt by the candle-flame, "Love" is moved by inner warmth to the candle-light of the soul; and the open casement, which leads to the garden of the working brain, reforms the bleak separation in "La Belle Dame" between barren lakeside and secret granary. This new bourne or threshold (a characteristic image of Keats) is one of invitation and communication, not exclusion. Finally, the reverential opening address to the goddess Psyche—with the god Cupid—becomes at the end of the poem, through these various "working" transmutations, the intimate personal invitation to "thee"; and "Love" returns partly to being an abstract noun, transferable to a more personal circumstance. Psyche and Cupid in the sense of gods or internal objects have faded into the background, having fulfilled their mediatory function of infusing their qualities into the poet's mind.

CHAPTER SIX

"Song-and-dance" and its developments: the function of rhythm in the learning process of oral and written language

Suzanne Maiello

Preliminary remarks on rhythm

Singing and dancing are both rooted in rhythmicity. In music, rhythm is the element that organizes and structures the melody and the body of its underlying harmonies. In dancing, the rhythm determines the moment when a movement begins or ends or changes direction, and when the dancers' feet leave or meet the ground. We shall see how the rhythmic elements in song-and-dance have a holding and sustaining function, and at the same time introduce discontinuity and change.

"In the prehistory of the race", Meltzer writes, "the first leaps of imagination ... were enacted in song-and-dance" (Meltzer et al., 1986, p. 184). This may be equally true for the "prehistory" of every human individual—that is, prenatal life.

A dream that the dreamer, a woman, associated with possible intrauterine experiences, may illustrate this. She dances with a man:

> We are in perfect harmony with the sound of music that comes from somewhere, our bodies moulded to each other. There is

nothing sexual about our closeness, no tension or excitement, just a deep and total sense of well-being. Our legs and feet are in such perfect agreement that they sometimes step out of the beat of the music, without ever losing their harmonious correspondence. The most wonderful of all sensations is to feel our steps moving in syncopation with the rhythm of the music while effortlessly maintaining their movements in perfect accord. [Maiello, 1995, pp. 28–29]

The common experience of a perfect union of two bodies dancing to the same music seems to have represented a sufficiently secure base for the dreamer not only to dare, but also to enjoy stepping out of the rhythm for a moment and thereby taking the first "leaps of imagination"—that is, making the first attempts of differentiation and creative representation. I suggest that mental development grows on the ground of a basic trust in an ongoing rhythmical object, which can, once it is securely internalized, also be playfully varied.

This chapter does not deal with the possible prenatal precursors of song-and-dance, where dancing might well be represented by the foetus's movements accompanied by the song of the mother's voice which reaches the unborn child in the amniotic bath, immersed in the ongoing rhythmical pulsating sound of her breathing and heartbeat. What is explored is the role of song-and-dance and its rhythmical structure in postnatal normal and disturbed mental development.

I suggest that the perception of the rhythmical sounds of the maternal organism during prenatal life may constitute the base that prepares the foetus to receive the sound and rhythm of the mother's voice, with its infinitely more complex articulations in terms of pitch, loudness, timbre, and rhythm. Her voice contains and conveys not only her own personal peculiarities, but also the musical line and rhythm of the language that will become the child's "mother tongue". This is where the "deep language structures" described by Chomsky (1972) could be rooted. It is worth noting that the foetus hears the low-frequency sounds of the body noises, including the heartbeat, about one month before its ear is tuned to the frequency that corresponds to the maternal voice.

The rhythmic prenatal "song-and-dance" experience is reproduced after birth every time the mother rocks the baby and sings a lullaby. But it is most significantly transformed and recreated at the breast, where the baby takes part actively in shaping the quality of this new relationship. When things go well, the baby's sucking and the mother's milk-flow adjust to each other and find a rhythm of cooperation and reciprocity. Mouth and nipple could be described as dancing to the rhythmical sounds of swallowing, together with the little guttural vocal sounds many babies produce as they suck.

The development of oral language

The first stage of language development, lalling and babbling, could be seen as a transformation of the oral experiences of rhythmicity at the breast, and at the same time as an active enriched re-creation and exploration of the rhythmical experiences at the level of "song-and-dance" in the uterine container.

Discussing a paper by Rhode (1982), Meltzer suggested that lalling was much more than "vocal experimentation to achieve mastery of the physical apparatus". In describing the events that occur in the "theatre of the mouth", he writes: "... lalling is to be seen as the vocal aspect of a more general phase in cognitive development in which the physical space of the oral cavity is utilized as the theatre of phantasy and play, a mid-point between external play and internal thought" (Meltzer et al., 1986, p. 179).

At this point, the rhythmic song-and-dance around the concrete nipple has developed into a song-and-dance experience around immaterial objects—that is, the sounds produced by the baby's voice itself. This corresponds, in Bion's terms, to the no-breast experience creating the space for symbolic thinking. In fact, following Langer's (1951) thesis of the musical base of language, Meltzer asserts that the song-and-dance level of language corresponds to "the most primitive form of symbol formation" (Meltzer et al., 1986, p. 181).

Rhythm is intrinsically part of language development. Not only is the voice of adults spontaneously more rhythmical when they talk to babies (nursery rhymes are the result of the intuitive attunement to the infant's need for rhythmicity), but the development of the baby's lalling and babbling itself is connected with its rhythm of breathing and depends on the alternation of inspiration and expiration, without which no vocal sound can be produced.

We shall see how the primordial rhythmical experiences at the level of song-and-dance have a fundamental function in the development of a feeling of relatedness with persons and things in both the external and the internal world and with language development. Rhythm in fact conveys trust through its reliability. At the same time, it introduces the principle of separation in the originary chaos of fusional at-oneness and thereby represents the first element of discontinuity and differentiation, described as a kind of prenatal "biological clock" (Mancia, 1981). Analytic thinking, counting, arithmetic, and mathematics are inconceivable without this basic structuring experience.

Through two examples, we shall try to understand the function of a rhythmical "song-and-dance" object in mental development in general, and more specifically at particular stages of learning.

Observation material of a little girl's first attempts to transpose oral language into its written form will show us the vicissitudes of rhythmical elements; clinical material from the psychotherapy of an autistic child will allow us to think about such children's lack of a primordial song-and-dance experience in and with the world, and to connect this lack with their learning difficulties.

From "song-and-dance" to "song-and-sign": on learning to write

Returning to Meltzer's formulation of the baby's lalling sounds in the mouth being somewhere in the middle between external play and internal thought, I suggest that verbalization grows out of vocalization. Both have intense communicative value and are meant for a listening ear. What verbal speech adds is a clearer articulation, in accordance with the need and capacity to convey more differentiated feelings and thoughts.

When a child masters oral language, the next step in its development, in Western culture, is the attempt to write. If lalling is "play with sounds in the mouth", speaking can be described as vocal communication aimed at conveying meaningful messages through sequences of specific sound-rhythms belonging to a shared language. Writing, which at the beginning is often accompanied by vocal sounds, reintroduces a kinaesthetic element: the movement of the hand on an external support. Meltzer's intuition prefigures this development when he completes his image of the "first myth-making leaps of imagination being enacted in song-and-dance" by saying that from that level there is "only a short step to their graphic or sculptural representation as gods and spirits" (Meltzer et al., 1986, p. 184).

This is the transition we now observe in a 4-year-old girl's first attempts to write.

"Giulia" had been drawing complete human figures for a few months. At some point, she began adding graphic signs that resembled letters of the alphabet (Figure 6.1). This drawing was commented on by her as representing "Giulia and the name". Both the number and the shape of the graphic signs

FIGURE 6.1

FIGURE 6.2

were haphazard, but she knew somehow that writing had to do with naming.

In a drawing she made a few months later, the human figure was smaller and without arms (Figure 6.2). It seemed to have lost importance in comparison with the two graphic sequences, which were large, more central, and surrounded by frames. Giulia explained that the signs below were meant to mean "For grandmummy", and the signs above, "Giulia Martini", her name. This time, she checked whether she had written the words "correctly". Her criterion was that the number of *signs* had to correspond to the number of *syllables*, and not, as the adult reader would expect, to the number of *letters*. "For— Grand-mum-my" was rhythmically right. In fact, four syllables corresponded to four signs. But when she checked her name, for which she originally had also written four signs, she discovered an error. She read, from left to right: "Giu-lia Mar-ti . . .". The last syllable was missing. She needed a fifth sign and added it on the left. She read once more, again from left to right: "Giu-lia Mar-ti-ni". Now, she was satisfied. It did not matter that the single signs did not correspond to the same syllables as before.

A month later, she went a step further in her exploration of the correspondence between oral and written language. She had found a typed letter in her father's waste-paper basket and followed the line of the signature with her felt-tip pencil. On the same sheet of paper, she "wrote" what she explained to be her father's name, in two subsequent phases.

This time, she pronounced the syllables *during* the process of writing. While her hand "danced" his name on the paper, her voice "sang" the syllables that compose it: "Fio-ren-zo" (Figure 6.3A). The three movements corresponded to the three syllables that composed his name. The correspondence was between *song* and *dance*. When she had finished, she wanted to read the signs. But since the first two movements of her hand had produced only a change in direction and not a separate graphic unit, the signs at the visual level were only two. She read: "Fio-ren . . ." and discovered that the name was incomplete. At this point, she had recognized that it was not possible to maintain the correspondence of dance *and* song *and* sign. She added the third sign (Figure 6.3B), this time in the direction of flow of her writing hand. It was composed of two movements, like the first sign, although Giulia knew it had to represent only one syllable. She read: "Fio-ren-zo".

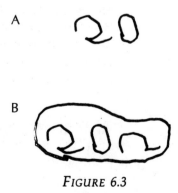

FIGURE 6.3

FIGURE 6.4

There had been a shift in priorities. Giulia had dropped the criterion of the *"dance rhythm"* and maintained only the correspondence between *syllable song* and *graphic sign*.

A few months later, when writing her little friend's name, she no longer counted the syllables but the letters, B-A-R-B-A-R-A, although she did not know the alphabet yet (Figure 6.4). There were seven signs for seven phonemes. This was the moment when Giulia also left the rhythmical base of syllable words, which had lingered on in her first attempts to write, and to explore written language with its different rules and criteria. After renouncing the kinaesthetic rhythm in her writing movements, she also dropped the criterion of the *"song rhythm"* of the syllables.

At this point (Figure 6.5), she had learnt the graphic shape of many letters, but could not yet return back from "sign" to "song". She acknowledged her inability to read and asked her mother to tell her what she had written. The mother read for

FIGURE 6.5

her: "OIAURBP" and "MIURBP". Giulia laughed whole-heartedly and repeated these funny words. But then she pointed to one of the letters and said, correctly: "This is R".

A month later, she proudly showed a drawing that represented herself standing on a pebble ground under a blue sky. Next to her image, in capital letters, she had correctly written her name (Figure 6.6).

Discussion

Giulia's material allows us to follow the complex mental processes that underlie the capacity to transform oral language into the corresponding graphic representation.

Giulia went through this learning process with active curiosity and joyful initiative, but, at the same time, her attention was, in Meltzer's terms, "patient, receptive, awaiting the advent of the 'unknown'" (Meltzer et al., 1986, p. 182). She could not foresee what would result from her graphic signs, but her basic internal "rhythm of safety" (Tustin, 1986) allowed her both to wait with confidence for the "new idea"—her wish to produce written language—to develop and manifest itself, and to abandon, one after the other, the elements of *dance rhythm* and of *song rhythm*.

At the beginning, syllable writing allowed Giulia to transpose the rhythm of oral language into its written form. A syllable is the result of the combination of a vowel with one or more consonants. "Syllable" in fact means "taken together". It could be described as a "combined object" in the process of language development—that is, the result of a primary integration of sounds. Giulia's written syllable words may represent a new edition of the basic experience of linking and matching vocal sounds that a lalling baby explores in the theatre of the mouth. The little girl seemed to have been able to abandon the rhythmical elements in the process of learning to write because she felt sufficiently anchored in an ongoing internal and interpersonal rhythmicity for her to explore new levels of symbolic representation.

Piontelli (1993) describes how children between the ages of 2 and 4 years are concerned with giving meaning to preverbal and possibly prenatal experiences and to express them in play, verbalization, and pictorial representation. But at around the age of 4, the representations of the past undergo a profound change.

I suggest that Giulia is at precisely this latter stage of transition in her development when she makes her first attempts to write. The successful outcome of this transition probably depends on the capacity to forsake basic rhythmical experiences rooted, in part, in prenatal life. I suggest, however, that these primary levels of experience are not lost, but continue to be expressed in our body

FIGURE 6.6

language, in the flow of oral language, in dreams, and in love-making, and they re-emerge in poetry, music, and the figurative arts.

Autism and the absence of "song-and-dance"

Many autistic children do not suck at the breast and do not go through the stage of lalling and babbling. Later speech is either absent or adhesively echolalic. Without the normal mental process of projection and introjection, there is no internalization of what Meltzer describes as "speaking objects from whom and in identification with whom . . . the musical deep grammar for representing states of mind can be learned" (Meltzer et al., 1975, p. 193).

There is no shared experience at the level of "song-and-dance". These children lack the basic "rhythm of safety". The endless solipsistic repetition of movements or sounds is different in its essence from the basic rhythmicity that guarantees a feeling of going-on being and results from the coming together of two elements—breast and nipple, song and dance, vowels and consonants—and is open to variations and syncopations. The autistic children's stereotypies are meant to maintain sameness by preventing or dismantling consensuality and reciprocity and shut out any experience of meeting otherness.

Without the primary interpersonal experiences of musical rhythms, these children lack the "song-and-dance" basis on which oral language grows. The absence of differentiation in space and time makes non-imitative speaking, writing, and counting impossible. Harris Williams asks what happens when children are ". . . for some reason deprived of human company during the playful, musical 'lalling' stage of life, such that they can never after become fluent in language. They could learn the cerebral 'referential' use of language . . . but never the poetic or symbolic—the music of communication" (1997, p. 5). This statement is particularly relevant in autistic and post-autistic states.

The clinical material that follows shows the importance of the first rhythmical experiences at the level of "song-and-dance" in a little patient's struggle to enter the human world.

"Rosetta" had severe autistic features when she started psycho-therapy at the age of 5. At the beginning of our work, when she recited parts of her favourite video stories with an artificial high-pitched tone of voice her speech was fluent and articulated, but the odd word or sentence she might utter with her own voice was blurred and had such a fleeting and liquid quality that it was usually gone before I could grasp the cluster of sounds that she had emitted.

In another paper, I described how

> a similar phenomenon of clustering occurred in the time sequence of our verbal interaction. In a normal dialogue, two speakers talk and listen alternatively, following a spontaneous rhythmical pattern of reciprocity. With Rosetta, it happened that when we had been silent for a while, she would start speaking at exactly the same moment as I did. I would stop, in order to hear what she was saying, but she would stop at the same time. I would then listen and wait for her to speak again. If she remained silent, I would at some point say something about my wanting to hear what she had wanted to tell me, but she would start speaking again the very moment I did, and again I could not hear what she said.
>
> The absence of rhythmical alternation had the effect of non-communication. It was as if we were both deaf, and in a way also mute. The potential dialogue broke down, because Rosetta lacked the experience of rhythmical reciprocity that develops in time. [Maiello, 1997]

At the age of 7, in her third year of psychotherapy, she began tolerating some awareness of separations and the passing of time. In the last session before a brief holiday, she looked at my wristwatch and asked when her mother would pick her up. She put her ear to the watch and listened. After a while, she looked up and said: "toc—toc—toc". She bent her head again, lightly laying her ear to my chest. When she got up, she said: "the heart".

One year later, her keener awareness of reality had increased her vulnerability. Before another one-week break, I wrote the "yes-days" and the "no-days" for her. She was more conscious now of the frustrating irregularity of the weekly rhythm of her sessions, which became more unbearable at the time of an approaching break. She muddled up the names of days and months, and the number sequences of dates. Her fragile awareness of the structure of time collapsed, and she wetted her pants. At the end of the session, she drew the outline of her hand and, on top of it, the outline of my hand. I was left in doubt as to whether she felt that her hand could be somehow contained in mine during the break, or whether she had flattened back into her adhesive state.

On her return, she was totally absent and inaccessible and endlessly repeated her stereotyped activities of being a dog on a leash. Towards the end of the second session, I took an unusual initiative, telling her that I would now write her name. She got to her feet, sat down at the table, underlined her name, and said that she wanted to write "papà" [daddy] (Figure 6.7). She wrote a capital P. It was not imitative, because there is no P in her name. It was her own internal daddy-letter. (It is interesting that an important step in Giulia's learning experience also occurred when she tried to write her father's name.) Rosetta wrote two more letters that *are* part of her name, a kind of B and the A with a rounded top, different from mine which had straight lines. She drew two more Ps and an A, which seemed to continue the sound-image of "papà", and then connected the Ps with a line at the base, saying that they were holding hands.

My active intervention had resulted in Rosetta's abandoning the autistic leash that tied her to her delusional world. There had been an interaction between the two of us as separate

FIGURE 6.7

people. She had shown me for the first time her ability to write a letter of the alphabet and to recognize it. As to the connection between the two Ps, I was not sure whether it represented a meaningful link between two separate units connected by holding hands, or whether it showed her difficulty in being on her own for any length of time without falling back into adhesive modes of functioning that brought about the loss of meaning of the original daddy-letters.

Before the following long holidays, the calendar became an important issue. This time, I decided to represent the holiday period by a bridge that stretched across the paper over the time of our separation. On its curved line, I began to write the name of the first month, which I pronounced slowly to accompany my writing hand. Rosetta's voice took over. She dictated the months correctly, our eyes and my hand following the line of the arch or the bridge.

In the very last session, she sang the chorus of Beethoven's Ninth symphony from beginning to end, with the words. Her voice was rhythmical and in tune. Her class teacher was probably preparing the children's show for the end of the school year. There was a recurrent passage that ended with "Joy". While holding the note as long as she could, she raised one hand with the help of the other and held it up with a gleeful expression. The text said something about "singing together". Rosetta stopped to ask me to join in and sing with her. Every time we reached the point of "Joy", she wanted me to raise my hands as well.

Towards the end of the session, feelings of anxiety and sadness around our separation could emerge. She took a handkerchief to dry a tear that she thought she had seen rolling down my cheek, and she drew an open mouth on the calendar, which she quickly cancelled again with a scribble. The last thing she did was to trace the letters of the months of our separation across the bridge of her calendar and to fill in all the empty spaces in the "closed" parts of the letters.

After the holidays, she produced many drawings and dared more often to face unsatisfactory results. One day, she asked

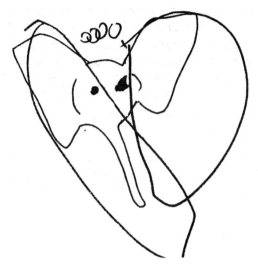

FIGURE 6.8

me to draw Dumbo, the little elephant. When I had done it, she took the pen from my hand and, in a rhythmical cadence, said: "du—du—du—du", her voice accompanying the movement of her hand, which slowly wrote four signs above Dumbo's head, from right to left (Figure 6.8).

Up to that time, she had had great difficulties in numbering. When she tried to count something on her fingers, they would move at a pace that was dissociated from the rhythm of her counting voice, and she felt the result to be meaningless. From that moment onwards, Rosetta eagerly counted the five light bulbs on the ceiling of the hallway to my practice when she came to the session. The rhythm of her words now reliably matched the movements of her pointing finger.

Towards the end of the last session before another one-week holiday, Rosetta told me a nursery rhyme that she had learnt at school. It was about the days of the week, whose names were decomposed into their syllables during the song and recomposed at the end. Clapping hands was part of the song.

She knew that we would meet again on a Monday, and she asked me to count the days with her. We did so, in unison, raising our fingers to the rhythm of our voices, from one to ten. I carefully watched that it was her voice that lead the way, not mine. I adapted her nursery rhyme to our situation, and together we said that we would meet again on "lu-lu-lu", on "ne-ne-ne", on "lu–ne–dì" [Monday], and clapped our hands, our own and each other's alternately, to the rhythm of our voices. Rosetta wanted to repeat this many times.

On her return, she happened to say something in a rhythmical way. This made her remember our Monday-rhyme. She asked me to repeat it with her. At this point, it was sufficient to do it once for her to feel that she had managed to bridge the gap of our separation.

Discussion

I suggest that there was a turning point in Rosetta's therapy when she discovered my ticking watch and then turned to my heartbeat before a separation. Her ability to begin to explore rhythmicity in interaction showed that, at some deep level, there had been a shared experience of a rhythm of going-on being, which allowed her to expose herself to a non-controllable "not-me" rhythm. In addition, her spontaneous association of a mechanical time-measuring instrument with an alive human heart was a moving and promising moment in our work.

From there, she seemed to pursue her unconscious search for experiences that could help her to create or reinforce a primordial rhythmic object at the "song-and-dance" level.

Much singing in unison, and much tracing of letters that I had written, had been necessary for her to become capable of producing what I would describe as her first "song-and-dance objects"— the chorus of "Joy" and the Monday-rhyme—in an interpersonal relationship. After that, she could make her first attempt of rhythmical writing and explore the area that leads from "song-and-dance" to "song-and-sign". When she tried to write Dumbo's name, her voice produced the syllable "du" in rhythmical correspondence with the movement of her hand, the graphic sign representing visually the sound that she was pronouncing. The rhythmical repetition of sound and movement occurred in an atmosphere of serenity and made me think of the dancer's enjoyment in the dream that I mentioned at the start of this chapter, when her feet moved in harmony with the music.

From the graphic point of view, it is worth noting that this was the first time that Rosetta had drawn open and empty shapes which were playfully related to one another. Usually, her graphic signs had stood lonely in space, she had meticulously sealed every circular shape at its closing point, and she had almost invariably filled empty spaces with colour.

The open "du-du" signs had a "song-and-dance" precursor in the "lu-lu" syllables of the Monday-rhyme, which had helped Rosetta to tolerate our brief separation without her inner space collapsing. She may momentarily have felt like the disconnected syllables of the Monday-rhyme, repeating herself in a sequence of sameness, but then the rhyme was recomposed at our reunion into a meaningful word, accompanied by the rhythmical clapping of our hands.

For encounter to become possible, there must be some tolerance of both openness and emptiness. Although the moments of communication with Rosetta were fragile and fleeting, she had started exploring experiences of joining and linking at the level of "song-and-dance" which were meaningful to both of us.

Concluding remarks

Meltzer states that "the most primitive form of symbol-formation" (Meltzer et al., 1986, p. 181) finds expression at the level of "song-and-dance". Etymologically, a "symbol" results from two units having been "thrown together"—in other words, from the experience that two elements meet in a meaningful way. Symbols "cannot be understood simply in one direction, but must be seen to enrich both members so linked" (Meltzer, 1983, p. 78).

I suggest that song and dance are meaningfully linked by their common rhythmicity. They go back to pre-symbolic experiences in prenatal and early postnatal life and represent the ground from which symbol formation develops.

As to the mental level of "song-and-sign", it is important to distinguish between signs and symbols. I am not suggesting that graphic signs *are* symbols, but the signs are the expression of the mental processes of symbolization that lead to the faculty of transposing oral language into its written form. Bion states that there is a moment in mental development when the visual dimension with its illuminating power overrides its "aural mental counterpart" (1965, p. 90).

In terms of my considerations, this is what occurs when, after the abandonment of the preponderance of the rhythmical element, the transposition of "song-and-dance" into "song-and-sign" opens the way to more abstract forms of expression of symbolic thinking.

CHAPTER SEVEN

Clinical notes on the organizing function of time during puberty

Paolo Carignani

It is my intention to present in this chapter some ideas on the development of the perception that preadolescents have of the passing of time. To do so, I refer to the theories that Freud, Klein, and Bion had about the concept of time; furthermore, I try to explore some of Meltzer's contributions on the subject. Starting from this theoretical background, I discuss some clinical material from the psychotherapy of an 11-year-old girl.

In a report commissioned by the Organisation of Economic and Cultural Development, Meltzer and Harris (1976) suggested that there could be four kinds of attitudes that the individual, the family, or the social group can maintain towards the passing of time. These four attitudes were described by means of four operative concepts: timelessness, oscillating time, circular time, and linear time. Each of the operative concepts corresponds to a different way of perceiving time and to the development of a different mental condition:

> Timelessness tends to promote sensuality and the pleasure principle into a dominant position in values, favouring a

mindless acquiescence in the compulsion to repeat that disre-
gards prior evidence of consequences.

Oscillating time favours attitudes of apathy, for it sees
the world as being controlled by overwhelming inanimate (or
anthropomorphized) forces and structures of perfect resilience. As day follows night, every action has an equal and
opposite reaction. Nothing therefore can or need be done to
alter anything. . . .

Circular time. The concept of circular time generates attitudes of cynicism. "Plus ça change, plus c'est la même chose"
. . . forms may change, but the substance of the human condition remains the same. There is neither good nor evil (but
thinking makes it so), and one may therefore stand on the
sidelines, enjoying the fruitless struggles and passions of the
unwise.

Linear time. He who sees time as linear . . . must travel and
observe, whether in the inner or outer world, to enjoy a too
brief life-space, inheritor of a beautiful estate that must be left
even more beautiful. [pp. 401–402]

These four concepts seem to describe exhaustively both the
different capacities to perceive time and the different mental functions to which these capacities relate and that in some way they
produce. The four concepts were presented by Meltzer and Harris
in a developmental order, from those representing more primitive
mental functioning to those leading to states of increasing awareness. In this chapter, I would like to inquire whether the four
concepts might be considered also as stages of growth and development in the psychotherapeutic process and in what way the
change in the perception of time can be used as a means of communication between patient and therapist. It is also my intention
to describe the use I made of what Meltzer affirms in his paper
"Adhesive Identification" (1975): "[The] processes connected with
confusion about time and attitude toward time could now be noticed more in the phenomenology of the consulting-room and
brought into the interpretive work" (p. 302). I endeavour here to
observe these processes specifically in work with a preadolescent
patient who was terrified by the approach of puberty. The observation follows two main lines of research: the first inquiring into
the mental functions that enable us to perceive the passing of time,

the second considering the role that perception of time has in the organization of mental processes. Before doing so, I would like to consider a few theoretical points.

Theoretical background

The first point of inquiry can be expressed with a question: what enables us to perceive the passing of time? Freud stated on several occasions that for the Unconscious, time does not exist (1914c, 1915e, 1918b [1914], 1920g, 1950a [1892–1899]):

> The processes of the system *Ucs.* are timeless; i.e. they are not ordered temporally, are not altered by the passage of time; they have no reference to time at all. [Freud, 1915e, p. 187]

Freud seldom enquired into the origin of the formation of the concept of time. In *Beyond the Pleasure Principle*, while describing the functioning of the *Pcpt.-Cs.* (Perception–Conscious) system he stated:

> Our abstract idea of time seems to be wholly derived from the method of working of the system *Pcpt.-Cs.* and to correspond to a perception on its own part of the method of working. [1920g, p. 28]

In another paper he stated:

> Our perception of time seems thus directly related to the particular kind of perception that the *Pcpt.-Cs.* has of itself: based on discontinuity and determined by the periodic non-excitability of the perceptual system. [1925a (1924), p. 231]

In other words, Freud stated that it is just the discontinuity of the functioning of the *Pcpt.-Cs.* system, or rather its perception of itself, which is responsible for the origin of the mental representation of time.

Klein considered the question of time marginally. Her statement about her patient "Fritz" seems to be the more significant:

> The unconscious equation of sleep, death and intra-uterine existence was evident in many of his sayings and phantasies, and connected with this was his curiosity as to the duration of

these states and their succession in time. It would appear that the change from intra-uterine to extra-uterine existence, as the prototype of all periodicity is one of the roots of the concept of time and of orientation in time. [1923, p. 99]

We see that Klein believed that the personal development of the conception of time derives from the perception of a discontinuity in one's own experiences. I think that it is possible to compare Freud's point of view with Klein's: according to Freud the origin of the idea of time derives from a discontinuity in perception; according to Klein it derives from a perception of discontinuity. Should we then assume that the discontinuity that can originate the perception of time, and the adaptation to it, belongs to the structure of the perceptive system of the human being, or rather that it is introduced by the introjection of the experience of physical discontinuity (life and death, sleep and wakefulness, intra- and extra-uterine life, etc.)? This is the first question that I attempt to explore while discussing the clinical material.

The second question is: what is the function that the perception of time assumes in developing the mental structure, in giving it its organization, in establishing a dynamic relationship between the individual and external reality? The perception of time, or, in Piaget's words (1946), the development of the notion of time, is something that appears from early childhood and, together with the perception of space, acquires vital importance in originating the equilibrium of mental development. Time and space are mental categories which organize the mind and relate the individual to his or her world, both internal and external. In child analysis we often see that the conception of time and its organizing function can be violently attacked by children who aim at destroying those limits and at annihilating the anxieties connected with them. In her "Notes on Some Schizoid Mechanisms", while describing the splitting processes, Klein added a footnote in which she expressed her agreement with W. C. M. Scott's ideas when he "stressed the importance of the breaks in continuity of experience, which imply a splitting in time rather than in space" (Klein, 1946, p. 6n). This is the second point I shall be keeping in mind when discussing the clinical material.

I present below excerpts from my work with an 11-year-old girl. I think that preadolescence is a crucial age for the development of the idea of time, as it is an age in which so many violent psychic and physical drives appear simultaneously. I think that self-perception, during the process of puberty, becomes the perception of oneself in the passing of time and makes possible a new definition of the individual. In this period of life, the conception of time as "circular" (typical of the child) is transformed into "linear", and this facilitates the preadolescent's acceptance of his or her physical and hormonal changes. I hope that these exerpts from the clinical material will enable me to throw some light on the emergence of a powerful awareness of time and on the function that this awareness can have for the development of thought.

Clinical material

The girl, "Rita", began psychotherapy at the age of 10 years. She was in a state of great mental confusion and had developed many symptoms such as permanent enchopresis, compulsive masturbation, and severe scholastic difficulties. Rita was unable to sleep in her bed at night and needed the reassurance of her parents' room and bed; she had a confused perception of herself and was in a permanent state of internal excitement. The excitement was closely related to Rita's defences and hindered the emergence of thoughts about the difficulties of growth. Rita's fragile defences barely protected her from deep anxieties of disappearing or being annihilated. One of the consequences, as her parents said, was that Rita was late in developing, and this, still according to her parents, made her uncomfortable when she compared herself to other girls of the same age.

The first thing that Rita did in her sessions was to pretend that she was an invisible and bodiless ghost, and she asked me to search for her in the room without ever finding her. One could think that as pubertal development approached, Rita's body menacingly imposed itself on her attention. Rita's game was about denying in all possible ways that she had a body. These defences,which seemed to produce the anxiety of disappearing and becoming invisible, were observable in the first months of the therapy and were followed by a continuous attempt at interrupting the functioning of her mind in an effort of self-protection: time, space, Rita herself seemed to be in a suspended condition.

During the first year of psychotherapy, Rita gradually became "visible". As the therapeutic process dealt with the conflicts related to her deeper anxieties, it became possible for Rita to look into these conflicts, therefore to become more aware of her own life and take some responsibility for it.

The short period of therapeutic work that I discuss in detail took place about 15 months after the beginning of psychotherapy. Rita was giving signs of good progress in many aspects of her life: her enchopresis had disappeared completely and masturbation diminished sensibly. She had also changed in her relationship with her family and was finding school less difficult. During the sessions, nevertheless, Rita began again, after a holiday, to play excited games in complete annihilation of space–time perception. The more significant game was "The Midnight Witch": it consisted of making the room completely dark and of saying, in a sing-song voice, the following rhyme:

> It is one and everything is fine
> It is two and everything is fine
> It is three and everything is fine
> . . .
> It is eleven and everything is evil.

At this point, Rita began to look for me in the room and I was supposed to hide. Eventually by touching me she would "find" me. Then I had to be the one to say the rhyme and to search for her. Rita was greatly excited as she played, and her game—possibly because of her excitement—did not last long. But beside the excitement there was her communication: "It is eleven and everything is evil." Rita was 11 by now, and I thought that one might understand her statement in two different ways: on the one hand, one could think of her deep suffering and of her difficulty in coping with her anxiety; on the other, one could think that she was inclined to push her thinking to its extreme consequences—"everything is evil"—as an extreme defence.

"Everything" and "nothing" were in some ways equivalent: if *everything* was evil, there was *nothing* to do except protect one-self with an exciting game, so that one would not be thinking of one's painful experience. In this way the space–time coordi-nates were lost and all possibilities of thinking about herself annihilated. Time, the time of the sessions, the time of her age, was extended until it lost all meaning. It was suspended so that all the years of her life could only lead to that fatal "It is eleven and everything is evil". If we go back to the development of the concept of time focused upon by Meltzer and Harris, I think we might say that Rita, at that time, was halfway between time-lessness and oscillating time. By making the space dark, Rita annihilated spatial coordinates and therefore was left only with the sense of hearing or even more the sense of touch, this last probably evoking her maximum excitement and causing the end of the game. Then came a new beginning: the whole sequence was possibly related to her compulsive masturbation.

My attempts at helping Rita to understand that by this game she was trying to protect herself from her fear of disappearing produced scarce results up to the moment at which, on one occasion, at the end of this game I suggested that Rita had a catastrophic idea of the passing of time: the passing of her years could lead only, according to her, to an inevitable trag-edy. She knew from her experience that her "everything is evil" was not true, but that, in reality, some things were better and some things were worse and that time had lessened her anxieties and not augmented them.

The distinction I was trying to introduce in this way seemed to penetrate her unconscious defensive theory and enabled her to begin to find in herself some new internal reference related to an awareness that some things were getting better: her rela-tionship with her parents, with the school, and, as she once said, the fact that she felt "better" than before. Rita quickly accepted my suggestion, and her game came to an end. Encour-aged by the results, I modified my interpretations significantly: instead of just underlining the quality and intensity of the anxi-ety related to the passing of time and of the conflict between her wishes and fears connected with growing, I suggested that she could find, in her own experience, some areas of functioning that were progressively improving. I suggested also that she could use for deeper and more complex aspects of her growth the same mental processes that had enabled her to make significant progress in her life at home and at school.

The perception of time was beginning to become essential as an internal reference for Rita. In a session that followed a successful mathematical test at school, Rita expressed for the first time the following thought: "If school were to finish now I would pass!" She was thinking of her school results of the first few weeks of the last term. I told her that school would not finish now, but that if she used the time left before the end of the school as she had used the time so far, working and studying her lessons, then she might pass.

One could think that Rita was seeking further comfort in an omnipotent phantasy (school could not really finish "now"), but I believe that this statement represented a significant change in her understanding of the passing of time. The recognition of temporal aspects seemed to enable Rita to discriminate between the scholastic results she had already obtained and the ones she still had to obtain in order to pass. It also enabled her to find comfort and derive new strength from the results she had already obtained, so that she could struggle forward towards new achievements. The pattern could repeat itself: Rita could rely on the experiences she had acquired and cope with more courage and decision with future ones. It seemed that Rita's theory (about everything being evil and about there being nothing to do) was losing strength when she acknowledged that she has acquired new capacities. The perception of time appeared on her mental horizon and became essential for her growth.

Acknowledgement of time in the session

In this same period Rita began to give evidence of recognizing significantly the time of the sessions. In the past she used to be 5 or 10 minutes late. Now she began to come in on time, sometimes even early. Eventually she proudly began to wear a

watch and inspected it from time to time, to see how much of
the session she had left. The anxiety was reduced by Rita's new
capacity to recognize and distinguish the different features of
her life and to tolerate the psychic pain, and this enabled her to
use the time of her session thoroughly. Furthermore, every
minute seemed to become extremely important for her, and the
watch had the function of informing her of the time that she
still had left. Rita began to pay more and more attention to the
importance that the passing of time had in her development: in
one session she spoke of time as of a measuring scale situated
between birth and death, to count the "time" of living. On the
following day, after she had gone with her class to visit the
Botanical Gardens, Rita told me that she had been greatly impressed by the sight of two trees: the tree of life and the tree of
death. Rita spoke of her interest for the two trees: so special, so
rare, so attractive but at the same time so different. She explained that they were "close, one in front of the other, as if one
couldn't exist except in the presence of the other". Rita seemed
to be expressing that when the potentiality of life emerges,
the idea of death also emerges with vigour. While Rita was telling me about the trees, she interrupted her tale to tell me,
with great emotion, about another episode: at 12 o'clock, in the
Botanical Gardens, they suddenly heard a loud, deep explosion. It was the City Gun announcing midday and frightening
them all because, as it was raining, they thought it might be
thunder. Here again the time (midday) broke in as Rita was
forming her thoughts towards life. Life was explosively assert-
ing itself in Rita's mind, contrasted with the death anxieties
that only a few weeks before were present in her phantasies of
the Midnight Witch. As a consequence of this assertion of life,
Rita became able, towards the end of the session, to tell me
about an intense fear of her childhood days:

"When I was small I believed that the statue of Garibaldi, but
also other statues, were true people who had been embalmed
when still alive. Then I imagined they might come to life again.
I used to look at the statue and then I went backwards in time,
with my thoughts, and Garibaldi began to move on his horse.
. . . This happened to me always. Once I went by the Coliseum
and I imagined it was full of Christians fighting against the

lions. I could really see them through the holes of the Coliseum and I couldn't get rid of that sight. On another occasion I was close to the Roman Circus and I 'saw' the Romans with their chariots fighting. This terrified me; I was scared that they might all come back to life and that they would hate me: Garibaldi, Julius Caesar, the Ancient Romans. . . . Today this doesn't happen anymore, . . . that is, it almost doesn't, but it isn't as strong as before."

I told Rita that it seemed that she had stopped the time or was sending it backwards and felt menaced by the statues and by the historical heroes who had died several centuries before. I added that she had remembered her fears just as she was beginning to enjoy being with her friends, to like the feeling that she was growing, and to accept her growth and the passing of time.

Rita's acknowledgement of the passing of time came together in this session with acknowledgement of the danger into which she put herself by her manipulation of it. On the one hand, the perception of time could enable Rita to distinguish and think about the strength of her anxieties and of their representation. Rita could speak of her anxieties because she placed them in the past, beginning her tale with "When I was small" and finishing it with the admission of her own present anxiety. On the other hand, one could see in her hallucinations the danger that she was in when she attacked and destroyed the temporal context. Once time was annihilated (timelessness), ghosts could appear, even from a distant past, coming back to life and attacking her directly. The world could become crowded with people from the past, dead and petrified coming back to life, seeking vengeance upon her. I would like to emphasize that two important events took place simultaneously. In one session, time was powerfully asserted in Rita's mind: the midday gun announcing the bursting in of time, the bridge joining life with death. It was the same session in which she was able to speak of her deeper anxieties about the annihilation of time and consequent confusion between life and death.

In a session of the following week, Rita came bringing a photo album. They were the pictures of her birthday, six months before. With great emotion she showed me the pictures: she was obviously affirming the moment that more than any other represented the passing of time—her birthday. Time was not placed somewhere in the past or in the future; it had become also an area of passage, of movement, of growth. The last photo, bigger than the others, was not inside the album, Rita left it face down for a long time while considering whether to show it to me or not. In the end, she let me see it. It was the photo of her class at school. As soon as she gave me the picture, she asked me whether I could find her in the photo. The fear and the anxiety present in this question seemed deeply related to the anxiety with which Rita had begun psychotherapy: "Do I exist?", "Can I be perceived by others and by myself?", or "Am I lost in the background and confused with others?" The anxiety of annihilation which Rita revealed in the first months of her psychotherapy can now be analysed. Rita was now confident that she could be perceived and distinguished from the others, because she herself had begun to distinguish and perceive in a new way. She was no longer the invisible child of the first months nor the excited girl who needed to play "Midnight Witch" in order to feel alive. She could show me the signatures of all her friends on the back of the picture and tell me who each of them was, different, with their own features, more or less agreeable, more or less a friend of hers.

In the following session, Rita spoke about her childhood, about her anxieties during the trips to a country in the Middle East, a country at war, where she went with her mother and sister to visit her father, who was there for reasons of work. She told me about staying there and about coming back. One memory was stronger than all the others:

"My sister and I used to chase butterflies there. We followed them and caught them. On one occasion I managed to catch a big white butterfly. It was lovely and big, its wings were white and gold. I caught it but my sister told me that butterflies have a light powder on their wings and if I caught them with my hands they couldn't fly any more. I cried so much that day, I was terribly sorry, I stopped chasing butterflies ever since."

I told Rita that it seems that she was terribly frightened at the idea that the beautiful butterfly might never fly again. I added that, because of the fright, she seemed to have given up her attempt to get hold of herself and of her own capacity to go forward and grow. Rita told me that such a long time had passed and now she knew it well, but before she did not know and thought that growing was like dying.

What Rita seemed to convey was that there was something very small and very lovely and fragile that was in danger. The danger was represented by Rita herself. Here also, as in the case of the statues coming back to life, the anxieties could be named only if they were placed in the past. Time here, rather than creating a distance that would deny the anxiety, had the function of placing the anxiety at the right distance, so that it could be observed. The butterfly seemed also to represent the end of childhood and the entrance into puberty, where a game could have deadly consequences. It also stood, with its dangerous flight, for the development of Rita's feminine identity, for the explosion of physical sensations, generating new emotions and desires. It was connected with thoughts about eventually approaching a sexual identity, perceived at this stage as extremely menacing and fragile. The question of sexual identity brought her great uncertainty and fear, but the awareness that she reached of those feelings helped her to cope with the violence of the new, unforeseen experience. We can think of the sequence of these two sessions in this way:

1. discovery of herself as a person placed in time (the photo of the birthday) who, for this reason is unique, separate, and recognizable (the photo of her class);

2. memory of the first perception of the blossoming of her own feminine identity (the butterfly's flight) and fear of the dangers one might meet in assuming this identity (the damaged butterfly);

3. description of the acknowledgement of her own anxiety (her fright and decision that she would stop catching butterflies): if "growing up is like dying" then it is better not to grow.

The moment of the acknowledgement is also the moment of change, as we can see in the session that came after the story of the butterfly. Rita came and told me about an episode:

"On the day of my birthday I put a chestnut in the earth and for some time now there has been a little plant. I thought I had lost it and was frightened but today I found it again: it is quite tall but still very thin and fragile. It needs protection, but warm weather will help it and next winter it will be stronger and bigger."

During the rest of the session we worked at the theme of her growing up, of time passing. The fragile plant made her think of herself: she was beginning to grow. The attention that Rita could now pay to herself seemed to enable her to acquire the temporal perception as a hopeful perspective: time was not a menace any more to her physical and mental health, and it had become a means of making herself stronger and facing the "winter". The "winter" here probably represented the impending menace of pubertal development, something frightening for which she was trying to prepare. Only at the end of the session, a few minutes before leaving, did Rita admit with a sort of hidden satisfaction that in the morning she had looked at herself in the mirror and had discovered that her breasts were beginning to grow. One could see here, for the first time, the conception of time that Meltzer and Harris (1976) call linear time, where time is seen as "linear adventures in the infinite, always leaving behind what has been strenuously won" (p. 402). Rita had introduced herself into the linear conception of time, acquiring growth and development, instead of annihilation and backward motion, as before.

Discussion

I would like to discuss this clinical material in the light of the theoretical issues discussed at the beginning of this chapter.

The internal movement of which Rita became capable in these months took her nearer to the pubertal development for which she appeared to be so unprepared at the beginning of psychotherapy.

The pubertal development represented for Rita the possibility of thinking about herself as someone who was developing forward in time and was acknowledging Linear Time.

We can now go back to the question that we left open at the beginning of the chapter: does the appearance of the concept of time take place because of a person's perception of the discontinuity of life (Klein) or because of an increased discontinuity in the person's perception (Freud)? I believe that, as pubertal development approached, the theme of death appeared with an absolutely new strength in Rita's thoughts. Rita came to think of death as the natural conclusion of each life, and moreover—and this was the really important discovery—of her own life. Understanding this fact caused violent anxieties for Rita, but it also enabled her to establish some limits and boundaries, necessary for her to enter adolescence. Life has its natural end (the trees of life and death) imposed by nature, and Rita's perception of it brought her closer to a linear conception of time. For the first time, in other words, Rita had the perception of a discontinuity between life and death, and this discontinuity introduced her to the understanding of the passing of time, as propounded by Klein (1923, p. 99) in the quotation in the theoretical section above.

For time to become a structuring category for the development of personality during adolescence, it is necessary that it be recognized repeatedly and continuously. Here we come back to Freud and to his understanding of the *Pcpt.-Cs.* system and of its perceptive functioning, which Freud described as discontinuous. When Rita started to tolerate the frustration and the mental pain connected with the recognition of limits, she developed an attention towards her own reality, internal and external. I use attention in the sense described by Freud (and subsequently developed by Bion): the "activity [that] meets the sense-impressions half way, instead of awaiting their appearance" (Freud, 1911b, p. 220). For a long time, Rita had attacked and destroyed her sense impressions, to avoid facing external reality and recognizing its boundaries (the game of the Midnight Witch). When the necessity to attack the data originated by her sense-impressions progressively decreased, it became possible for her not only to await the appearance of the sensory and emotional perceptions, but even to "meet them halfway". Attention ("as the strings which hold the senses together in consensuality": Meltzer et al., 1975, p. 13) is a capacity that brings discontinuity with itself, creating restrictions and drawing boundaries in the world of space and time. Attention necessarily excludes from the conscious mind an immense amount of sensory data and concentrates just on a small, definite amount. We can describe it as the mental capacity that enables us to turn actively towards the *Pcpt.-Cs.* system described by Freud. I think that this capacity for attention, because of its inevitable discontinuity, produces an internal awareness of the linear passing of time. This extremely precise awareness introduces a new and very helpful element for the development of the adolescent mind.

Attention seems to play an essential role for the conquest of the concept of time, and this concept enables further progress in the process of growth. Bion borrowed from Freud the concept of attention and made it a column of his Grid, considering it a factor of the alpha function (Bion, 1962, p. 24). He even showed how extremely violent attacks against the perception of sensory data could lead to a disintegration of main thought processes, causing psychotic functioning. These attacks can sometimes be directed—as we have seen in the case of Rita—against one's own capacity to perceive the passing of time. Bion discussed this in his 1967 "Commentary" when he spoke of patients having a defective orientation in space and time:

> Most people accept that there is a realization which is adequately represented by the formulation "time is passing", but a psychotic patient may not be aware of that realization and may not behave as if the formulation "time is passing" represents a realization of any significance. [Bion, 1967a, p. 136]

As we can see, Bion is referring to the consequences of psychotic attacks against the perceptive apparatus. These attacks can, in my experience, be extremely severe during pubertal development when sensory and bodily impulses violently impose themselves upon the mind (Ferrari, 1994). But at the same time, as we have seen, this is a moment in development when adolescents can acquire a close relationship with the fundamental categories (space and time) which supervise the organization of the mind, just when these categories present themselves anew. We can say that, in this phase, time begins to appear not only as an internal quality, but also as an external one: adolescents seem to acquire a capacity to distinguish between subjective and objective time. They can begin to distinguish between their own subjective perception of the passing of time and objective, absolute, physical, unidirectional time. In the clinical example, the trees of life and death and the Midday Gun are temporal references concerning not only Rita but life itself. This is the fourth "operative concept" described by Meltzer and Harris (1976): linear time. Unidirectional time—that is, irreversible time—brings a better distinction between self and others, between one's own internal experience and experience with others, in a shared world. Rita's mentioning that her breasts are beginning to develop shows that the new dimension is accepted. The price that was paid in not accepting this distinction— to avoid the frustrations that the recognition of the passing of time might bring with itself—was the price of an intense disharmony in mental functioning, also described by Bion:

> The complexity of the problem is increased when it becomes clear with certain patients that measurements of time and space are based on psychic reality and not physical space or time; both measurements are possible only to the patient capable of tolerating frustration because both are derived from measures of frustration. If the personality cannot tolerate frustration, he prevents the development of any apparatus which measures it. Thus, if he is so many years, or so many minutes from his objective, he annihilates space or time which measure his frustration. The development of more sophisticated usages of this capacity, such as measurement of time or space, is thus prejudiced. A state is produced in which the patient is unwilling to admit awareness of distance or time. [Bion, 1967a, p. 210].

Bion's description seems to fit closely Rita's mental functioning during the initial sessions. The process that took place later was the process of beginning to tolerate frustration and mental pain and, as a consequence, of perceiving the limits imposed by reality (space and time included) not as impediments, but as delimitations enabling one to move in a knowable and known context marked with relatively stable reference points.

Conclusions

I hope that I have shown in this chapter how Rita moved from stage to stage in the conception of time: from timelessness to linear time. Meltzer (Meltzer et al., 1975a) described the different psychic organizations connected to the different conceptions of the passing of time: from the unidimensionality of timelessness to the four-dimensionality of acquiring a concept of linear time and irreversible time. I have also tried to describe in what way the conception that the patient has of the passing of time might become the subject of interpretations and in this way foster transformation. In the discussion that followed the presentation of the paper on "Adhesive Identification", Meltzer (1975) said: "The psychoanalytical method is beautiful for observing time disturbance and we see it all the time but we don't generally know what to do with it except to deal with it as resistances, if the patient comes late, or seduction if they come on time. They are wrong no matter what they do" (p. 305). It is my belief that Meltzer was bringing to our attention the limits of this mode of dealing with the question of time. I hope that I have succeeded in describing a possible way of coping with this subject in a different way.

CHAPTER EIGHT

The light meter, the thermostat, the tuner: the compositional aspects of communication with very disturbed adolescents

Roberto Bertolini

A 10-year-old boy commented passionately to his female therapist at the end of his therapy, "I shall never forget you, because you have taught me how to give the correct weight to things". In Banana Yoshimoto's 1989 novel about two adolescent girls, the main character, Tsugumi, says in what is apparently the last letter she will write to her best friend Maria, "I wonder all the time how, in spite of your stupidity, you always seem to know the correct weight of everything; it must be a mystery" (p. 49).

In these two situations, one real and one imaginary, a young patient and a very disturbed adolescent girl see the therapist and the friend as being capable of giving things their correct weight. They recognize their ability to inject a special dimension into their communications which they feel to be beneficial to their well-being. Both the patient and Tsugumi say that being able to experience this special quality in their communications has enabled them to feel deeply understood. By this they mean that when they find themselves in an atmosphere of mutual interest and sympathy, they are able to discover something true about themselves from the way things are given back to them. I believe that when we observe healthy interaction between a mother and her child we are looking, in fact, at something very similar to the two experiences I have described above.

We are impressed not only with the mother's ability to solve her infant's problems, but also with the way she shares with her infant her personal understanding of its state of mind. There is a particular mental dimension in her communications, unique to each mother–baby relationship, which has to do with the mother's ability to "explore" the various facets of her baby's more intimate experience, and to "compose" them in such a way that mutual understanding and growth are stimulated. She gives form to her child's anxieties, meets its needs, and modulates its omnipotence and omniscience. In the light of these observations, one begins to wonder just how far these qualities of the mother's mind, during her communications with her child in the early months and years of its life, might be considered fundamental to the infant's emotional development, the basis for his ability to think as well as for the development of a stable character and secure sense of identity in later life. I refer to these dimensions as "compositional" following Meltzer in his paper "Does Money-Kyrle's Concept of Misconception Have Any Unique Descriptive Power?":

> Existing theories seem to go some considerable distance to enable us to describe the "normal" course of development and the interaction of pathological aspects of the developing child vis-à-vis its intimate surroundings, both in its normal (or, better, "optimal") and "inadequate" aspects. But this is only taking into consideration the intentional aspects of the behaviour of figures in the environment. It is like describing a painting only in its iconographic aspects, without reference to the mysterious compositional qualities wherein its unique impact on the viewer reside. Similarly our powers of describing the analytic situation tend to be limited to the descriptions of the "iconography" of the analytic situation, throwing very little light on the development of the treatment situation and its overall impact on the lives of the analyst and analysand. [1981, p. 496]

If I have understood Meltzer correctly, I think that the 10-year-old boy and Tsugumi experienced a "compositional" dimension within the communicative interaction which led them to feel truly understood. Those mysterious qualities that we see in the way a good mother relates to her baby are, I believe, the same. In this chapter, I would like to show how observations of this "compositional" dimension in human interactions could greatly improve our ability to describe what really happens in analytic work with severely disturbed adolescents. As a result, we may be able to improve our understanding of what I consider to be the real drama of these patients: that of no longer being able to give form to themselves through the images that other people give back to them when they attempt to express themselves. My objective, then, is to establish a "centre of gravity" that is capable of composing their intimate experience creatively. This drama, clearly observable within the analytic situation following the development of the transference relationship, has been expertly described by Donald Meltzer and by Meg Harris Williams in *The Apprehension of Beauty* (chapter 7—"The Undiscovered Country: The Shape of the Aesthetic Conflict in *Hamlet*"):

> The problem of self-knowledge is simultaneous with that of self-expression. But self-expression requires some form of external resonance; and much of the drama of Hamlet is based on the hero's failure to find ... any intimate relationship whose answering reverberations will "denote him truly". The "antic disposition" is not only a guard but also the external indication of a search which never finds a containing form. . . . His shape seems ready made, to others and perhaps also to himself, until he is faced with the necessity of becoming a prince, as opposed to merely acting the prince through any of the various "actions that a man might play"—any form of acceptable role playing. [Meltzer & Harris Williams, 1988b, p. 86]

Like Hamlet, disturbed adolescents fail to find an intimate relationship whose answering reverberations "denote them truly" and allow them to feel understood. They are repeatedly thrown back into their "antic disposition". They feel inadequate and impotent when faced with the upheavals of their physical and emotional transformation and growth. They become frustrated by not being able to give form to themselves or being able to change reality in accordance with their needs and desires. During these critical moments they may easily be seduced by ways of thinking, feeling, and acting that deeply alienate them both from the adolescent community and from the truth and beauty of their own emotional life. Some adolescents drown in solitary masturbatory states of mind, forever on the brink of violence, some turn towards delinquent or drug-dependent groups, while others become victims of the unscrupulous. Only a few find their way to therapy (either through choice or because they have been sent), in the hope of discovering that their inner experience can be explored and composed in such a way that makes it thinkable.

I have included here some clinical material from the psychoanalytic psychotherapy of three adolescent patients who were no longer able to compose their inner experience in a way that they could think about. A specific dimension in their internal and external communications had been temporarily destroyed. I would like to be able to show how close observation of the interactions inside the psychotherapeutic sessions has contributed to a better understanding of their inner experience and at the same time improved the quality of my analytic attitude.

The light meter

G was almost 17 years old when he began psychoanalytic psychotherapy three times a week. He had been referred by his previous therapist, who had been seeing both him and his family for many years. During one of the last family therapy sessions he said that he wanted to start personal analysis because he had difficulty going to school, where he studied photography and graphics. There were many things that he wanted to explore on his own. He was often verbally and physically abusive to his brother, and he argued with both his divorced mother and his elderly grandmother each time they contradicted his opinions. He had also stopped seeing his father, who was living with another woman, as he felt attacked by his father's criticism against his religious ideas and voluntary work. He had also become very concerned about his tendency to stammer, which gave him a feeling of being handicapped.

The first time I went to fetch him from the waiting-room, I found him sitting on the sofa busily writing something in a small notebook. He was so wrapped up in his activity that for a time he did not notice that I was there. Everything about his body language and posture seemed calculated to impress me and show me how dedicated he was to our work. His clothes had none of the usual adolescent trappings, making him look like a small, old-fashioned boy. Beside him there was a professional camera and another small object hidden inside a black roundish leather box. After some time he stood up. Six feet tall and hardly looking at me, he uttered a shy, "Hello Sir!" As he was gathering his things he told me that the leather box contained a broken light meter. Inside the consulting-room, he took a seat in the opposite corner to me. He immediately began to read his notebook, flicking the pages backwards and forwards. He reminded me of a speaker delivering a speech from a haphazard collection of notes. I stayed silent for most of the time. Only once did I ask him to repeat something, because his voice had been drowned by the noise of the traffic outside. Here he interrupted me by saying that he was going to come to my point on the next page. The notes contained a chronicle of the most important events of the last few days, a recollection of his childhood memories, and some thoughts on his parents' personalities and characters. They were lacking in observation and detail and were so brief that it was difficult to understand what he wanted to say. His insights and childhood memories were presented as "flashes of revelations" (similar to God's revelation to Saint Paul on his way to Damascus) or as the last "fundamental discovery". They were thrown at me like flashes of light, but they did not throw any proper light onto the subject. The image of reality he gave me was flat and confused, rather like a photograph taken with the wrong light exposure. It seemed to me that G was projectively identified with an idealized all-knowing object and that he wanted to blind me with the "clarity" of his thoughts. Finally, he stopped reading his notes. At this point I asked him his reasons for wanting to start psychotherapy. After a long pause, he said that he was sad and confused because he had been left by his girlfriend and could not understand what had gone wrong. He secretly smiled inwardly. He added that at times he thought that it was all his fault, and that maybe he had offended his girl when he had attempted to stroke her breasts and have sex with her. He smiled again. Then he went on to say that his girlfriend was two years younger than him, so she might not have been able to understand him, she might not even have been "worthy" of him. Finally, he said that his girlfriend's mother had persuaded her to leave him because he was a member of a rival religious organization. In his attempt at giving meaning to this experience I observed that G moved from one conviction to another completely opposite one in the space of a second, showing that there was no room in his mind for two different meanings. In the same way, he oscillated between two poles in his self perception: one minute he was on stage in the limelight, the next he was completely hidden as if he were behind the curtains, in the dark. The light attributed to the other characters in the story was continually changed as well. They had either too much or too little light, too much or too little exposure. All this led me to think about the broken light meter in the leather box. It seemed to me that he had the wrong way of measuring or throwing light onto things in his attempt at building an image of his internal emotional experience. It was as if his internal light meter was not working properly.

During the course of therapy, it became apparent that every time there was a period of crisis or a great change in G's life, his difficulty in finding the correct light to capture his own or other people's experience became particularly intense. During his third year of analysis, for example, he had his final photography examinations. He started being difficult with his tutor, who was also his course teacher of photographic techniques. He had lost his trust both in him and in his judgement. G felt that the teacher changed his opinions too frequently and too quickly. In point of fact, G had become anxious because he had to prepare a portfolio of photographs under his tutor's supervision, and he was afraid of having to face his criticism. His teacher–tutor suggested taking some close-ups of a model, with a cityscape background in black and white. G was enthusiastic about the idea and got everything ready for the assignment.

When the time came, he forgot to take the light meter with him, and all the photos came out either bleached or black. The teacher was not at all pleased with him, but gave him another chance to repeat the exercise, this time using the meter. G found out that he had passed his exams, but he did not mention this to me. Some time later, he handed me two photos from his first photographic assignment as soon as he got inside the consulting-room. He then lay on the couch, without moving, waiting for my opinion of them. I looked at the two photos closely, but I could not see what they were of. I told him that the images looked vague and confused. He sprang off the couch and snatched them away from me, and he began looking at them from various angles to catch the light in different ways, trying to improve the clarity of the images. He treated his photos as if they were studies of light taken by an important photographer, in his attempt at convincing me that his tutor–teacher had been superficial in judging his work. Then he relaxed and told me that he had passed his final exams. After, he recalled a recurrent dream of the last few weeks:

In this dream he was in the classroom and had just completed his admission tests for the final exams. He could see the results on the teacher's class register. His marks kept changing all the time. His marks kept changing like the position of the arrow in a badly gauged light meter.

This time, unlike at the beginning of therapy, G recognized that there was something fake within himself that changed the marks on the teacher's class register in his refusal to recognize the light meter's function of finding the "correct light" for his subjects not only for his photographic assignments, but also for those of his internal world. From his being "confused" in the past, he was now deliberately "making confusion" in order to test the strength of my internal light meter.

Now G was able to recognize this deception and to differentiate it from his previous confusion because in some way or other he had introjected the function of my internal light meter. This meant that during the course of treatment, on many occasions he had felt that my way of illuminating his emotional experience had made him feel contained and understood. Unfortunately, it is not possible to give further examples of how I worked with this patient or to include more detailed material, as this therapy took place many years ago. However, in the two situations that I have described—the first one concerning the girlfriend, the second the photographic assignment—I remember that my inner experience in response to G's material suffered from the same lack of compositional quality as his internal and external systems of communication. I tended, for instance, to see too much light on one subject and too little on another—to illuminate things in a way that made them incompatible, or increased the split between infantile anxieties and manic defences against them.

The thermostat

Whereas G needed to repair his internal light meter in order to be able to contain and think about his mental experience, the second patient, B, was never able to find the correct temperature within his relationships. He was a young man in his early 20s, and he was addicted to heroin. His father brought him to our first meeting. The patient was straightforward and calm in his introduction. He was smartly dressed and his hair was short, identifying him as an upper-class adolescent. He settled himself comfortably on the couch straight away, like the "perfect patient". He said that he had come for psychoanalytic psychotherapy. He had recently found a small flat, which he was going to move into soon. Following an agreement he had made with his father and the psychiatrist who dealt with him pharmacologically, he wanted to have psychotherapy to help him through this change in his life. I asked him how he felt about it. He replied that he was afraid of being alone and free from any parental or other control, and that he was worried about falling back into the use of drugs and of being sent to a residential community. Then he added that he was looking for a job in order to earn enough money for his daily expenses, and that he wanted to take up his studies in sociology at the university, which he had interrupted during the last year. After a long, silent pause, he took an exercise book out of his inside jacket pocket and asked me if he could read some poems he had recently written. I listened to him until the session ended, without making any comment. At times, it was a struggle to keep myself awake, his reading was so flat and unemotional. Only the parts in his poetry that were exhibitionistic or pornographic were given some vocal emphasis. He clearly wanted to impress me with his poems, in the same way that G had with his psychological insights from his notes. He presented himself as a "fine connoisseur" of the art of seducing women, the geography of the female body, and the genitals. In fact, as I later found out, he was very much alone and longing for an intimate relationship with a girl. At the end of the session, I explained that I would need five sessions in order to get to know him better, which would also give him time to see how I worked, before making the decision to embark on psychoanalytic psychotherapy.

B came to his second session furious with an old lady he had met on the bus on the way to the consultation. She was heavily laden with two plastic bags full of fruit and vegetables she had bought at the nearby open market. She had blocked the exit of the bus for the entire journey. He felt superior to her because she looked like a poor working-class lady. He could not tolerate her blocking the exit; he was afraid he would miss his stop near my consulting-rooms and not get off the bus in time. I immediately thought that his emotional reaction towards the working-class lady had some infantile significance, and that he had transferred onto her something that had been stimulated in him during his first interview with me, and which belonged to an inner experience. He might also have felt hurt and thwarted by my lack of enthusiasm for his poems and by my decision to set a limit to the number of sessions instead of starting psychoanalytic psychotherapy immediately. After this tirade against the "working-class lady", he recalled a dream he had recently had.

In this dream his grandmother threw herself out of the window and killed herself. He was standing at the window looking down on the street and saw people gathered around the body. Then he ran down the stairs and out of the building. He joined the small gathering, trying to see the dead body. He then left the scene feeling absolutely detached and quite unemotional.

Before falling into silence for the rest of the session, he explained that the grandmother of the dream was his maternal grandmother, with whom he spent most of his time during the day because his divorced parents—and in particular his mother, who was an MP—were very often out of town. Through his dream and the tirade against the old lady, the picture of himself that he gave me was of a cold, determined young man. I felt that this was not the whole truth about what he was feeling deep inside. The dream told the story of a sudden tragic departure. Was there any link between the fact that he was leaving his grandmother's house to enter his new flat? Maybe he had begun to feel that he was going to miss her but could not, for some reason, give a home to this feeling within himself?

The episode of burning rage towards the old lady perhaps told a similar story. There was something mysterious in her appearance, laden with the two plastic bags full of fresh fruit and vegetables, that attracted his attention and triggered off feelings of warmth that he could not contain within himself. In spite of his apparent coldness and excitement, I could detect the warmth of some of his dependent infantile parts towards his grandmother, and towards the therapist, represented by the old lady. On the other hand, it was clear that he could not stand being hindered or thwarted in his desire for freedom. He wanted to be able to go on his way whenever he wished, which really meant alienating himself with the use of drugs or pornographic material.

Towards the end of the assessment, two sessions later, he spoke about another dream. It showed that he had decided not to start psychotherapy immediately. He was ready to move into his new apartment, where he had already spent the last two weekends. He had been feeling a bit under the weather because of a slight temperature. He was expected to start a job as an assistant to a film producer. He had no qualifications for the job, which had been found for him by his father, but he felt very excited by the prospect.

In the dream he was in his new flat, but he was very anxious because there was a water leak in the bath. At the same time he noticed that the boiler was not working properly. The thermostat was faulty. The gauge indicated that the water was getting hotter and hotter. He did not want to call in the plumber, preferring to do the job himself.

He left the session a little early this time, as he had an appointment to meet his mother in the foyer of the parliament building. He was coming to terms with the anxiety caused by the fact that our sessions were about to end, by returning to his "antic disposition". He was trying to evade the idea that he would miss his grandmother, and that he deeply longed for a warm, intimate relationship. Inside himself he did not yet know what the word "mother" meant—that is, which mother he was going to meet. He was confused between the MP mother—a sort of queen mother—and a mother who knew him and could understand his infantile needs and anxieties and who had, perhaps, been too denigrated—like the working-class lady—to be appreciated or been killed like the grandmother in the first dream. He knew that his thermostat was broken, but he did not want me to repair it. By offering him the job as assistant to a movie director, probably precluding any chance of starting psychotherapy, his father offered him an inadequate, perhaps false, containment for his anxieties and his search for a secure sense of identity.

This material illustrates just how much this patient needed to explore and give form to his infantile feelings of dependency, and how much he feared to do it inside the therapeutic relationship. He did not know whether he could trust the therapist and the qualities of his mind that were symbolized in the two bags the old lady carried. Moreover, the last dream showed that he had become aware that there was something wrong with his internal thermostat. He was left either terribly cold, as in the dream with the grandmother, or hot, on the verge of melting in high temperatures, as in the dream about the boiler. I felt that the heroin, with its pharmacotoxic effects, reinforced the omnipotence of his virulent attacks against his internal thermostat. At the same, time however, heroin was a substitute for a real object. This object became, at times, an idealized sort of "mummy" that magically recreated a stable internal temperature based on a manic denial of both psychic and external reality.

The tuner

The following clinical observations are from the psychotherapy of a 16-year-old boy, L, who was slightly mentally retarded. He was an only child and lived with his mother and maternal grandmother. Recently his father had died dramatically after years of alcoholism. L was referred by his psychiatrist as he had expressed the idea that he wanted to kill his mother. He thought that she was responsible for his father's death. Moreover, on a few occasions he had approached small babies in public gardens and had grabbed their naked feet with the idea of rubbing them up against his penis.

During the first period of therapy, L spent the sessions talking non-stop. He filled the whole space with verbal communications, forcing various stories concerning his real life, his past, his relatives, the programmes he watched on TV, his reading, and his daydreams into me. In his story-telling, he jumped from one subject to another, often stopping in the middle of a sentence to start another one about something different. In this way he created a collage of verbal communications. He drew fragmented pieces of his experiences together which he enjoyed colouring with different tones of voice and a lot of theatrical gestures. Most of the time L seemed to be drunk on the stream of sounds and words he produced, while at others he became very active, frequently changing the content of his verbal communications, especially when he wanted to stop my verbal intrusions. He acted like a spiteful boy who was changing the channels of the radio by fiddling with the knob of the tuner. This collection of fragmented verbal communications seemed to create a supporting network for his fragile sense of identity, as well as being a barrier against his persecutors, who were projected into me and my words. He was alone and desperate and would have got lost if he had not been in analysis. He could not understand the significance of what he was doing, why he had become the speaker of a thousand channels. He kept "flat spinning" (Money-Kyrle, 1977) in this state of mind, not unlike G in his periods of crisis. He made me feel sleepy and unable to think, until two distinct patterns emerged from my close observation of his emotional orientation towards both myself and the analytic setting. In the first place, this activity increased after the weekends, and towards the close of each session. Second, he used a linguistic trick to cut up his sequence of verbal communications: he would intersperse his discourse with a "by the way . . .", either making reference to something new or adding a last word to the ongoing subject which changed or distorted its whole meaning. The "by the way . . ." was used in such a way that all the cut-up pieces became meaningless and lost their associative connections. As a result of these observations, I changed my therapeutic strategy with L. I confronted him firmly every time he was identified with "Mr By the way . . ."; at the same time, I kept his attention and interest on those fragmented pieces of his collage that I felt were very much linked to the way he was emotionally oriented in the session. I helped him *to tune into those signals,* to listen to what they were saying, until they reached a form that contained something meaningful for him. At the end of his first year of analysis, L told me that his maternal uncle had given him a radio transmitter for his birthday so that he could talk to other radio enthusiasts in the town. He was now able to do this thanks to the therapy he had undergone. He was very pleased with the radio even though he found it difficult to find a free channel or to select the correct wavelength for transmission. He added that he thought he might need a more powerful transmitter, fantasizing that the air was full of tyrannical or bad people blocking the lines, speaking over his voice, or melting down his little antenna with their powerful ones. He was now able to take part in an external reality through a complex network of communications that put him in touch with many different people. He was able to do this as the quality of his internal communications had been partially repaired. It had given him the sensation of " being", and the strength to abandon the delirious and lonely world of his collage.

Final remarks

These clinical observations from the psychoanalytic psychotherapy of three very ill adolescents illustrate that the fundamental ongoing conflict in the internal world of these patients, and which is projected into the analytic relationship, is one between two different ways of thinking. One stimulates the patient's ability to think and make him or her feel contained and understood, the other destroys emotional experience. The first originates from the mysterious compositional qualities of interactions and communications, the second from omnipotence and omniscience. Meltzer (1978a) calls these two distinct mental modes "exploring the mystery" and "solving the riddle" and considers them the essence of aesthetic conflict. Returning here to Hamlet's drama of continually being frustrated in his attempts at discovering his real inner self, Meltzer writes:

> Time and again, attempts to pursue the developmental mode of "exploring the mystery" are converted, through an instantaneous switch of energies, into the essentially destructive and violent mental mode of "solving the riddle": not just by the visionless characters but also by the hero. And this contrast between two distinct mental modes that are operating in parallel—exploring the mystery and solving the riddle—is what constitutes the texture of the aesthetic conflict throughout the play. [p. 85]

When this conflict does not resolve itself in favour of the development of the ability to think, it may lead to the development of thought disorders. Whenever the three patients failed to find an intimate relationship "whose answering reverberations would denote them truly" in a period of crisis, thereby losing any hope of

either being understood or knowing something true about themselves, they shifted to a mode of thinking that was extremely destructive of the meaning of their personal experience. The light
meter was substituted by flashes of light, the thermostat by the
pharmacotoxic effects of the drugs, the tuner by "Mr By the way
. . .". Each tenaciously held on to this mental activity in an attempt
to find comfort, a sense of security and erotic pleasure and to keep
the fear of being "thrown away", of disappearing into nothing, at
bay (Meltzer, 1992b).

This conflict between the two opposite modes of thinking is
immediately reflected in the responses of the therapist's mind, in a
way that mirrors the conflict within the patients. The therapist can
observe the same pathological shift within himself and thereby
understand its meaning. By being aware of this conflict in his
mental functioning, the therapist ought to be able give his patients
those compositional qualities that are necessary for keeping the
balance of their emotional life on the side of meaning, truth, and
beauty. This should be achieved through his communications, the
ways in which he explores his patients' material, and the answers
he gives to the patients. He must also be aware of the ways in
which the impact of each type of communication that sustains the
patients' experience of identity help the therapist to identify the
missing compositional qualities in his countertransference. His
technique can then be modified accordingly. The impact of "Mr
By the way . . .", for example, in my analytic work, made me
aware of L's difficulty in paying attention to those emotions under
the pressure of the transference experience, so that I had to keep
him tuned in until they reached a form that contained something
meaningful for him. The impact of B's cold determination made
me painfully aware that a warm, comfortable relationship capable
of containing his more dependent parts was missing in his inner
life. Unfortunately, B did not continue coming after the assessment sessions, so the opportunity of giving space to these feelings
within the analytic setting was lost.

The impact of G's tendency to throw flashes of light onto his
emotional experiences in his attempt at making them seem out of
the ordinary made me aware of the destructive consequences this
had on his ability to observe the complexity of his inner life, and

to compose it in a meaningful way. As a contrast, I showed him the pleasure that could be obtained from working with a good internal light meter.

The three cases discussed above all seem to suggest that each patient needs to experience, through analytic interaction, a well-defined compositional dimension that is rooted in his sensorial perception of those primitive body communication channels that are so active in the mother–child relationship.

CHAPTER NINE

Love and destructivity:
from the aesthetic conflict
to a revision of the concept
of destructivity in the psyche

Jean Bégoin

I first heard Donald Meltzer speak about the "Aesthetic Conflict" when he presented this new concept in Paris, at a meeting of the GERPEN[1] in March 1986, almost fourteen years ago. This paper became the second chapter in his book *The Apprehension of Beauty*, written with Meg Harris Williams and published two years later, in 1988. As did many others who were listening to Meltzer on this day, I felt that moment deserved to be considered *historical*, and I still think it was. Many elements were new in this concept, but what was most striking was his evident inspiration: we were listening to a *new* Meltzer—not so much in his theories, with which I had been familiar for more than twenty years, after having had supervisions and having translated his two first books into French—but especially in what I have to call his "spirit", a new way of thinking theories, comprising a newly integrated mixture of psychoanalysis, philosophy, and poetry. Actually, it would be more precise to say that we were present at the *birth* of a higher

---

[1] [A study group put together with James Gammill, Geneviève Haag, and other colleagues, created in 1974, that worked in France with Donald Meltzer, Martha Harris, and Francis Tustin.]

degree of integration of qualities we had in fact *always known in Meltzer* since his first papers and his first book, *The Psycho-Analytical Process*: a unique Meltzerian mixture of *science and art*.

Of course, there were also new psychoanalytic ideas in this very extraordinary paper of 1986. One of the most striking was the accent put on *love*, instead of libido, when Meltzer (1988) evoked the conditions by which an "aesthetic object" is constructed by "the ordinary beautiful baby" together with its "ordinary beautiful mother", the theoretical corollary of this being that "the aesthetic conflict and the depressive position would be primary for development, and the paranoid–schizoid secondary" (p. 26). *Love, and not hate*, was being given the first place in development, and a new attitude was possible concerning the old and so difficult problem of mental pain.

The enigma of mental pain

In "Aesthetic Conflict" (1988), Don Meltzer insisted that "the shift introduced by Bion in the Model of the Mind must cause us to rethink the whole problem of mental pain and the developmental process since infancy" (p. 8). As we know, since Freud invented it, the analytic process has become longer and longer, from lasting only a few months in those early days to more and more, years afterwards. It seems to me that it is because we are increasingly able to *perceive* and take into account the deepness of mental pain. Experience has shown to me that the end of the psychoanalytic process is often most difficult because the threat of stopping the analytic sessions *reveals* the existence of psychic suffering that had remained much more latent than the separation anxieties and their dutiful interpretation could have shown and resolved.

I found new possibilities of understanding these deepest forms of mental pain thanks to the work of Esther Bick on the psychic role of the skin and to the studies of Don Meltzer and of Frances Tustin on autism. Meltzer had already described as "terror" a kind of excessive paranoid anxiety that is *intolerable* by its very *quality*, and to be differentiated from other forms of persecution that can become intolerable by their intensity. Tustin succeeded in elucidating the *traumatic* nature of the fundamental anxiety of autistic children, which is the fear of an annihilation of the feeling of being, or "going-on being", as Winnicott said. Autistic barriers are barriers against the fear of the "black hole" of *primary depression* and against *nothingness*. These descriptions and concepts allowed me better to understand the mental pain experienced by my patients as resulting from catastrophic anxieties of separation (Bion) provoking a fear of psychic annihilation (Tustin). I understood that new parts of the self had been born during analysis, particularly new capacities to love; these new capacities were felt to be in danger of dying by the loss of the analytic link invested with the primary function of containing and detoxifying the excessive mental pain. This primary function is precisely what autistic children felt deprived of.

Following Klein, Meltzer (1967) has described the termination of the analysis, based on the model of weaning in infancy, as a mourning of the analytic link. For him, the evolution of "the psychoanalytical process" can be seen as having a "natural history" that follows that of the functioning of the psychic apparatus. In this sense, the end of the analysis would be of the same nature as the separation between children and parents when the children have become adult enough—and, one must add, when things have been good enough! And, of course, it is far from being always good enough! The lack of real autonomy is replaced by different forms of pathological dependence, which could until then have been more or less split off or denied, and these reveal themselves suddenly in full light and provoke dramas, as is typically the case during adolescence. I will give a short and most dramatic example, one that I shall never forget.

I received in consultation, a few years ago, a man who had just lost his son, about 20 years old. The young man had killed himself by defenestration, after a quarrel with his younger sister. The dispute started over something apparently very trivial: the possession of the family bathroom. The young man felt that his sister had spent far too long in the bathroom, and he pounded at the door, claiming the bathroom for himself. The noise of the quarrel made the father come and ask his son to keep quiet. Exasperated, the young man shouted, "I won't disturb you any more!"—and he jumped out of the window, smashing to the ground, where he was killed. At first sight, it did not seem that there had been a very severe pathology in this family. The father was an honourable man, a perfect representative of the French middle class, and apparently full of good intentions—but we know that the road to hell is paved with good intentions! This man had been totally caught off guard by the drama. The young man had, indeed, the father said, had difficulties in freeing himself from his family to become more autonomous. But he was a good boy, he had just been accepted in a professional school, and, the father added, "He was just about to jump into life". In fact, he jumped into nothingness!

We know quite well how intolerant narcissistic patients are to frustration, and suicide in adolescents is an extreme example of this. In that case, we can, of course, easily imagine, both in this young man and in his family, a mental pathology much more severe than it seemed at first sight. But it is not possible to be certain about this. (I did not have the opportunity to know more about this case, because I could not take the father in treatment and had to send him to a colleague.) Rather, I want to point out that pathology is, as is mental health, something that may or may not be *revealed*, according to life circumstances.

This example reminded me of the crucial importance of establishing, in psychic life, an internal object such as Meltzer described it in *The Psycho-Analytical Process* (1967) under the name of "toilet-breast". This internal object, sometimes represented in dreams by a bathroom, is the part-object into which the self can evacuate the *intolerable* excess of psychic pain, in order to allow the psyche to *survive*. So, such an object must have sufficient capacities to receive and to contain particularly the anxieties of primary depression, which threaten the very possibility of psychic life.

The use of "toilet-breast" appears as a projective defence which is part of the manic defences. In fact, the manic defences often appear to be based on masculine identifications, and, if they are not too massive, they are part of the normal mechanisms of psychic growth because they are quite necessary to protect the self from excessive and too dangerous depressive feelings that would prevent any development. Moderate manic defences can allow some sufficient and protected space suitable for the progressive elaboration of depressive affects, which are contained in other parts of the personality, generally in the feminine identifications. So, psychic bisexuality is very soon, by the means of identifications, implicated in the struggle against mental pain. In the above example, it is striking to see the bathroom being the object of a real *struggle for life* between the brother and his sister.

From the traumatic theory of growth to an aesthetic one

The importance given by Freud to traumatism in the psychosexual development of the child has long remained rather puzzling to me. In *An Outline of Psycho-Analysis* (1940a [1938]), he sums up his conclusions about the evolution of the child as essentially a series of traumas in relation to the environment: trauma of seduction by the mother, trauma of weaning, trauma of the threats of castration. It is only when I realized more fully the decisive role of the economics of mental pain in intersubjective relations that this way of theorizing seemed less enigmatic to me. For instance, I came to understand the *fantasy of seduction* as essentially based on the necessity to project one's desires into other people, under the principle that the one who loves is the one who suffers. In fact, seduction is the way *par excellence* of evacuating latent pain and radically preventing it from becoming manifest, when there is no toilet-breast available.

The hypothesis of a death instinct *inside the organism* seemed to result in a theory of a double polarity of instincts *inside the psyche*, so that the trauma was situated strictly inside the self, as an inevitable and permanent conflict between two basic instincts. The relation with the environment would be traumatic only because these instincts would reinforce the inevitable phantasms of a "bad object", while good experiences would reinforce the phantasms of a "good object". This is, at least, how Klein used the Freudian bipolarity of instincts, which she accepted totally and even systematically developed. However, she estimated that Freud did not, in the factors of resolution of conflicts like the Oedipus complex, give enough importance to the *positive feelings* that the child felt towards its environment, especially towards its *father*. But, even with this very important correction, can we really conceive a general theory of psychic development that would give only a secondary role to *human interaction* in the genesis and growth of the psyche?

When we begin to speak not only of development, but of the "genesis" of psychic functions as well, we enter the modern period of the evolution of analytic theory. This was set forth by Bion in *Learning from Experience*, in which he presented the first analytic theory of the conditions of the birth of the psyche, based on the capacity of the mother to receive and contain the first anxieties of the baby. With the idea that the mechanism for this was a "normal" form of projective identification, *mutual* in the child and in the mother, Bion gave the first theoretical description of Winnicott's concept of the clinically "good-enough" mother.

But even more important is the next step, the totally new and original description by Meltzer of the basic psychic conflict, under the name of the *"aesthetic conflict"*. This is no longer related to the supposedly innate instincts of life and of death, but to the conflict resulting in the libidinal and epistemophilic drives directed towards the "inside" of the mother. Meltzer does not give a very clear and precise definition of the nature of the conflict. He uses poetry rather than theory to evoke the ineffable feeling of it inside the reader by communicating his own "feeling" about it, using juxtaposition of clinical material essentially based on dreams, and literary allusions. He writes:

> The ordinary beautiful devoted mother presents to her ordinary beautiful baby a complex object of overwhelming interest, both sensual and infra-sensual. . . . But the meaning of his mother's behaviour, of the appearance and disappearance of the breast and of the light in her eyes, of a face over which emotions pass like the shadows of clouds over the landscape, are unknown to him. . . . [1988, p. 22]

So, we can understand that the baby's epistemophilic drives would come into conflict with the investment of the mother as an *"aesthetic object"*, a primary object of love and admiration when the baby discovers the outside world after birth. Meltzer states:

> He (the baby) cannot tell whether she (the mother) is Beatrice or his Belle Dame Sans Merci. This is the aesthetic conflict, which can be most precisely stated in terms of the aesthetic impact of the outside of the "beautiful" mother, available to the senses, and the enigmatic inside which must be construed by creative imagination. Everything in art and literature, every analysis, testifies to its perseverance through life. [1988, p. 22]

The concept would deserve a very long discussion. I shall briefly mention only three points

The concept of enigmatic object

The object described by Meltzer is an enigmatic one, as he says explicitly:

> The mother is enigmatic to him (the baby); she wears the Gioconda smile most of the time, and the music of her voice keeps shifting from major key. Like "K" (Kafka's, not Bion's), he must wait for decisions from the "castle" of his mother's inner world. ... For it is the human condition. What man knows the heart of his beloved, or his child, or his analysand, as well as he knows the heart of his enemy? [1988, p. 22]

It seems to me that one must differentiate between *enigma* and *mystery*. The French analyst Jean Laplanche also speaks now of the first relation to the mother as essentially "enigmatic". In my opinion, an enigma, like the typical one of the riddle of the Sphinx, is always very persecutory because it contains a very large amount of terror in the face of a latent pain, which can be a danger for psychic life itself. It is the danger of intolerable feelings of depression; their nature was stated by Klein's young autistic patient, "Dick" (Klein, 1930), when he saw the pencil shavings, and said "Poor Mrs Klein!" The concept of mystery implies, rather, a deep respect for insufficiently known but very important matters concerning life and death, and above all the creation of life.

It seems clear that Meltzer wants to indicate the differentiation between aesthetic and idealized object, when he speaks of
the "ordinary" beautiful devoted mother and her "ordinary"
beautiful baby. And I prefer to think, like Meltzer, that the paranoid–schizoid position is only secondary and not primal in development, which implies that the first object must be *more mysterious
than enigmatic* to be introjected as a "good-enough" object.

The concept of "reciprocity"

Meltzer has given a great importance to the concept of "reciprocity". There are clinical examples where the reciprocity of the
investment between the child and its environment was not good
enough, but where it was quite impossible to know whether this
lack of reciprocity came from the mother or father or whether it
came from the baby. So, it can often be impossible to decide which
of the two—mother (and father) or child—first considered the
other as an "enigmatic" object. I would think that it is the very
character of "early interactions" that it becomes quickly impossible to differentiate the role of one from the other, so much so that
the primary investments and identifications have a predominant
character of mutuality and reciprocity. Thus, we must speak of
interaction as something different from the ordinary concept of
object relations. In this sense, I think that what makes for successful early object relations is neither wholly on the side of the child's
investment, as admiring as this may be, nor wholly the mother's
love for the child (even when contained by the father's love), but
their interaction when this is harmonious enough. The aesthetic
feeling described by Meltzer seems to me to be the result of the
beauty of the encounter between the mother and the nascent capacities to love in the baby, contained by the father. Such a wonderful
encounter seems quite necessary to *confirm* for the baby its being
able to "go on being", because, in more theoretical terms, the mutual investment of the parents' attention and care *weaves a psychic
intersubjective substitute* for the containing function of the mother's
body, lost at birth: it is the symbolic equivalent of the containing
role of the skin, described by Esther Bick (1967).

This accomplishment has a twofold aspect. The first one is a
defensive and anti-traumatic function (the Freudian protective

shield). It carries what I have called a "basic security", composed of the trust derived from being sufficiently protected from annihilation anxieties, and which is the first step towards the sense of identity.

The second function derives from the libidinal aspect of a beautiful-enough encounter between baby and mother-and-father, and it constitutes the *pleasure of being alive*, thanks to the aesthetic investment of the object which permits sufficient *self-investment*. It is the very great merit of Meltzer to have added this aesthetic dimension to primary investments, which greatly enriches our comprehension of them, compared with Freud's ironic description of "His Majesty the Baby" as the projection upon him of the naïve or perverse narcissism of the parents.

Cognitive and affective development

Systematic observation has revealed the existence of very unexpected capacities or "abilities" in the baby. It becomes clearer that cognitive and affective developments are, in the very beginning of postnatal life, very linked and almost impossible to differentiate. We can think, however, that it is necessary to distinguish the sensual aspects of the relationship with the object, which are neurophysiological and cognitive, from the affective and more or less aesthetic investment of them which will determinate the psychic personality of the subject.

The most beautiful example of the possibility of revival of the sensual and aesthetic aspect of the primal object is certainly, in French literature, the famous memory of the madeleine in *A la recherche du temps perdu* ["Remembrance of Things Past"] by Marcel Proust. Let me remind you how he movingly described the obstinate search for the forgotten memory, whose mnemic trace had been unexpectedly awakened by the taste of a madeleine dipped in a teacup:

> But no sooner had the warm liquid mixed with the crumbs touched my palate than a shiver ran through me and I stopped, intent upon the extraordinary thing that was happening to me. An *exquisite pleasure* had invaded my senses, something isolated, detached, with no suggestion of its origin. And at once the vicissitudes of life had become indifferent to me, its

disasters innocuous, its brevity illusory—this new sensation having *had the effect, which love has,* of filling me with a *precious essence;* or rather this essence was *not in me, it was me.* I had ceased now to feel mediocre, contingent, mortal. [Proust, 1913, p. 58]

Is this not a wonderful and lively evocation of what we laboriously try to define in more abstract terms: the memory of the primal interaction which establishes the basic security and the pleasure in being alive, when it is based on mutual love—that is, *to be able to love and to feel being loved.*

Proust goes on searching:

Whence could it have come to me, this *all-powerful joy?* I sensed that it was connected with the taste of the tea and the cake, but that it *infinitely transcended* those savours, could not, indeed, be of the same nature. [p. 58]

The author makes a very clear and crucial differentiation between the sensation itself and the emotional investment of it. This corresponds to the differentiation between cognitive and affective development, but we can see, at the same time, how much these two lines of development have to be sufficiently integrated, one with the other, to be able to resist the splitting that occurs when mental pain is intolerable.

Proust goes on:

Where did it come from? What did it mean? Where could I apprehend it?

And he tries to drink a second mouthful, then a third one, to try, but vainly, to re-find the origin of this " exquisite pleasure" which seemed to him to be the essence of himself, as a rebirth of his feeling of identity and pleasure in being alive.

Then, he stops and he thinks:

It is time to stop, the potion is losing its virtue. It is plain that the truth I am seeking lies not in the cup but in myself. . . . I put down the cup and examine my own mind. It alone can discover the truth. But how? [p. 59]

And Proust begins a wonderful self-analysis, of which he gives an unforgettable narrative from which I shall quote only a few sentences:

Seek? More than that: *create*. It [the mind] is face to face with something which does not yet exist, which it alone can make actual, which it alone can bring in the light of day ... I place in position before my mind's eye the still recent taste of that first mouthful, and I feel something start within me, something that leaves its resting-place and attempts to rise, something that has been anchored at a great depth; I do not know yet what it is, but I can feel it mounting slowly; I can measure the *resistance*, I can *hear the echo of great spaces traversed*. Undoubtedly what is thus palpitating in the depths of my being must be the image, the *visual memory* which, being linked to that taste, is trying to follow it in my conscious mind ... [pp. 59–60]

And suddenly the memory revealed itself. The taste was that of the little piece of madeleine which on Sunday mornings at Combray ... my aunt Léonie used to give me, dipping it first in her own cup of tea or tisane ... [p. 61]

And Proust concludes, for the time being, this "search" with such a beautiful sentence that I can never read it aloud without a powerful emotion:

... when from a long-distant past nothing subsists, after the people are dead, after the things are destroyed, taste and smell alone, more fragile but more enduring, more immaterial, more persistent, more faithful, remain poised a long time, like souls, remembering, waiting, hoping, amid the ruins of all the rest, bearing unflinchingly, in the tiny and almost impalpable drop of their essence, the immense edifice of remembrance. [p. 61]

A revision of the concept of psychic destructivity

Now, the question is: how are things when environmental conditions are not good enough and the aesthetic aspect of primary love cannot be created? What are these "unimaginable anxieties" (Winnicott) and these "annihilation anxieties of the sense of being" (Tustin) made of? It seems to me that one can say that instead of the creation of the sense of *Beauty* which derives from mutual love, its *negative* takes place—Horror—which is the negative of the admiration and bedazzlement of love.

Horror has been represented in mythology by the figure of Medusa, who had a paralysing and mortal power. Of the three Gorgons, daughters of sea divinities who lived in Far Occident, not far from the Kingdom of the Dead, Medusa was the only one whose glance could kill. She was represented as a monster with a woman's head, whose hair was made of snakes, whose enormous and dangerous teeth were protruding from her gaping mouth, and whose face was so *horrid* to see that it *petrified with terror* those who were unlucky enough to meet her. To be able to defeat and kill her, Perseus had to use Athena's shield in order to fight her without confronting her glance.

Psychoanalysts like Pasche and Racamier have used the myth of Medusa to illustrate the terror of what they call *"the unrepresentable"*. We can understand what they mean, but I would prefer, with Elisabeth About, who too has worked with Meltzer and who has written a book, *Rencontres avec Méduse*, to speak of the terror of the "black hole" of primary depression, which indicates the horror of the abortion of psychic life.

Actually, I am now defining a *"narcissistic object relation"* as a relationship with an object which is felt and invested by the subject as being able to accomplish, *in interaction with* the subject, certain functions necessary for his or her security and development. The main character of such a relationship is to be the *matrix of potential change and psychic growth*.

When it fulfils its function, this matrix is the *container*, in Bion's terms, of change and growth. It is particularly necessary in order to allow the subject to contain and elaborate *the unknown*, which implies confronting at every new step in development both new aspects of life as well as depressive feelings of having lost the past ones.

On the other hand, when this matrix presents aspects that are too pathological because there is a too inharmonious interaction between the subject and the object, it fails to accomplish this function and becomes, in accordance with the concept introduced by Meltzer, a *claustrum* that imprisons the potential capacities of change and growth.

The perspective introduced by Meltzer with the concepts of "toilet-breast", "aesthetic conflict", and "claustrum" obliges us, in my sense, to completely revise the psychoanalytic theory of psychic destructivity, even leading to a complete reversal regarding the classical position of two basic instincts. When conditions have not been good enough and, particularly, when there has not been harmonious enough interaction between the child and his environment, *the pain in not being able to grow* will be too intense and will release a *core of despair* more or less hidden in the depths of the human being. In my opinion, mental pain is fundamentally depressive, because it is essentially the *pain of being unable to develop*, which has the meaning of a feeling of psychic death. That pain remains generally latent, because there are many and more and more complex defences against it. When it is recognized as such, which can occur only if conditions make it *tolerable*, as in a therapeutic situation, it can be transformed by thinking and then be used for psychic growth, which is a *creation*, as Marcel Proust felt and has said. The part of it that remains *intolerable* constitutes a more or less secret core of despair very deep inside each of us, and this can result in *violence* or in the so-called *psychosomatic diseases*.

Narcissism revealed itself first, like always, through its pathological forms. In my experience, pathological narcissism reflects the *violence* of defences against despair. People who have not found an object good enough to have permitted the creation of a basic security keep inside themselves *"unborn parts"* of their self. The expression has been created by Bion in relation to the "caesura of birth", but I use it in a different sense. We know that there are patients who often dream about savage and terrifying animals, like lions, tigers, spiders, and so forth. I think it is too simple and even false to consider these as deriving purely and simply from destructive drives coming from the death instinct. I think, rather, that this destructivity reveals the internalization of the failure of developmental interaction, which constitutes a real *abortion of the creative container–contained relation*, source of the normal narcissism of self-investment. This abortion of potentialities of development is accompanied by a *reversal*, in a negative way, of self-investment, which depends on the economics of mental pain. If there is no toilet-breast available, the object becomes a persecutory object with which the subject is obliged, for his or her *survival*, to identify: this primal identification with the aggressor is essentially a *survival* technique preventing *suicidal depression*. These pathological projective identifications constitute the *claustrum* described by Meltzer, and they oppose development in imprisoning the subject who *rejects his or her own self*, which he or she experiences with *horror*. Paranoia can result from this abortion of self-investment. The paranoiac not only feels persecuted by the external world, he or she also feels persecuted by his or her own unborn self. I recently heard from a colleague about the horrible story of a man who could not bear the divorce asked for by his wife and who killed her with a revolver; however, before trying to commit suicide, he also killed their two boys by hitting them on their heads with a hammer, as if he had tried to crush concretely his own intolerable mental pain projected into his children.

Klein had seen, in her child analyses, the existence of annihilation anxieties. But she seems to have spoken of it as if it were essentially the fear of physical death. For instance, in her paper "The Theory of Anxiety and Guilt" (1948), she writes that she "was led to apply Freud's hypothesis of the struggle between the life and death instincts to the clinical material gained in the analysis of young children", and she says: "Following this line of thought, I put forward the hypothesis that anxiety is aroused by the danger which threatens the *organism* from the death instinct; and I suggested that this is the primary cause of anxiety" (p. 275, emphasis added).

In fact, as I have already said, we must differentiate between the fear of physical or psychic annihilation, under the weight of depression. Physical death can even be wished for and acted out, as in the above case, to put an end to unbearable psychic torture. So-called psychosomatic diseases can be considered as somatic expressions of latent and split-off forms of suicidal depressions.

I shall give a short example of the shift in perspective which I propose by quoting the way that Klein illustrates, in the same paper, her point of view about the death instinct:

> A five-year-old boy used to pretend that he had all sorts of wild animals, such as elephants, leopards, hyenas and wolves, to help him against his enemies. They represented dangerous objects—persecutors—which he had tamed and could use as

protection against his enemies. But it appeared in the analysis that they also stood for his own sadism, each animal representing a specific source of sadism and the organs used in this connection. The elephants symbolized his muscular sadism, his impulses to trample and stamp. The tearing leopards represented his teeth and nails and their functions in his attacks. The wolves symbolized his excrements invested with destructive properties. He sometimes became very frightened that the wild animals he had tamed would turn against him and exterminate him. This fear expressed his sense of being threatened by his own destructiveness (as well as by internal persecutors). [1948, p. 276]

That is a very impressive description of the imaginary world in which this child lived! The paper is later than "Notes on Some Schizoid Mechanisms" (1946), but Klein expresses herself only in terms of sadism, to illustrate her thesis about destructivity and the death instinct. It is clear to anyone that this child is in great danger, but I would rather express it in terms of an enormously late development in constituting and investing his self-image. What Klein calls sadism, according to the classical terminology of stages of development of the libido, seems to me to have to be understood, rather, as the *negative investment* of this child's own functions and physical organs which reflects his being non-invested by his internal objects. Certainly such a child lives in a terrible and persecutory feeling of *loneliness*, as if he could trust absolutely no one to help him develop a better self-image. He feels totally alone to face his internal rejecting objects, trying desperately to tame his fragmented body, which remains a *stranger* to him and which he fantasizes as a heteroclitic horde of savage animals. He has to use them as allies, the only ones he can use in his immense inner loneliness, to fight what he calls his enemies, the most dangerous one being doubtlessly the depressive feelings that could invade and annihilate his psychic life, were he not continually fighting against them for his *survival*.

We can encounter cases where *space* and *time* are felt as terrifying persecutors. It is the interpretation that Samuel Beckett gave to time in the works of Proust. Beckett was only 24 years old when he wrote, in 1930, a short monograph on Proust. It is a very extraordinary book, quite fascinating, seeming almost like a paper from Bion! However, they had not yet met, a meeting that Didier Anzieu thought very important for both of them—maybe some kind of mutual identification? Anyhow, Beckett (1931) wrote this about Proust:

> The Proustian equation is never simple ... it is convenient to examine in the first place that double-headed monster of damnation and salvation—Time. ... Proust's creatures are victims of this predominating condition and circumstance—Time; victims as lower organisms, conscious only of two dimensions and suddenly confronted with the mystery of height, are victims—victims and prisoners. [p. 1]

I was quite amazed when I first read such a direct evocation of bidimensionality, as if it were a Meltzerian description of the world of autistic children, and of the difficulty to elaborate a third dimension, with reference to pathological projective identifications and the claustrum! Beckett goes on to describe the persecutory aspects of time:

> There is no escape from the hours and the days. Neither from to-morrow nor from yesterday. There is no escape from yesterday, because yesterday has deformed us, or been deformed by us. The mood is of no importance. Deformation has taken place. ... We are not merely more weary because of yesterday, we are other, no longer what we were before the calamity of yesterday. [pp. 2–3]

He then expresses a sense of absolute loneliness, meaninglesness, and absence of any "good" object:

> The good or evil disposition of the object has neither reality nor significance. The immediate joys and sorrows of the body and the intelligence are so many superfoetations. ... Such as it was, it has been assimilated to the only world that has reality and significance, the world of our own latent consciousness, and its cosmography has suffered a dislocation. [p. 3]

So, a concept of catastrophic change, to finish with, and then nothingness:

> ... We are disappointed at the nullity of what we are pleased to call attainment ... [p. 3]

This is a very impressive description of a psychic world without space for development (bidimensionality) and in which Time is seen as an inexorable predator. Beckett makes us perceive the latent *horror* of a permanent *threat of annihilation of psychic life*, which rules such a world. It only leads to nothingness and nonsense, the *absurd*, which will become more and more the central theme of Beckett's work. For him, ". . . the Proustian solution consists . . . in the negation of Time and Death, the negation of Death because the negation of Time. Death is dead because Time is dead" (p. 56). Beckett mocks the *"regained time"* of Proust; he maintains that "Time is not recovered, it is obliterated" (p. 56).

In fact, Proust's position is quite different, as he succeeds in rediscovering the *aesthetic memory* of the object to overcome his depressive feelings of loss and destruction and to *recreate his own self*. As he says at the end of his reflection, when he

> . . . was searching the cause of this felicity, of the character of
> certainty with which it imposed itself. . . . So many times, during my life, reality had disappointed me because, at the moment I perceived it, *my imagination, which was my only organ to enjoy beauty*, could not apply to it, in accordance with the inevitable law which wants that one can imagine only what is absent. . . . But let a sound, a scent, already heard or breathed in the past, be heard or breathed anew, both in the present and in the past, real without being actual, ideal without being abstract, instantly the permanent and usually hidden essence of things is freed, and *our true self* who, sometimes for a long time, seemed dead but was not entirely so, awakes and revives in receiving the divine food which is brought to him. [Proust, 1990, pp. 178–179; translated by J.B.]

Indeed, the aesthetic emotion has the deepest links with the recognition and re-creation of the love for life. The French language does not possess as many words as English, an inconvenience that has, however, an advantage: The French word *"reconnaissance"* means recognition as well as gratitude, a good integration of cognitive and affective development, or so one can hope. We must, in this vein, thank Donald Meltzer for reminding us of such important matters and for having helped us to understand them more clearly.

CHAPTER TEN

Reflections on "aesthetic reciprocity"

Gianna Williams

I intend to focus this chapter on the theme of aesthetic reciprocity in the context of the aesthetic conflict as it was described by Meltzer in *The Apprehension of Beauty* (Meltzer & Harris Williams, 1988a). I will begin by quoting Meltzer's attractive and imaginative conjecture about the proto-thoughts of the newborn:

> I have always found my world basically congenial ever since I began to find it interesting. When I was a fish I just swam about and had no thoughts. But once I found my friend placenta we explored and shared our findings. . . . We decided to leave (placenta and I) though we both suspected we were being forced to emigrate to make room for some newcomer. I felt pretty angry for this usurpation for I had lived there since the beginning of time, after all. . . .
>
> My body became suddenly dense and heavy, immovable. I heard myself not humming but screaming. They must have thought I was screaming at them, those huge and beautiful creatures, so strong they could lift me with one hand while I couldn't even lift my head. *But it was the beauty of one that*

overpowered me and I could see from the way she looked at me that I was tiny and ugly and comic. [pp. 43–44, emphasis added]

A little later in the same narrative:

Then she showed me *the most beautiful thing in the world* to blind me, I suppose, so that I should not see the abyss. Quite kind, really. My mouth stopped screaming and started sucking the anaesthetic stuff with which I was to be put to sleep. Very humane. I could die laughing and crying and dreaming of being huge and beloved by her. [p. 44, emphasis added]

Although in the "proto-thought of the new-born" (p. 43) Meltzer suggests that the very first experience of the infant blinded by the beauty of mother is one of feeling ugly and comic, elsewhere in *The Apprehension of Beauty* he refers to Winnicott's definition of "the ordinary devoted mother and her baby", and he says that Winnicott "could have spoken in the same idiom of the 'ordinary *beautiful* devoted mother' and 'her ordinary *beautiful* baby'" (emphasis added). He says that Winnicott was right to use the word "ordinary", with its "overtones of regularity and custom, rather than the statistical 'average'". "The aesthetic experience of the mother with her baby", he says, "is ordinary, regular, customary, for it has millennia behind it, since man first saw the world 'as' beautiful." Meltzer describes also how the observer of aesthetic reciprocity between mother and baby is overwhelmed by a feeling of awe. "No flower or bird of gorgeous plumage imposes upon us the mystery of the aesthetic experience like the sight of a young mother with her baby at the breast. We enter such a nursery as we would a cathedral or the great forests of the Pacific coast, noiselessly, bareheaded" (p. 16).

This description reminded me of the observation of a mother and baby who were both capable of sustaining the pain of experiencing one another as precious. The baby, aged 2 months, would move away from the breast after the first few hungry sucks and look up into mother's eyes (this happened repeatedly), giving her a white smile as his mouth was full of milk. The gratitude and reciprocal appreciation that came across in that observation, when the baby was still so tiny, gives support to one of the very important statements made by Meltzer in connection with the aesthetic conflict. He suggests (and I will return to this point) that depressive feelings and the experience of an object as infinitely precious and beautiful are *primary*. He even hypothesizes that "proto-aesthetic experiences can well be imagined to have commenced in utero when the infant is 'rocked in the cradle of the deep' of his mother's graceful walk, lulled by the music of her voice, set against the syncopation of his own heartbeat and hers" (p. 17).

In the play of lights and shadows that permeates *The Apprehension of Beauty*, I have focused so far on the play of lights. The play of shadows is certainly present in a clinical example given by Meltzer in the chapter on aesthetic reciprocity. He talks about a case he supervised in Italy with Martha Harris, the case of a little girl, "Claudia", who was born brain-damaged and whom Meltzer describes in the first consultation "lying in mother's arms drooping like a battered little rag doll, her squinting misshapen face hung loosely, drooling, eyes lifeless, a painful contrast to the delicate and elegant beauty of her mink-coated mother" (p. 44). It was very difficult for Claudia's mother to look at her as "her ordinary beautiful baby". Meltzer describes a number of aspects in the treatment of this patient, but I found particularly poignant the description of the time in the treatment of this child when the aesthetic reciprocity begins to be restored. The therapist does *not* settle for the child's perception of herself as an ugly, ridiculous little clown. Meltzer says that the therapist catches a glimpse of what he defines as the child's "cloud of glory, her enquiring spirit" (p. 56), and that Claudia is now exhibiting "some of the daily beauty in her life which inheres in her quest for knowledge and understanding the qualities which make her a beautiful little patient for her therapist" (p. 54).

This might often enhance the mother's capacity to *discover* an interesting baby. I do not think, sadly, that my experience of infant observation has confirmed that the "aesthetic experience of the mother with her baby is ordinary, regular, customary". I have seen repeatedly, though, how the presence of an observer deeply interested in the baby has enhanced the mother's capacity to look at the baby with different eyes. Meltzer would perhaps suggest that observations should start at the moment of birth, and then one would undoubtedly catch a glimpse of aesthetic reciprocity. He says that:

There could be countless babies who do not have ordinary devoted beautiful mothers who see them as ordinary beautiful babies, and who are not *greeted by the dazzle of the sunrise.* Yet I cannot claim with conviction that I have ever seen one in my consulting-room. Not even in my extensive experience of schizophrenic patients and psychotic children have I *failed* to find evidence of their having *been touched by the beauty—and recoiled wildly from it,* as they do again and again in the course of analysis. There is much evidence (cf. Spitz) to suggest that being thus untouched is not compatible with survival, or at least with the survival of the mind. [p. 29]

I shall now make reference to a patient, "Matthew", an adolescent boy whom I treated for a very long time and whose recoiling from an aesthetic experience probably took place at an early age.

Matthew's mother had been very ill after he was born. She had to stop breast-feeding him quite abruptly, and Matthew was looked after by his grandmother. He had always excelled in his studies, but he seemed to have a memory of his childhood and early adolescence as a time of "splendid isolation". He started treatment aged 18, chiefly as he wished to be helped with an excruciating migraine which paralysed him at times. (It is interesting in terms of the material that I am going to present that he referred to it also as a *"splitting* headache"). Matthew was no longer living in splendid isolation. He had had, by the time I first met him, a number of short-lived sexual relationships with both girlfriends and boyfriends, the relationships with girlfriends being more markedly sado-masochistic than the ones with boys. With boys, at times he joined in the "drag" scene, which provided an irresistible attraction for him. He told me, for instance, that he had dressed up as Goldilocks, with a blonde wig and enormous balloons for breasts. He thought I should find it funny that the blonde wig made such a striking contrast with the tiny dark moustache he had grown (indeed, a striking caricature of the combined object).

At the time of the drag scene, he brought me a dream that I think speaks for itself:

Matthew was inside the crater of a volcano. There was bubbling lava, smoke, and everything looked very dark. He was not in the lava but on firm ground. There was a smell of sulphur (little was left to my imagination). A group of men dressed in drag were dancing South American dances. Matthew was dressed up as Carmen Miranda. [No, he did not think that I was Latin American—perhaps Spanish, maybe Italian.] *There were tanks in the crater, but no shooting was going to take place because the men in the tanks were spellbound looking at the dances.*

Couples, and in particular feminine beauty, were caricatured and denigrated again and again in a world that leaves little doubt about a possible connection with the claustrum, if we think of the crater bubbling with sulphuric lava. There seemed to be no paternal function to protect the mother from Matthew's attacks. The ineffectual men were "spellbound by the dances".

The beauty of the object was gradually allowed to emerge in Matthew's dreams, but he could only admire the maternal object if he were in total possession of her. Very close to a holiday of mine, he had the following dream:

Matthew inherited a very beautiful Italian mansion. He was the sole owner. He described in great detail the banqueting-room, high ceiling, large and tall windows surrounded by white stucco, light shining through them onto statues of men on horseback lined up in front of the windows. There was electricity but it was produced by two old generators and he was going to replace them with his own modern system. The garden looked very beautiful, more English than Italian. Matthew was going to get the peasants from the village to grow beautiful Mediterranean types of vegetables. They were going to work for him. There was a room at the top of the house with a sliding roof, and one could lie there and sunbathe.

There was indeed an overall feeling of light and beauty. Matthew moved his hands (which he rarely did during his sessions) in a very animated way while describing the beams of light coming through the windows and the glass becoming iridescent.

I do not talk about this dream as an example of an aesthetic experience about the beauty of mother's body. Matthew's state of mind was very manic and did not at all convey the feeling of his being in awe. He conveyed the feeling of being in total projective identification with the beautiful mansion/mother. The other children were out; perhaps they were the peasants in the village. They may get a share of the beautiful Mediterranean vegetables, but Matthew was definitely *the sole owner and squire.* He owned the banqueting-*room*, perhaps the breast, the top room open to the sunshine of strong emotions (or perhaps the image of a mind open to the light of new ideas?). He did not think much of the light produced by the "old generators"/ parents. He replaced it with "his own modern system". Matthew seemed totally identified with a matriarchal mother of many peasant's children all depending on her and the fruits of her garden. The many equestrian statues appear to be the effigies of this rich mother's many men.

After this holiday, which dealt a severe blow to Matthew's perception of being the squire and owner of the beautiful mansion, I found him very sedated and he was able to tell me that he had felt very lonely during the holiday. He was struck by the fact that when I returned I was very suntanned. He said that I must have been abroad and had gone far away because "there hadn't been much sunshine over here", unless perhaps I had discovered a sunny spot in England—"but you don't tell *us* about it". He seemed to perceive himself as out there, one of the patients, one of the children, and in the second session he brought a dream about a suntanned couple:

He was travelling in Turkey, alone, on his bicycle (not motorbike). In a very beautiful place, probably Ephesus, he met a man and a woman who looked full of life and interests and seemed very close to one another. They were a middle-aged couple, both very suntanned and they were kind to him. He visited some of the sites with them. Then they left in their car and he was alone with his bicycle.

He had no doubt that the dream was related to my suntan. He said that he could never expose himself too much to the sun because he burnt easily. He said that I had obviously got the sort of skin that can soak the sun in, perhaps because I was born in a sunny country.

In the context of this dream, where the sun-tanned couple was described as full of vitality and interests and "they seemed very close to one another", I felt that exposure to the sun probably had the meaning of an intense emotional experience, something to do with the "passionate intimacy with another human being" (p. 29) that Meltzer describes as often so frightening. Matthew felt that he was not equipped to expose himself to the dazzle of the sunshine (he burnt easily). In the "dream of Ephesus" (incidentally, a place he knew to be associated with mysteries, not ugly secrets), the parental couple, no longer uglified, was perceived as having capacities that he lacked. The parents also had the capacity to withdraw, without being cold or unkind to him, to the nuptial chamber of their intimate relationship, and he—no longer sir or squire of the castle, very clearly outside the object at this point—experienced the full impact of his loneliness.

I felt very touched in the session of the "dream of Ephesus", when Matthew described his birthday present from his mother. It was a most beautiful, warm jumper which she had knitted weaving *two* different strands of wool together, but she had not had enough time for him. She had not got around to knitting the sleeves of the jumper . . . two sleeves missing . . . not enough time for him, and I had been away for two weeks basking in the sunshine and left him in the cold. Matthew's appreciation of feeling understood in this session, the "cloud of glory of his enquiring mind" (p. 56), his wish to be helped to give a meaning to his pain, evoked a feeling in the counter-transference that I prefer to describe with Meltzer's words: "for in the interplay of joy and pain engendering the Love (L) and Hate (H) links of ambivalence it is the quest for understanding, the K link, that rescues the relationship from impasse" (p. 28).

In spite of Matthew's fear of exposing himself to the sunshine, he was *not* in this session recoiling from the beauty of the analytic experience. There was between us a truthful feeling of aesthetic reciprocity. Meltzer would suggest that such feeling was not found for the first time but recaptured, that it would be true for Matthew, as Meltzer thinks it is so for all babies, that the "aesthetic impact is what greets his emergence into the world outside the womb . . . ".

What follows is a revolutionary statement that is implicit in the universal primacy of the aesthetic conflict described in *The Apprehension of Beauty*. I had only touched upon this theme earlier in this chapter:

> The depressive position would be primary for development and the paranoid–schizoid secondary, the consequence of the baby's closing his perceptual aperture against the dazzle of the sunshine. In Plato's terms he would hasten back into the cave. [p. 28]

And earlier in the chapter:

> I think that Melanie Klein was wrong to assume that the paranoid–schizoid position in object relations was anterior to the depressive position. This preconception coloured her language and distorted her thought about the processes of development. The depressive position was "reached", or "attained" or "achieved" by three months, she thought; and the evidence for it was a noticeable change in the baby's eyes. [p. 26]

Many, but I am afraid not all, infant observations over some thirty years of my acquaintance with this method of learning make me feel inclined largely to share, albeit not unconditionally, Meltzer's view and his admittedly drastic review of Klein's theory of development. An ecstatic and awe-inspiring feeling of aesthetic reciprocity between mother and baby can bowl over the observer in the earliest observations. I have, nowadays, become particularly sensitive to the first signs of recoiling from this overwhelming experience in mothers and babies, clinicians, and patients alike.

It is not surprising that the session of the "dream of Ephesus" was followed by one where Matthew recaptured his full talent for contempt. It was, by then, easier for me to keep my hope alive through a series of countless and, at times, heartbreaking fluctuations.

In the treatment of patients who *recapture*, as Meltzer suggests, rather than *acquire* the perception of their object as beautiful and precious in the transference, this experience is often accompanied by powerful phantasies of control and total possession of the object. At the core of this phantasy, there is a wish to rob the object of its essence. When this wish becomes conscious, this can bring about waves of depressive anxiety and regret.

A very attractive, very disturbed, and very verbal little girl, whom I treated and wrote about a long time ago, gave me a striking and extremely appreciative summary of my job description with the following words: "My digestive system is not very good. You digest the food for me and give me back what goes into my bloodstream" (Henry, 1969, p. 55).

Little "Sarah", who was 7 years old at the time, knew more about Bion than either myself or my supervisor in those remote days. Sarah literally drank my words, and she was endowed with an overpowering attraction for the K link. "Please talk, my ears ache", she told me in a session when I was puzzled, intrigued, and unusually silent. But the very attractiveness of the analytic work (and heaven knows if I experienced aesthetic reciprocity in my work with Sarah) was claiming for a time total ownership of me. The very attraction of the object risked turning it into a fragile one, because Sarah so much wanted to possess it and control it. She intended to put sellotape on my mouth at the end of a session so that I wouldn't talk to other children (let alone to the very hated father) until she returned for her next session. She wanted to "tear a ladder in my tights so that she could come right inside". On one occasion she delegated the mission to little soldiers that she made out of plasticine. She said she was going to put them in my mouth so that they would *debone me* so I couldn't move until she came back—the most graphic image of robbing me of my shaft, my backbone, of the father. What if she couldn't put the bones back in the following session? Wasn't she lucky that I was not going to let her get away with that project? (I did not mince my words in my interpretations in those days). Sarah was able to sustain, at a later stage, deep feelings of regret for what she might have done to me if I let her or Mr Henry let her. She also couldn't believe, for a time, that her mother, who had a hysterectomy because of gynaecological problems, may not have been damaged by her virulent attacks: "Perhaps", she said, "when I was inside my mum I kicked so hard that I made her incapable of rebabying."

Patients like Matthew took much longer than Sarah to reach the stage of recapturing depressive feelings.

I have found, with some adolescents, that a desecration of the beauty of the object takes the form of what is apparently a most passionate erotic transference.

"David", a very disabled 18-year-old I treated intensively for six years, had not perceived himself as an ordinary beautiful baby for his mother, whom he described to me as his extraordinarily beautiful mother. He was born without arms from the elbow down. When he was 6 months old and his single mother returned to work, he was put in a children's home where he spent seven years, apparently because his grandmother did not wish to care for him. Mother visited him every week in the children's home throughout those seven years.

When I started seeing David, his most beautiful dark eyes gripped me with a desperate plea not to look at his "bits missing", as he referred to his arms. He was at the time having a passionate affair with a married woman twenty years older than himself. In his first session, he asked me if it was true that patients always fall in love with their analysts: he had read something about it in a Sunday newspaper supplement. He started sending me passionate love poems in the weekend gaps. He could, fortunately, be encouraged to bring to his session his words and his poems. His dreams did indeed belong to the analytic setting, and some of them were somewhat daring. I will quote one of them:

About three months after the beginning of treatment, David had a dream in which *he came to visit me in my home. We were supposed to have a session, but he asked me if he could kiss me, and I said he could. I was wearing a sexy silk dressing-gown and it felt very intimate. Then my husband returned home with our two children. David told me where to hide and I obeyed. He then spoke with my husband and explained that we were having a session and he should not really meet people from my family, as he was a patient. My accommodating husband went quietly upstairs with the children.*

My predicament in this dream is not very different from the one Sarah wished to consign me to in her phantasy of getting me "deboned" by her plasticine soldiers. I was helplessly at the mercy of my patient, without a father or a backbone/father to set limits and to protect me. I was an extremely fragile object, rendered fragile by David's ingenious possessiveness.

This boy desperately needed to be held and could only begin to lie on the couch and let go of the grip of his eyes on me after two years of treatment. He told me, after the wave of erotic transference was over, that he used to have a recurrent dream when he was a child: *he was sitting on mother's lap and was sliding from mother's lap. He couldn't hold on to her and she was not holding on to him.* Obviously, David's attempts to seduce his object were to be understood also as a desperate need to hold on with all his means, but what safety, what containment, could be offered to him by a foam-rubber, pliable mother coupled with a half-witted father? What help could this object be to him?

I have focused in the description of the early days of my work with David on the *fragility that is inherent to the patient's desire to possess his object.*

This is an aspect that particularly interests me, as it seems to be *engendered by the aesthetic experience, but greatly to reinforce the aesthetic conflict.*

One of the aspects of the aesthetic conflict—the precariousness of the object—has been beautifully captured by many poets. I quote from John Keats's "Ode to Melancholy":

"for Truth is Beauty, Beauty that must die."

and Walter de la Mare's "Fare Well":

"Look thy last on all things lovely,
Every hour."

Meltzer says indeed that the apprehension of beauty "contains in its very nature the apprehension of the possibility of its destruction". There is a dread of the fragility of a precious object that *cannot* purely be confined to the fear of the damage brought about by one's possessiveness.

The core of the aesthetic experience, though, according to Meltzer, resides "*not* in the transience but in the enigmatic quality of the object". He quotes from elsewhere in Keats's "Ode to Melancholy",

"joy whose hand is ever at his lips, bidding Adieu"

and he says:

It is a truthful object that is always reminding the lover of the transience or a tantalising one like "La belle Dame sans Merci"?

The aesthetic conflict is different from the romantic agony in this respect: that its central experience of pain resides in uncertainty, tending towards distrust, verging on suspicion. The lover is naked as Othello to the whisperings of Iago, but is rescued by the quest for knowledge, the K link, the desire to *know* rather than to *possess* the object of desire. The K link points to the value of the desire *as itself* the stimulus to knowledge, not merely as a yearning for gratification and control over the object. *Desire makes it possible even essential to give the object its freedom.*

Again, this concept can be found in a very poetic form, in William Blake's words:

"he who binds himself to a joy doth the winged life destroy, he who kisses joy as it flies lives in eternity's *sunrise*."

It is quite striking to see how often the *sunshine* or *sunrise* appear in patients' material (Matthew is a good example of this) in connection with an aesthetic experience. It is a metaphor also often used by Meltzer in *The Apprehension of Beauty*, and indeed it is present in the poem by William Blake I have just quoted.

I shall now refer briefly to a little boy who had plentiful reason to experience "uncertainty tending towards distrust and verging on suspicion" for his object.

"Darren" was 5 years old when he started treatment with Rosy Duffy. Darren had had a loving and happy relationship with his young mother until he was 18 months old. He was then (and this coincided with the birth of his sister) totally rejected and severely physically abused by his mother over a two-year period until he was removed from home. I will not talk about the very arduous work that Rosy was engaged in for many years with a child who had become totally entrenched in the grips of an internal gang. While in the grips of the gang, Darren was fiercely attacking links and hated thinking. He interfered with Rosy's thinking in countless ways, and he attacked with a vengeance her paternal function, whom he referred to as "Mrs Daddy Duffy". About three years into the treatment, Darren spent a number of sessions drawing road maps, and he said to Rosy, "all these roads link things up, I like things to be clear", and he added: *"I knew you were thinking just then—sometimes when I see your face thinking, I am thinking too."*

This seems to me the most beautiful recapturing of an aesthetic experience in a child who had so many reasons to be suspicious of his object. I quote from Rosy's paper (Duffy, 1995) on Darren:

> There were of course huge reactions from the gang after this wonderfully hopeful declaration. I had used the word mind in my conversation with him, he then spat at me "'mind', mind, fucking rubbish mind, that's all you ever fucking think about, there's no meaning, peaning, reaning, beaning", and in a later session, "every time you say: 'think' I'll hurt this Mrs Rag Doll Duffy".

It is, in my experience, very frequent indeed that the initial recapturing of aesthetic reciprocity may be followed by *desecration* and a *need to spoil* which is *directly proportional* to the pain engendered by the intensity of the aesthetic experience.

This appears to me to be one of the moments, in treatment, where it is most essential to interpret the defences and, *at the same time,* interpret the anxieties defended against.

One has, indeed, to bear the onslaught as Rosie did until Darren could return to say to her again, "please help me to think thoughts", as I had to do with the resurgent wave of contempt in

Matthew, after the session of the "dream of Ephesus", before we could return to better times. But I think that one has also to find the way to convey, with different words, to different patients, that the onslaught has something to do with the pain of allowing something beautiful in the relationship to survive, that one may feel that it is better to kill it as it could so easily get lost anyhow.

In *The Psycho-Analytical Process*, Meltzer (1967) describes the "last-ditch fight" that often takes place on the threshold of the depressive position. His later hypothesis that the depressive position is not *reached* but *recaptured* in the turmoil of the aesthetic conflict makes it even more understandable that such an experience should be so turbulent, characterized not just by fluctuations but by powerful storms, as it is a great gamble to return to a place that one has run away from.

I would like now to conclude with a reference to a very hopeful case. I quote from a paper by Annette Mendelson (1997) about "Joseph", a child who is now 5 years old. Joseph has been exposed probably more than most children I have treated myself or heard about in supervision to the experience of the fragility of his objects, but he has amazingly retained an object-seeking capacity.

> "Joseph is the third child of refugee parents who fled to this country seeking political asylum from their native Uganda. He was born two years later. . . .
>
> Terrible atrocities which took place between rival tribes in Uganda resulting in imprisonment and the torture of his father and the torture and rape of his mother were to have devastating consequences. In their escape to England they left behind their young daughter whom they were never to see again. Already traumatised by her experiences in Uganda and grieving for her lost daughter, Joseph's mother gave birth to a second child Nathan some months after their arrival here.
>
> Tragedy struck the family once more with the discovery that mother had contracted the HIV virus possibly as a result of rape during her imprisonment. Through vertical transmission (that is transmission of the virus to the baby through the placenta), the baby was born HIV positive. Mother's pregnancy with Joseph 2 years later escalated the progress of her disease and before Joseph was born, she was already suffering from full blown AIDS. (Joseph was not HIV positive). At the same time the health of Nathan had deteriorated. Such were

the circumstances awaiting Joseph, the new baby, at the time of his birth. Over the next three years, Joseph was to experience no less than 18 changes of carers, the first of these occurring when he was ten days old. A number of these were temporary placements arranged formally with the help of Social Services now involved with the family. Others were arranged informally by the mother for a few days here and there with various friends. All these changes were because of mother's and brother's illness which necessitated periods of hospitalisation and because of mother's inability to cope with the vigorous demands of a baby and later a toddler when she herself was burdened by her own disease and her son's. The first experience of death came for Joseph at the age of two when his brother Nathan died. At the age of three, almost a year after Nathan's death, Joseph and his mother and father were referred to the children's team of the Traumatic Stress Clinic for an assessment. Only one week after the assessment took place, Joseph's mother died. Joseph was moved again this time to live with a Ugandan woman called Leah who was a friend of the family. Like Joseph's parents she too had been a victim of torture and had witnessed terrible violence in Uganda.

About one year after the death of his natural mother, Joseph was to lose also foster mother Leah whom he had by then learned to call mummy. She also died of an AIDS related illness."

There would have been so much grounds for this boy to recoil totally from seeking precious relationships. I find it very puzzling to this day that he has established, from the start, such a strong bond of trust with his therapist in spite of a very large number of breaks and interruptions due to the upheavals in his life during nearly two years of treatment. As I said, the therapist's name is Mendelson, but it is certainly significant that Joseph turned this into "Mrs Medicine", an obvious indication, as Annette suggests in her paper, that he was thinking of her as an object who might help him to feel better.

I would like to quote a particularly moving sequence where one sees how this child is not only able to sustain the experience of aesthetic reciprocity with his therapist, but is also able to recapture with her help the image of a beautiful mother in his mind. The session took place after the "second mummy" had died.

> "Joseph . . . fetched a piece of paper and asked me to draw his two mummies together "do them holding hands like they did when they were alive" although I wouldn't normally draw for a child in a session Joseph was so intensely absorbed in this process of trying to understand or remember, I yielded to his insistence. I drew as he quietly instructed me, telling me to be very careful: when I had finished, he said he would colour the picture himself and he chose bright and vivid colors. Whilst involved with this he went through all the parts of the body saying "mummy was like this when she was alive" and so on. With the picture finished he told me it was *special* and he folded it and put it into his box."

As I was very puzzled by the resilience of this little boy, I sent (with Annette's permission) her paper to Dr Meltzer and subsequently spoke with him about it. He felt that Joseph was a robust little boy who "makes one think twice about crediting or blaming parents. A child who is able to shift his hopefulness to a new source and has an ability to shift to a new object without being unfaithful to the old one." What one sees in this child is rather wonderful and gives one hope for human nature. Meltzer also said that hearing about a child like Joseph helps to demonstrate the presence of something rather mysterious and, he added, that one is not called upon to explain everything but just to describe.

CHAPTER ELEVEN

Beckett:
dramas of psychic catastrophe

Margaret Rustin and Michael Rustin

Donald Meltzer has demonstrated how a psychoanalytic perspective can illuminate works of contemporary theatre in his essay on Pinter's plays, published in *Sincerity and Other Works* (1994). We shall be drawing on some of his ideas in our discussion of Samuel Beckett [1906–1989], who was Pinter's most important forerunner and exemplar in the contemporary drama. Anthony Cronin's (1996) biography of Beckett refers to Pinter's admiration for Beckett and his friendship with him.

What are Beckett's plays about?

Even forty-five years after the first production of *Waiting for Godot*, the question of what Beckett's plays are about remains a challenging one, though many people—including Beckett himself—have thought that this was not necessarily a productive question to ask, since it threatens to lead one away from the plays themselves. We might see this as analogous to Bion's distinction between knowing about and getting to know. But the question arises because of Beckett's break with our previous expectations of what a modern play was supposed to be—that is, a representation of a more-or-less familiar patch of social life (usually taking place in a house or a room) with characters who are at least in part identifiable versions of social types that we recognize. This apparent correspondence between the staged play and recognizable social and domestic reality had become especially the case for modern drama in the work of its great masters, such as Ibsen, Chekhov,[1] and Miller. Indeed, part of the achievement of modern dramatic writing had been to invest with tragic dimensions the experiences of characters whose social identities were not so different from those of the majority of their audiences.

But in *Waiting for Godot*, Beckett put onto the stage two nondescript characters, Estragon and Vladimir, who had little in common with those conventionally represented in the theatre. They are in some respects like vagrants (with ill-fitting boots, sleeping in ditches, eating raw turnips, radishes, half-eaten chicken legs), yet some of their routines are like those of circus clowns. The play has no plot or action to speak of, except that of "waiting" for Godot, whose identity is a mystery and who in any case does not come. The absence of action or plot—the extreme difficulty of Vladimir and Estragon in doing anything, even moving from the spot—is what distinguishes the action of this, and of Beckett's other full-length plays, *Endgame* and *Happy Days*, from most previous drama.

This is a more extreme dramatic strategy than that of Chekhov, Beckett's main forerunner in his attention to the "real time" or "here and now" of his characters' interaction with one another on the stage. In Chekhov's work, what happens, or does not happen (the failure to sell the cherry orchard until it is too late, for example), is mostly moved by the states of mind of his characters and their relations with one another. Beckett is more radical than Chekhov in that Vladimir and Estragon, Winnie and Willie, Hamm and Clov are in a world in which virtually nothing can

---

[1] Chekhov, however, as Richard Gilman (1995) has pointed out, is one of Beckett's major forerunners in the ways that his plays give preference to the depiction of often paralysed states of mind over conventional action.

happen at all, since they have lost the capacity for agency. Another way of putting this is to say that Beckett is representing characters who are trapped in their own mental states.

There are three questions one can ask about this dramatic method. The first is: why does Beckett choose to depict characters with such vestigial social identities, in all of his plays? A second question is: what are the mental states in which these characters are in their different ways imprisoned? And a third is: why should these distinctive *mise-en-scène*, and the mental states that are explored in them, have such continuing resonance? Clearly we have to understand the mental states in order to understand why Beckett chose to represent them as he did, and why it is that audiences should feel, over nearly fifty years, nourished and enriched by their representation.

We begin with some further reflections on *Waiting for Godot*, then offer some thoughts about *Endgame*, and finally turn to *Happy Days* (Beckett, 1986).

Waiting for Godot

Estragon and Vladimir appear to have virtually nothing, except the clothes they wear. They have no project, except, at Vladimir's insistence, to wait for Mr Godot, who has promised to see them and who seems to offer some kind of indeterminate hope. They are vulnerable to attack—Estragon says that he has slept the night in a ditch and has been beaten up by ten men. They have nothing to eat except the assorted scraps that they carry in their pockets. Estragon's boots hurt him. Vladimir finds urination acutely painful. They repel each other through their smell. These are images of infantile helplessness and persecution. Clowns likewise represent for the audiences extreme physical vulnerability and liability to attack, failure, and humiliation of all kinds, reminding us of our own memories of vulnerability, though encoding this in the relatively safe external form of the clown, whose underlying sadness is, however, often made evident. Beckett was, in fact, an admirer of Buster Keaton and cast him in his only film.[2]

---

[2] The story of this episode is told in Cronin (1996).

However, these figures have other imaginative referents. One should hardly forget that this play was written in the years just after the Second World War, when Europe was full of displaced persons and the victims of war. There are fragmentary evocations of death and disaster throughout the play, references to "billions of others", "dead voices" that make a noise like wings, leaves, sand, or ash, voices for whom "to have lived is not enough".

Estragon and Vladimir express a shared memory of more deaths than any mind can bear to think of, but which makes it impossible for them to think of anything else. They share the burden of these thoughts, as if what could not be thought at all by one might perhaps just be bearable if the two of them share the task. Suicide is no good to them, they recognize, unless both of them can die, since unless there is someone with whom to share their terrible thoughts, to live on would be unbearable.

Theirs is a strategy of bare psychic survival, and their dialogue is its main resource. The rhythms, repetitions, flow of ideas, irony, playfulness, and rejection in their talk gives some containment to the anxieties and terrors that beset the characters. The audience, brought into the dialogue as spectators of these bizarre events, is also caught up in subtly shifting identifications. The point of Beckett's choice of Chaplinesque or Keatonesque figures as his two central characters must have been that audiences could identify with them as stylized representations of ordinary vulnerable citizens in a senseless world. The play's frequent silences, abruptness, and apparent inconsequence creates unease and anxiety as it disrupts the normal theatrical expectation of a seamless and naturalistic flow of dialogue and action. It is the release of this unconscious anxiety in the audience that underlies much of the humour of the play. (Humour and anxiety, as Freud understood, are closely connected.) It is important in staging it that the despair and desolation—the dead and dying objects—that underlie the comedy remain real presences: laughter must be only a partial escape from unbearable mental pain.

There is, we think, some gradual movement towards greater hopefulness and perhaps recovery as the play proceeds. Pozzo's blindness and new vulnerability is less terrifying than his arrogant bullying—Vladimir and Estragon no longer have to worry about violence from that quarter. The concluding comic exchanges of the play, around the macabre subject of their hanging—they don't have a rope, they need each other's help to hang, their rope breaks, Estragon's trousers fall down when he takes out his belt— have the effect of containing their despair, and, of course, the audience's. What the audience is perhaps left with is that these two—traumatized victims of terror and disaster—have just about survived. And they occupy our minds insistently.

Our belief is that this play has to be seen in part as a response to the catastrophes surrounding the Second World War. While there are references to philosophical and religious themes, the sufferings evoked on the stage seem altogether more tangible than these, although the echoes of these discourses provide some fractured language in which the near-destruction of life and hope can be represented.[3] There has perhaps been some reluctance to acknowledge these actual horrors in some critics' insistence on more metaphysical interpretations.

Vladimir, Estragon, Lucky, and Pozzo are a collection of names which evoke the turbulence of postwar occupied Europe. They appear to be beset by guilt as well as by fear and hopelessness, though it may be the guilt of survivors, and a sense of general complicity, as much as of perpetrators. Vladimir's discussion of the one of the two thieves on the cross with Christ who was spared, according to one Gospel, expresses his sense of identification with this guilty victim. Will one of them be spared, he is asking, but, also, what crimes have they committed? Athol Fugard told his actors, when he was directing *Waiting for Godot* in South Africa in 1984, that "Estragon and Vladimir must have read the accounts of the Nuremberg Trials, or else they were at Sharpeville, or were the first in at Auschwitz. Choose your horror—they know all about it" (quoted in Graver, 1989, p. 103).

Of course, they seem hardly capable of doing anything, but we learn more of what this state of mind might mean when Pozzo and Lucky come onto the stage.

---

[3] The tree that has put forth leaves in the second act calls to mind Revelations 22:2, which describes "a new heaven and a new earth": "In the midst of the street of it, and on either side of the river, was there the tree of life, which bare twelve manner of fruits, and yielded her fruit every month: and the leaves of the tree were for the healing of the nations."

Pozzo holds Lucky as his slave on a leash. He controls him by the threat of the whip. Lucky has been turned into a wholly abject instrument of his master's will, picking things up, putting them down, fetching and carrying them, in a way that makes clear that his continuing total obedience is his master's purpose for him. This demonstration of a broken will, of the turning of a person into a sub-human being, is surely an evocation of the fate of the victims of the ghettos and concentration camps.[4] At one point, Lucky is instructed to keep a few paces away from Pozzo, as the SS required their camp victims to do.

Estragon and Vladimir witness this treatment of a victim even worse off than themselves, and they display different reactions to it. This includes some sympathy for Lucky and protest to Pozzo. But they discover that Pozzo has something—food—that they want, and his self-confidence and bluster is in any case intimidating. Estragon's gesture of trying to help Lucky leads to his being kicked in the shins. That is the end of any sympathy for him. Pozzo explains as a matter of obvious fact that pain has to be lodged somewhere, and that Lucky has just got rid of a bit of it into Estragon.

These events are made to seem an ordinary enough part of Vladimir's and Estragon's lives. They are thus represented as ordinary, powerless, witnesses to and accomplices in abuse and atrocity. No wonder they experience guilt, impotence, and hopelessness. Lucky's fate could easily be theirs, and even observing Lucky's fate is destructive enough.

As one of Pozzo's two exhibitions of his damaged capabilities, Lucky is made to dance. For the other, he is made to think—that is, to make a speech in which thinking is supposed to take place. The speech draws incoherently on a variety of cited references. Its underlying theme, however, in so far as one emerges, is that man in spite of apparent consolations and activities, and of academic knowledge, "wastes and pines, wastes and pines". The speech culminates with repeated references to "the skulls", and "labours left unfinished". The emerging image is of total desolation, and of a mind destroyed.

---

[4] Beckett had a friend and Resistance comrade, Alfred Peron, who died soon after his release from Mauthausen.

The end of this speech produces a brief moment of triumph for the others, as Lucky's hat, symbol of his thought, is crushed. Vladimir and Estragon then cooperate with Pozzo in trying to restore Lucky—by propping him up—to some measure of servile functioning. Not only has Lucky's mind been destroyed by his experiences, whatever they are, and its destruction publicly exhibited, but the sense is that these established kinds of thinking (philosophy, scholarship, citations) and activities ("the strides of physical culture the practice of sports such as tennis football running cycling . . .") have lost all meaning and worth.

There is another kind of thinking that does go on in this play, and which provides the basis for its residual hopefulness. This is the thinking embodied in the conversations between the two friends, Vladimir and Estragon. Even the worst that can befall, Beckett seems to say, is made more bearable by its being shared.

The two friends have moments in which they can help each other, offering to share the meagre food available (turnips or carrots) and achieving some understanding of each other's states of mind. They are often verbally in tune with one another, even if they appear to start off with a difference of opinion.

Their anxieties and uncertainties—about what day of the week it is, about whether and how to kill themselves, about being beaten up—are all alleviated by the fact that they can put them into words, know that they are understood by each other. Their double act is the disguise, the outward form of the joke that conceals the desolate truths that it is the main work of the play to share with its audience. The "charming evening" which is "worse than being at the theatre" wrenches our guts as we laugh. The exchange of words is likened to a game ("Come on Gogo, return the ball, can't you, once in a while?"), but the underlying matter is deadly serious.

The problem, to which Beckett's method in this play was a solution, is what has been described as the impossibility of representing in art the terrible sufferings of catastrophes such as the two World Wars and the Holocaust. Beckett lived through the war in Occupied France.

It seems crucial to Beckett's method not to allow his audiences the mental comfort of references to circumscribed, recognizable events. Definition, narrative, description would all be defences, ways of pushing away anxiety, onto some named "other", in a place, a nationality, a recognizable "type" of some kind. A symbolic containment of the horror needed *not* to be available for its true meaning to be conveyed. The strangeness of these Beckett characters, the surreal quality of the scene and the dialogue, evokes the impossibility of sharing an understanding of catastrophic events such as those of war, persecution, and torture.

We could say, using Bion's terms, that a loss of contact with good objects, and the experience of the environment as wholly unreliable and persecuting, engenders a sense of "nameless dread".

Al Alvarez in *Beyond All This Fiddle* was one of the first to write about the emergence of a postwar literature that sought to do justice to the extremes of emotion and experience of our time. Beckett, with his exceptional sensitivity to mental pain, and his gift for representing the essence of this, was the pioneer in theatre of this exploration. After him, with Pinter and others, it became possible to recognize that bizarre and extreme states of mind were common features of our social world. It is, however, noteworthy that with Pinter, too, the exploration in his writing of psychotic states of mind has been accompanied by his increasing sensitivity to political atrocity. Dramatists, who need a theatre, are perhaps particularly aware of the importance of external containment.

Although there remains some vestigial structure of night and day in *Waiting for Godot*, its characters exist in a disordered relation to time. Estragon, Vladimir, and Pozzo torment each other with the uncertainty of whether they can remember what took place yesterday, or recognize each other when they meet again, and are tormented by the unending unchanging quality of their states of mind. The play investigates the response to a small change in this environment: at the beginning of the second act, the tree has sprouted a few leaves. Spring (hope?) has perhaps surfaced in this dead landscape. Vladimir's response is to sing a song about a dog stealing a bone and being beaten to death by the cook and the other dogs. It is clear that it is dangerous to allow hope to emerge: a dog who sniffs out a bone and believes he can get nourishment is in for trouble. Not only does the cook fail to respond to the dog's hunger, but all the other dogs unite in murderous rage because of their own deprivation. No one can therefore feel safe. It seems that it is better not to notice the leaves or smell spring in the air: one will only provoke the envy of the others and end up worse off than ever.

This bleak situation underlies the problem that Vladimir summarizes thus: "What is terrible is to have thoughts." There are repeated attacks on the possibility of thinking both within and between characters. For instance, Lucky's monologue, with its crucial remnants of thought which could provide meaningful clues to the catastrophe that they are living, is the cue for the others to steal and crush his hat, representing the head from which the mangled thoughts have come. The intolerance of the reality that his words have made real for his hearers is thus enacted. The routine that follows, with Vladimir and Estragon passing the hats back and forth as they try them on for fit, registers their confusion as black comedy.[5]

The place to which the characters have retreated is, of course, rife with infantile anxieties, though they struggle to hold these at bay through their immobility. Beckett shows us the fundamental fear of the void, of falling out of contact with a supporting internal or external object. There are many episodes of actual falling, responded to at times with concern and an attempt to pick up the one who has fallen, and at others with cruel delay in responding. "When we wait with folded arms," says Vladimir, evoking the image of the stony parent who fails to respond. The panic that the characters experience provides a theatrical representation of the infantile terror described so well by Esther Bick. Vladimir asks Pozzo: "What do you do when you fall far from help?" Of course the answer can only be that he waits. Meltzer's work on the defensive use of intrusive identification to evade the terror of the dependence on an object is visibly exemplified in the relationship between Vladimir and Estragon. "There you are again at last," says Vladimir, as Estragon reappears and falls into his arms. They are "playing" at Pozzo and Lucky, but it is deadly serious for each of them if they cannot maintain contact with the other. "Where were you? I thought you were gone for ever", Vladimir continues,

---

[5] Beckett once began rehearsals of the play with Lucky's speech, saying that this was the key to the play (Graver, 1989, p. 49).

and when they are separated again a few lines later, Estragon says, "I'm in hell".

The version of mutual dependence that their relationship ex-emplifies is a parody of a benign tie between parent and child. For their hell is as much in being together as in being apart. "Get up till I embrace you" well expresses their contradictory feelings, as they both love and repel each other, moving swiftly from a com-forting embrace to hostile rejection: "You stink of garlic."

They have brought this relationship of ambivalence to a fine art, playing much of it out as a game and managing their depend-ence on and aggression towards each other in this way. *Waiting for Godot* gives one of the most resonant expressions of the image of a couple joined together in hopeless mutual dependence.

Even though there is some development in an otherwise re-petitive and static state of affairs, the characters remain trapped by their unbearable pain. In Act Two, Vladimir tenderly helps Estragon to go to sleep, and he comforts him when he wakes up in panic. But Vladimir, though kinder to Estragon than in the paral-lel scene in Act One, still cannot bear to hear about Estragon's nightmare, and he proposes walking off instead. Estragon's anx-ious complaints finally drive Vladimir to furious rejection of the "bellyful of lamentations".

Their suffering is engendered by the act of waiting which the play sets out to investigate. They are waiting for someone else to intervene and make a new direction possible. When an infant has to wait for too long, the problem of trusting in Godot/God, mother and father can be extreme. Vladimir and Estragon do not hang themselves, and their knowledge that they are waiting is evidence that they are not wholly trapped in the claustrum-type of world (Estragon even speaks of being in "another compartment"). They wish to meet up with someone outside this.

The image of birth offered by Pozzo is relevant in this respect: "They give birth astride of a grave, the light gleams an instant, then it's night once more." The brief gleam has not been extin-guished, so death has not completely won, despite the dreadful confusion of creation with the grave. The baby is being born mo-mentarily into a world of light (a mother looking at her baby with love), and this image has not been entirely destroyed by fear and hatred.

Endgame

Endgame is the bleakest of Beckett's plays. The sense of imprisonment of the characters in their relations with each other and in the physical space they inhabit is almost total. The absolute greyness of the room's interior, added to by the colourless world that Clov briefly describes when he peers through the small high windows, takes us into a bleached-out world lacking much potential for elements of discrimination, and depleted of vitality and the means to sustain life. Dry dog biscuits may be all that remains in the larder, there is no blade of grass in the landscape, a real dog is replaced by an incomplete toy replica. The appearance of a flea provokes panic and a determination to exterminate this disturbing sign of life as speedily as possible. What has happened to humanity?

The setting stirs echoes in our minds of the prison cell, of a house whose inhabitants have moved away or died—the rags covering Hamm's face and the dustbin-lids remind one of dust-sheets over abandoned furniture. In terms of literary associations, Sartre's *Huis clos* and Koestler's *Darkness at Noon* come to mind. If we attempt to locate this place somewhere in time, might we consider a place of exile in Stalinist Russia as offering an external analogy to the internal landscape depicted in the play? There are references to the barren land, to the steppes, in stark contrast to the Ardennes or Lake Como, beautiful places known in the past when Nagg and Nell were alive in the world and had not yet been consigned to their dustbin-prisons. Now, though so close, they cannot see each other and can only communicate through speech . . . one might think of prisoners in their cells tapping or calling through the cell walls to establish a link with another live being.

Beckett's awareness of the horrors of Stalinism must have been growing in the early 1950s in common with intellectuals throughout the West. The Algerian colonial impasse may be another background preoccupation—the master–slave relationship described by Hegel was powerfully exemplified in the French settlers' relationship to their Arab subjects, and the future of Algeria troubled all France throughout this period.

Hamm, in his wheelchair, blind behind his dark spectacles, and unable to walk, is as incapacitated as Nagg and Nell—in a state of identification with the dead internal objects that these figures embody. The dustbins are called ashbins, perhaps expressing Beckett's sense of the deadness they contain: the ashes of a crematorium, the ash left after the fire has burnt up all that is combustible.

The relationship between Hamm and Clov is a present-day version of Hamm's picture of the relationship he has had with his parents, as we gradually learn. Its circular sado-masochistic structure is at the heart of the state of impasse depicted in the play. Victim and tormentor fit together in a horribly perfect unchanging system. Each day is as every other. There is no movement through time, no change, just repetition. Pleasure has become attached to the infliction of pain. For example, we can hear the delight in Clov's voice at the idea of inserting the catheter into Hamm. There is awareness of this perversity: "No one that ever lived ever thought so crooked as we." Triumphant glee and sadness vie for expression in this sentence.

Hamm is desperate to assert his omnipotent control—via the whistle, via his position as the master, via his knowledge of the combination that can unlock the larder. He gets in a terrible panic if anything seems to suggest that his control is not absolute: he must be right in the centre of the room in his chair, and obsessional anxiety torments him as he demands adjustments this way and that. He has to occupy the central position, linked in the infantile mind to the nipple that crowns the breast and gives access to the breast's contents, like the key to Hamm's larder, because only thus can he inflict the pains of hunger and helplessness on the others. Nell must be told that there is no more pap (baby food). The dread being held at bay is that if Hamm were not himself the controlling tyrant, he would be subject to such tyranny himself. Later, in the poignant conversation with Nagg we learn of Hamm's sufferings as a baby: left to cry, ignored by the parents. At first, it seems as if at least father is going to respond to baby Hamm's night-time distress, even if mother has shut him out of her mind, but this too then turns out to be a pipe-dream. Hamm's revenge on the parental objects in his mind is what we observe in the play: they are shut away, no food, warmth, comfort, human touch, no possibility of moving (like babies who cannot yet go to find the longed-for person), an endless recreation of the infant's loneliness and the terror of abandonment and death.

This picture only emerges in fragments: Beckett's language brilliantly captures the nature and consequences of the minute splitting of experience which has been used to destroy what has been unbearably painful. The minute fragments defy reconstruction into meaningful shape or narrative. Instead, we have ash, "smithereens", "a bit of all right"—only bits, not wholes. Linked to these processes of destruction via minute splitting are the jokes, a desperate effort to create something lively out of the faecal indeterminate world of fragmented objects. For example, the story of the tailor and the making of the pair of trousers is an elaborate anal joke which follows the narrating of the marriage at Lake Como, with its potential for generative sex, which has been attacked in rage and envy. If we can laugh enough at the tailor story, we may not notice the catastrophe that is taking place: instead of a couple together who might produce a baby, we have a brilliant display of verbal masturbation. The competitive infantile self can produce enough shit to drown the oedipal pains that might otherwise have to be suffered.

The relentless attacks on couples are perhaps the hardest parts of the text to bear: Nagg and Nell are not allowed to reach to kiss; they "crashed in their tandem" instead of going somewhere, having a real adventure in the world, or being allowed to link up in a creative intercourse; baby Hamm and his mother are not brought together in the night; the destitute father and his young son are not allowed to be together. The horrible cruelty of this child abandoned at Hamm's command (a brutal instance of identification with the aggressor) is at the root of the vicious point-scoring between Hamm and Clov: Clov threatens to leave, in which case Hamm would become the abandoned helpless starving child, as at the end when he is left to die. Most of the time Hamm and Clov are hand-in-glove (is this joke worthy of Beckett?) in destroying meaning: the discovery of the flea is the epitome of this. It must be destroyed as otherwise "Humanity might start from there! Oh God." Couples are held in a state of suspended animation (like Nagg and Nell in their bins), with all creative contact broken off. The children, represented by Hamm, are then identified with the deadened depressed objects and cannot move, see, or feel. The sight, hearing, and memory of Nagg and Nell are failing. Nell dies, and Hamm is also gradually dying. In psychoanalytic terms, we are observing the consequences of projective identification with destroyed internal objects whose state of near-death is consequent on their imprisonment in the child's phantasy. Meltzer's book *The Claustrum* (1992a) describes this state of affairs, and the type of claustrum relevant to this text is very obviously the rectum.

All this killing of creativity, of links, and of awareness of pain has reached a climax in the play because the painkillers have run out. Awareness of Hamm's psychic state is not bearable for him. There is a poignant reference to the fontanelle, the tender vulnerable spot on the baby's head when the protective skull is not yet fully in place and where even a tiny touch could do great damage. The images of horror in the play, like the child never fetched by its father and left to starve, expose us as watchers to feelings of our nerve ends being as exposed to traumatic shock as the fontanelle of the baby. Beckett's delicacy of mind seems to us important in protecting his audience from being exploited when they are opened up to the levels of psychic pain he is describing.

Let us gather together some of the important features of the reduced world of which Hamm is the tragic ruler: it is deeply boring. "I love them, the old questions, the old answers." We are in a timeless world of repetition, where deadly familiarity is the most that can be hoped for. There will be no New Year. It is immobile: there is a conversation about setting off on a journey— "Let's go from here . . . South"—but quickly the idea of going to the sea becomes impossible: the travellers would encounter sharks. The sadism that rules within the prison-room is feared outside it: if Hamm and Clov were to make a dash for freedom, they have no doubt that they would become victims in their turn. It is dirty: filthy handkerchiefs, sex reduced to anality. As Hamm puts it, "we're down in a hole". It is dominated by distor:ed perception, as in the story of the madman who can only see ashes. It is heartless: helplessness is systemically projected and then mocked. A dog implores for a home, baby Hamm cries for mother, Clov begs for food. It is deeply uneasy: there is always a suspicion that procreation may creep back in somehow. The small boy, the fleas, are reminders that the upside-down world in which the perverse has triumphed might be challenged by evidence of another reality, however blind to this the protagonists have made themselves. So there is a terrible lack of security. In political parlance, that is why so-called security police are then needed so badly. The grandiosity of Hamm's opening speech is perfectly paralleled by the devastation of his last lonely soliloquy.

Psychoanalysis ponders on the meaning of the death instinct and the fear of death in the infantile part of the personality. This play provides an extraordinary tableau of the death instinct triumphant in its characters but, of course, imagined by its author, whose capacities of mind and language thus represent the continuing struggle of the life instinct to assert its power. It also offers some very moving understanding of our primitive fears of physical deterioration and death. In the dialogue between Hamm and Clov, after the shared fantasy about sailing off on a raft is disrupted by the fear of sharks, Hamm questions Clov about his bodily powers—his eyes, his legs, which Clov says are "bad"—and Hamm's vicious rage builds to a chilling climax.

The dialogue continues with its cruel teasing interchanges replacing the unbearable desolation that Hamm has delineated, and, a few pages later, the terrible speech in which Hamm tells the story of the man who begged in vain for food. This reveals how the failure to pity, to feel for each other, to sustain life, leaves Beckett's characters in an inner world dominated by despair and failed reparation.

Such grief would be felt, if the bitter laughter stopped, that it would drive men mad. *Endgame* is about an extreme state in which the terror of encountering the reproachful ghosts is defended against by a deadly game which only intensifies the persecution.

Just as Ibsen was probably exploring aspects of himself in *John Gabriel Borkman,* so *Endgame* may in part be seen as a harsh self-exploration of the mind and work of the writer. Hamm is trying to tell a story, and Clov is prompted to ask him about it, to keep it going. Clov is forced to be the feed-man in this bleakest of Beckett's comic routines, with Hamm's reference to "technique" as what keeps him going.

Under this parody of narcissistic writer's talk is a deeper story of the malevolent control that the writer may feel he tries to exercise through his mind. We do not really know what has happened and what has been imagined or invented by Hamm. Did a man come pleading, was there a child left to die, how did Clov come to be there at all? All our revels now are ended, Hamm says, when Nell dies, but in fact the scene is more reminiscent of *The Tempest* than *A Midsummer Night's Dream*. Instead of a beautiful island, Hamm and Clov inhabit a hell-hole, in which all sign of procreation and love is hated. Your move, says Hamm, reminding us of the chess game in *The Tempest*. And among the props is a gaff (a pole used to spear fish), serving as a vestigial staff, though this cannot even move Hamm's chair. This writer's mind is filled with omnipotence and hatred of life, killing parents and children alike, creating characters only in order to control and humiliate them. But just as the play of language brings some glimmer of hope in these dramas, so also in *Endgame*, as in *Godot* and *Happy Days*, a vestige of life survives, as Clov manages to leave, pushed to escape perhaps by Mother Pegg's death and his recognition that whilst he and Nagg can mourn her, Hamm cannot.

Happy Days

Happy Days is unusual in Beckett's work in having a central female character. The play is set in blazing light on scorched ground. Centre stage is Winnie, buried up to her waist in a mound. At the back of the mound is her husband, Willie, who spends most of the time invisible to the audience, hidden in his burrow. This powerful image takes us straight to the theme of the play. Here is a marriage in which communication has almost dried up, despite the wonderful haunting eloquence of Winnie. The two are so near and yet so far from each other, hopelessly trapped in heart-rending near isolation. Being characters in a Beckett play, they are committed to surviving, though with ever-present thoughts of death, represented by the gun in Winnie's bag, and their survival is based on a residual capacity for thought and feeling, including shafts of brilliant humour. What catastrophe has taken place?

We can consider this at a number of levels. We might see the landscape as a world in which life has been almost extinguished, a post-nuclear world. As Winnie remarks, "flesh melts at so many degrees". There are also powerful echoes of seaside narcissistic loneliness. Winnie's parasol/umbrella evokes a beach scene, her

all-important bag is like a beach bag full of the necessary equipment to maintain her glamour while she cooks in the sun. As the
bell rings to wake her for the day, we might think of an old people's home, with the partially helpless inhabitants hanging on
desperately to the remnants of their old selves, waiting endlessly
for something to happen which will provide them with a sense of
being persons who mean something to someone else. Winnie remembers, perhaps enviously, that Willie has a marvellous gift in
being able to sleep through the bell, not wake up to the anxieties
about deterioration with which she struggles as she cleans her
teeth, does her hair, reconstructs her face, and puts on her hat,
ready to face the world. The intense light is holy but also hellish.
There is something it is very important to see, but it is truly terrifying to do so. Winnie's pain is clearly in her mind, and the hell-
ishly bright light makes her feel in need of medicine to deal with
her loss of spirits. She empties the bottle, and the audience feels
the anxiety of how she will be able to endure her position without
such magic potions.

Winnie's attempt to order things for herself is in counterpoint
with her flow of disordered recollections. The "happy day" she
would like to have is undermined by thoughts of hogs, castrated
male swine, as Beckett reminds us in due course. A sexual catastrophe has taken place. The play explores this in Winnie's memories and in the present relationship between Winnie and Willie.

The picture of the woman who is sinking further into the
dried-up ground despite repeated appeals for help to an impotent
husband brings to mind an infant's image of desolation—the
mound–breast is not alive with the intercourse of mother and father but instead a place where parental figures cannot reach each
other and are increasingly weakened by this failure of restorative
contact. The bell that wakens Winnie might then be linked to her
maternal preoccupation with an infant who needs to be attended
to—an external infant calling her to provide maternal care, or an
infantile part of herself still holding on to life (in contrast to
Willie's marvellous gift for ignoring the demands of living) and
calling her to attend to the state of her mind and body; an infant
who refuses to lie down and die, as she refuses to pull the trigger
on herself. Winnie longs for help—to be seen, to be heard, to be
acknowledged, as she tries to sustain life—but her partner is in a

much more deteriorated state. Willie spends most of his life stuck up the backside of the mound. His predominantly anal preoccupation interferes massively with his capacity to communicate with Winnie. Pornographic postcards, his snot, titbits from the newspaper occupy his mind. He reads out advertisements—"Opening for a smart youth", "Wanted bright boy"—which refer both to homosexual invitation and to the child that Winnie, and perhaps he too, may have wanted but could not create. "Lift up your eyes and see me", she says. Such biblical references are frequent in Beckett and underline the possibility of salvation which human relationship offers us, but which can also be refused. When an emmet (an ant) and eggs are noticed by Winnie, evidence that life remains in mother earth, Willie's brilliant joke about "formication" brings the couple together in laughter, and Willie finds a moment of joy in Winnie's mirth.

But this joke simultaneously reminds us that all sex is for him illicit, dirty, a subject for jokes. The text suggests that Willie's impotence and retreat to masturbatory preoccupations may be rooted in the unbearable realization of his incapacity to make a difference to her. In the play, we are a long way down the line, faced with ageing and loss of faculties and hope, but the couple's history seems to turn, in part, on the significance of the little girl Mildred, of whom Winnie speaks. One aspect of what we learn about Mildred suggests that she represents Winnie's terrified frigidity, the part of herself unable to engage in mutual sexual exploration, the woman Willie could not reach.

Beckett's imprisoned Winnie, who used to have the use of her legs and, in the course of the play, loses the use of her arms and any vestige of bodily freedom, is an image of a mother cut off from father. The problem is "visible flesh", says Winnie, and we can thus suggest that the son/sun has been enraged by a vision of intercourse. The infantile vengeance is represented by the burning up of mother and father and the remorseless gazing at this vision. The exposure of their sexuality is ruthless and full of hate towards father. The claim is that father is a dirty bugger when he enters mother. Mother is presented as narcissistically preoccupied but is shown in a more tender light because her attention to herself is clearly seen as replacing the love she craves. Winnie is still wonderfully beautiful in the play, and the infantile disaster confronting us is perhaps that described by Meltzer as a potential response to the encounter with mother's beauty. The too-bright light that is so hard to bear (or to forget once one has seen the play) is the infant's experience of being completely overwhelmed by too brilliant a vision. The audience has to struggle with this intense brightness with the overtones of exposure, helplessness, and absence of protection (not even shade is available) and the realization that theatre depends on intimate exposure.

In the second act, the childhood background of Winnie's distress is probed further. As her need for contact with another person to sustain her conviction in her own existence is heightened (a neat reversal of Descartes' axiom), a troubling figure reappears in her thoughts. Charlie, the Reverend Dr Carlos Hunter, has emerged from Willie's newspaper "found dead in a tub". Charlie the priest is remembered as a seductive figure. Winnie's anxiety increases, and she speaks of the earth losing its atmosphere—a phrase encompassing post-nuclear devastation, a sense of the loss of liveliness and hope, and a horrible glimpse of a world disconnected from the universal order of things. Beckett's talent for sketching endless nightmares in a phrase is extraordinary. Winnie's thoughts wander to the Browning-gun, turned into her pet, the Brownie. "Happy days" are those when there are sounds to interrupt her monologue.

Winnie begins to tell the story of Mildred, a little girl who explored forbidden territories in the middle of the night, undressing her beautiful doll beneath the table and then terrified by a mouse running up her leg. Mildred, perhaps primarily a little-girl aspect of Winnie, is curious about the mysteries of mother's body and horrified to discover that it is not all hers to possess. Is the mouse perhaps a perception of father's penis which moves between mother's thighs, or of the baby they might make in intercourse? The awareness of parental sexuality bursts into Mildred's mind in an unbearable way; she screams and screams, and perhaps we can sense that the infantile disaster of the too-bright maternal breast is re-evoked and ossified by the oedipal encounter. Winnie goes on to speak of the bitter pain of her marriage. Willie had seemed a source of hope—his love might pull her out of the fragile retreat in which she was perhaps already stuck, but Winnie is herself deeply imprisoned inside objects pictured in ways that make development, movement, and growth almost impossible. Winnie's Willie is a denigrated penis that cannot rescue her. For Willie, the failure of the marriage involves a despairing retreat; for Winnie, it involves the repetition of a degraded version of sexuality consequent on the shocked withdrawal from encountering the overwhelming unknown. At the play's close, there is an acutely painful restatement of the impasse: Willie emerges from his hole, all dressed up for a dance, and murmurs "Win" as he scrabbles unsuccessfully across the mound towards her, only to slip back; Winnie sings a dancehall lyric about love, and they look at each other and smile. Their humanity remains poignantly alive as they each acknowledge that this moment of contact sustains their existence. Their infantile anxieties have not been surmounted and their sense of damage is huge, but the characters share with their audience the emotional power of the truth of their lives. They do not believe in the romantic dream, but they understand why they cling to it.

In this play, Beckett's despair about the human condition is modified not only by the extraordinary wit and intelligence of the text, but also by the pity and understanding of the characters for each other.

Beckett's deep sympathy is with a woman who is holding together the remnants of her existence. She has, we infer, lived by a code that required her to take most of the responsibility for her and her husband's life, with little love or comfort from him. Her sense of herself depends on her sense of attractiveness, which she has to sustain in the absence of anyone who will, for most of the time, acknowledge it. What courage and fortitude is required for someone to survive in so isolated a situation.

Towards the end of the play there is a brief moment of companionship when Winnie sees Willie stir, and she wonders if he may come closer to her. She is able to capture his desire to see her, and Willie starts to crawl towards her.

The resonance of the play arises from the fact that its dramatized excess of deprivation and loss, which seems to be fast approaching a state of living death, evokes more recognizable and ordinary deprivations and states of damage. As we have mentioned, among these are the nuclear holocaust, the vulnerability of age and sickness, and a callous public world in which others are regarded as if they were despised objects in a freak-show. The intensity of the play comes from its juxtaposition of Winnie's love of life, which she evokes intensely in her audience, and the psychic pain that she bravely suffers, with the extremity and enormity of her plight. The play has the quality of a homage towards a maternal object—everyone's maternal object—who has suffered so much unrecognized and uncomplaining pain.

CHAPTER TWELVE

Living in intrusive identification

Carlos Tabbia Leoni

I t is difficult for me to unite the term "living" with that of "intrusive identification" as I consider that the relation between both is practically exclusive. The "living" of projective identification is a mere reflection or a parody of the "living" in relation with the objects. "Living" being able to tolerate the conjunction of the "links of relationship" with the "anti-links"— anti-emotion, anti-knowledge, and anti-life (cf. Meltzer et al., 1986)—favours not only the development of the mind, but also the capacity to experience love, joy, hope, pain, aesthetic pleasure, conflicts, and so on, all of which is impossible while one is "living in intrusive identification". One only *lives* outside the object. Inside the object one only *survives*, only *lives badly*.

"Living inside an object" is an omnipotent fantasy correlative to "intrusive identification" in an internal object,[1] transformed into

---

[1] The internal objects (part, total, combined) represent above all the parents, siblings, and persons who surround the subject in the present time (Heimann, 1942), and they provide a sense of existence and identity; one of the internal objects is the superego.

a "claustrum"; this fantasy differs from the communicative function of projective identification. Some of the queries that emerge
from this nuclear theme are the following. Is claustrophilia[2] an
omnipresent fantasy? Does the object of the claustrophilia always
become a claustrum? Into which internal objects is the intrusion
carried out? What is the motive that drives one to lose one's life in
order to attain a pseudo-existence? What are the consequences of
intrusion for that part of the *self* that penetrates intrusively into the
object? My contribution will be centred on this latter query. I
would like to present, using different material, what happens to
the intrusive *part* that seeks, to a varying degree, to live inside the
other. In this chapter, I show the relationship of the *self* with its
objects, or the paralysation of the *self* as a result of masturbatory-
intrusive attacks on the internal objects; subsequently, I discuss the
mental state of the inhabitants of the claustrum; and, finally, I
illustrate all of this with the clinical material of a *borderline* patient.

One could reformulate the claustrophilic *motivation* giving as
an example a "joke" attributed to Cantinflas (a Mexican come-
dian): "What do we come into the world for?—to suffer? If that's
the case, we're going back!" The subjacent fantasy of return–intrusion–confusion[3] with the object seeks to eliminate pain, implicit in
the differentiation subject–object. But, the *price* paid for avoiding
mental pain is high. Once the patient has worked his or her way
inside the internal object, he or she remains *trapped* there. Meltzer
pointed out in a seminar[4] that once Jane, the patient he was discussing, had penetrated the object, she remained *separate* from
other people by a glass division, referring to the glass divisions of
the compartments where she worked, inside which she adopted
the necessary social behaviour but was *incapable of maintaining intimate social relations.* Inside the object *one is protected from the world,
but one also loses it*—like the Wolf Man, who felt fortunate to have
come into the world protected by a foetal lining, a veil that hid
him from the world and hid the world from him (Freud, 1918b

[2] To be understood as the anxious search for an object for different purposes, such as to feel sheltered inside it, to deposit in it objects that one wishes
to preserve, to occupy it, dominate it, exploit it, ruin it.
[3] Freud himself analysed the fantasy of return to the mother's womb as a
denial of castration in the case of the Wolf Man.
[4] Unpublished paper presented to the Psychoanalytic Group of Barcelona.

[1914]). The flight from the world in intrusive identification is so great that *there is neither any contact with reality nor any idea of psychic reality (internal–external); there is a lack of the idea of nature, and reality is anthropomorphized; one does not live sufficiently in the external world, therefore access to meanings and value is banned; time, if it exists, is circular.* Meltzer (1992a) enumerates other consequences of intrusion: ". . . the intruding part of the personality suffers from anxieties that are contingent on the fact of being uninvited. He is a *trespasser,* an *impostor,* a *poseur,* a *fraud,* potentially a traitor. But he is also an *exile* from the world of intimacy, from the beauty of the world, which at best he can see, hear, smell, taste only *second-hand* through the medium of the object" (p. 72, emphasis added). The intruder feels as much a prisoner as Segismundo in *La vida es sueño,* by Pedro Calderón de la Barca [1600–1681], in his tower:

> . . . I know so little
> of the world here in this tower,
> my cradle and my tomb.
> I was born here (if you can call it
> being born), knowing only
> this rugged desert, where I exist
> in misery, a living corpse,
> a moving skeleton . . .
>
> [*Life Is Dream,* 1st day, scene II: in Honig, 1993, p. 297]

Upon entering inside the object ("cradle"), his situation changes radically ("tomb"), and as a result he remains devitalized ("living corpse", "moving skeleton").

Through Samuel Beckett's *Endgame* it is possible to illustrate not only the world of the inhabitant of the claustrum while he remains inside it, but also the state of the internal objects and the consequences for the *self.* The action of the play, of only one act, takes place in a dilapidated setting, separate from the external world; in the scene we find Hamm (H), the son, permanently seated in a wheelchair, blind, with his face covered with a dirty rag (at the beginning and end of the play); his partner is Clov (C), the servant, who is permanently standing; both are devitalized and daily represent a parody. At one side of the scene in the background there are two rubbish bins with a cover; in one lives Nagg, Hamm's father, and in the other is Nell, the mother.

The imprisoned intrusive part of the *self* has its own representation of the world (although it is not a delusional[5] representation), with which it maintains a relationship through veils. Therefore, in *Endgame* the *external world* is represented in a paranoid way because for Hamm (H, 15),[6] outside this room, on the exterior there only exists death; however, this representation responds to the fact that this part of the *self* was never in full contact with either the external world from which he feels he has remained absent (H, 47), or the internal world. As he resides within an object, he feels that he forms part neither of the world of objects nor of that of relations but that, on the contrary, he experiences a feeling of remoteness and surprise before daily life, which, according to him, passes by in foreign hands. He has gone into *self-exile*. The *intermediary elements* (equivalent to the senses) with the external world are represented in *Endgame* by two small windows placed in the highest part of the walls and which remain covered with curtains and through which it is practically impossible to see anything except a desperately grey landscape (C, 26). The only one who displays mobility and some possibility of looking outside this room is Clov, the servant. However, through second-hand observations, or observing through another, like Clov, very little information can be incorporated on account of the limited contact with the world and, as a consequence, distorted and aberrant thoughts are produced (C, 16). The *internal world* that correlates to this diminished capacity to observe the world would be represented, in the first place, by the same setting in which the whole play elapses: deteriorated, useless, dirty, piled-up objects. One very representative element of this anal-claustrum world is the inexistence of time, because for Hamm and Clov (C, 13) it is always the same time. For them there are never any changes, everything is always the same (C, 33), because as there is scarcely any incorporation there is neither development nor conflict. All life is an anaesthetizing and routine representation of nonsense sprinkled with an occasional haughty *boutade* that intends to simu-

---

[5] Because it has not abandoned the gravitational attraction of the objects, nor has it sought refuge in nowhere.

[6] The number next to the letter that identifies the character corresponds to the page in the English version translated by Beckett himself (Beckett, 1988).

late authority (C and H, 16). However, once the (manic) petulance deflates, Hamm (H, 30) is able to make out that he is living down in a hole, as if he were alluding to the rectal compartment of the invaded object.

The *couple* formed by *Hamm–Clov* represents aspects of the same *self*. *Clov* would represent the *instrumental-adapting aspects* developed through trial and error, and which are only useful in order to operate in the world of facts; for this reason, Clov has no qualms about admitting that he has never thought (C, 30). This part of the personality is characterized by *lacking authentic interests*. It is a *slave* to the tyrannical aspect of the *self* and for this reason permanently waits for Hamm to whistle to him (C, 12); he will wait forever as for Clov–Hamm time does not exist, and therefore he will never die (C, 14). As there is no concern for death, this part represented by Clov is only interested in reaching *an inanimate, devitalized, dementalized state* where all could remain still, unchanging, and where the only scant pleasure arises from the contemplation of the silent, deaf, and gloomy routine. Complementing Clov is *Hamm*, who with his eyes all empty and white (H, 13) not only is blind, but, besides this, covers his face with dirty rags (foetal lining?). Hamm would represent the narcissistic nucleus of the *self* which rejects contact with the objects and remains immobilized like Narcissus before the lake, but who proudly proclaims that the only life is at his side (H, 45). This part hates anyone who draws near his haven because he could be questioned or upset and he therefore orders the extermination[7] (cf. p. 103 of the original French version: Beckett, 1957) of anyone who attempts to draw near his grandiose refuge. Such great hate towards the world of objects increases his paranoid anxiety, which makes him fear the proximity of the people that surround him. For this reason, he orders Clov not to come near him, because he gives him the shivers (H, 24, 26, 43).

Hamm's relationship with his parents illustrates the relationship of the *self* with its internal objects. Nagg and Nell, infantilized, degraded, with their legs mutilated, are alone in their rubbish

---

[7] This expression is omitted in the English edition (Beckett, 1988); however, the whole scene is an aggressive reaction (C, 49) against anyone who draws near.

bins. This is a way of dramatizing hate towards the parents, which entails the natural consequence of the parents–rubbish falling on the ego. Therefore, Hamm (p. 89 of the French edition), after describing his parents as impoverished and dead, subsequently feels that he himself is freezing, like the destroyed objects. He will also die of darkness (H, 48), like Mrs Pegg, for not oiling the lamps, for not rehabilitating the objects. As a consequence of the omnipotent control exerted over the parents, whom he keeps separate, preventing them from having any kind of mutually reparatory intimacy, Hamm *cannot establish true intrapsychic or interpersonal relationships*. Hamm not only has no partner but when he tries to get close to Clov, the latter rejects him. Clov (C, 44) wishes neither to kiss him nor to touch him (C, 44); so then Hamm tries to defend himself by asking for his (felt!) dog. This scene suggests the isolation and the *privation of all intimacy* correlative to the attack on the parents, as the substratum of the sado-masochistic and sterile relationship dramatized by Hamm–Clov.

What is the particularity of the attack that can be described in *Endgame*? And through which means is the attack being produced? Hamm, on several occasions, directs verbal aggressions to his father, particularly those referring to the father's genitality, which is degraded to the level of fornication between scoundrels (H, 15, 35) Such is the hate that Hamm–Clov feels towards parental intercourse and fecundity that he even reproaches him for having engendered him. The hate towards children and siblings is what leads Hamm to reproach his parents for his own birth, thus confirming what Bion (1959) claims when he refers to the hate that certain persons experience towards everything that links to the couple and the fruit of this same link.

In *Endgame*, there are signs of *urethral attacks on intercourse*. There is a scene in which the parents recall their honeymoon at Lake Como and laugh, remembering anecdotes. Hamm then gets furious and screams for them to keep quiet, until the scene finishes with the parents each shut away in their respective bins. Hamm then feels that, as his anger subsides, his desire to urinate increases (H, 22). Later, in an amusing scene in which Clov struggles to free himself of a flea that has got in between his genitals, Beckett makes a play on the French words *coïte* and *coite* (which in English have been substituted by *to lay* and *to lie*), presenting the conflict that would arise if the flea were copulating instead of remaining still. It is at this moment that Hamm urinates and Clov gives his blessing to this evacuation. In both scenes, therefore, *Hamm urinates when faced with references to the couple's life and intercourse*, whereby what is emphasized is the primacy of urinating over copulating and relating. In this context, urinating would have the same function as Hamm's screams at the parents' account of their honeymoon: that of interrupting the relationship.[8]

At another moment of *Endgame* and in a sad dialogue (18–19), Hamm's parents refer to their own processes of deterioration and laughingly recall the accident that they had had while they were riding a tandem and they had lost their shanks. However, their laughter progressively diminishes until they both end up expressing that they feel cold, to the point of feeling frozen (19). They are frozen with sadness—sadness that arises from the fact that in that accident *they lost autonomy*, which is what led them to living in these rubbish bins and holding themselves up on their stumps (15), as their legs were amputated in the tandem accident. The choice of this vehicle is not devoid of meaning, as a tandem is a bicycle for two people who sit one behind the other. This suggests to me that *the tandem is an infantile representation of the parents' intercourse* (cf. intercourse *a tergo*), which would have been attacked intrusively through *bimanual masturbation*. The consequence for the internal object/parents is mutilation and degradation, and for the son— by identification—it is paralysis: Hamm is always seated, Clov, always standing. The envious–masturbatory attack on the parental couple entails the impossibility of creating an internal and external fertile couple. This Hamm–Clov attack is the clearest expression of the narcissistic personality that inhabits the claustrum.

If the patrimony of the *self* is composed of devitalized, denigrated, controlled, etc. internal objects, the person will not be able to think, experience happiness, feel alive, or establish contact with the world of objects, but rather, on the contrary, will feel banished from life, carrying around an arrogant appearance of reality, without being able to feel emotion, with the danger of becoming frag-

---

[8] As in the case of the Wolf Man, where evacuation interrupted intercourse (1918b [1914]).

mented, experiencing fear, feeling persecuted by hostile objects, and remaining on the fringe of time. If the lamp is not oiled, one will die of darkness—darkness such as Hamm's or that of the Wolf Man hidden in his foetal lining. It's a defeat: *Endgame* lost (H, 82)!

The blind Hamm and Mrs Pegg died for not oiling the lamp, and Segismundo knows little of the world because upon being shut away inside an object–tower he only has access to a dismantled, barren world, which makes him feel miserably dead–alive. *Knowledge is banned in all these spaces.* Another way of representing the impoverished and blinded condition of the part of the personality which carries out the intrusion is, according to my interpretation, Plato's allegory of the cavern *(Republic,* VII, 514a–521b). A parallel could be established between the sequences, motivations, and consequences established by Plato in this allegory and the fantasy of intrusive identification in the object. Just as, on account of their imperfection, the more the souls drink from the Lethe the more deeply they fall into sensitive reality, represented by the cavern, so the part that intrudes into the object (for the different motivations mentioned above) loses the relationship with the world of objects. In both cases, there is a change of condition (from the intelligible world to the sensitive one and from the world of objects to the claustrum) on account of intolerance to pain.

Plato describes the immobilized inhabitants of the cavern as being asleep, *having forgotten what things are like in reality,* and who regard as true only the shadow of the objects. These inhabitants would be in a state equivalent to that which governs thinking not through observation, but mediated through news agencies—looking with others' eyes and *lacking true knowledge and freedom.* The part of the personality trapped in the object, as it is unable to develop concepts, only increases its greed, while at the same time it tries to keep away from overwhelming truth and takes refuge in the shadows;[9] so then the subjects consume but do not experience

---

[9] The painful flight into the shadows was represented in the following clinical material of a patient, who in a productive session, and looking at the plants which can be seen from the couch, said: "The sun is so beautiful shining on the balcony plants! How many tones of green!" He paused and went on associating: " I had lunch at a restaurant where lorry-drivers usually go, where they serve food 24 hours a day. It was full of noise and smoke, and I was

enjoyment, accumulate but feel empty: they are only full of the shadows reflected by the others. It is the echo of the thoughts of those they idealize, but they do not know the value of ideas: they believe that the goodness of the objects resides in the fact that the other uses them. They know the best restaurants but lack a sense of "taste". They can become presumptuous experts like the cavern dwellers, skilful in discerning among fleeting shadows. However, it is not difficult to discover how their *grandiosity* tries to cover up their *boredom*. Plato considers the world of the cavern an equivalent to the hell of the Greeks, seen as a world of *darkened existences*. The part of the personality that lives in intrusive identification resides in a peculiar world, in a kind of distorted and *pale reflection* of the world of relationships between objects. The intruder is as much a prisoner of a world of words without meaning in themselves as is someone *lacking in the experience of contact* with objects/containers possessing the qualities pointed out by Meltzer (privacy, exclusiveness, comfort, and delimitation: Meltzer et al., 1986, chapt. V) and who has been thrown into a closed hellish world like that illustrated by Sartre in *Huis clos*: a world of exiles from intimacy, who only carry a past composed of "facts".

The analytic process of claustrum patients is as painful and slow as is the liberation process of the cavern's prisoners described by Plato, because they must be freed from their chains as well as cured of their ignorance; because the grandiose specialist in differentiating the wandering shadows is nothing but an *ignoramus*.

Some clinical material may help to illustrate the previous considerations.

"Jordi" presented himself before me as a brilliant professional leading an isolated life centred on masturbation; at the time, he resided in the home of a prominent politician. He was brought up in the bosom of a large family.

---

sitting at a table just underneath the TV, so I couldn't see the screen, but I was looking at the expressions on the faces of all those surrounding me while they were watching the film." Upon not being able to tolerate the beauty of the world, he regressed to the cavern (anal-claustrum) in order to look at only the reflections.

In the course of the analysis, what appeared was his yearning to *establish a sensual relationship with me*, expressing desires to touch me, through his verbalizations or dreams. However, the possibility of establishing contact with me was altered by his intrusive aggression. In a dream *"he saw a naked woman, who excited him, and there was a man who got excited with her; he saw the man's large penis, and when this man was about to penetrate her, Jordi confused himself with him, seeing in fact his own erect penis"*. What soon became manifest, as in the dream, was his yearning *to penetrate the internal maternal object* through the confusion penis–child. *The part-father–penis–object was only like a battering ram used to penetrate the interior of a mother felt to be only a mediator so that Jordi could get hold of his own penis.* This was correlated by the predominance of masturbatory fantasies about small women desiring the large penises of King Kong-type men. These fantasies were fed through pornographic films which favoured his *voyeurism*; this condemned him to passivity (he lacked interests and friends and practically did no work) and to a non-existent genital sexuality. At this stage, in which the external world practically did not exist, he spent his time planning his *masturbation*. At the beginning of the analytic weekend he would hire a pornographic film, and sitting in his armchair or lying on his bed, always covered (like Hamm?), he would reach a climax and then fall asleep. He practically did not leave his bed, remaining surrounded by the radio, TV, newspapers, books until the following session. Jordi considered his masturbation to be a recourse that protected him from disaster. Living outside, in the world of objects, was "tormenting" (a proof of this was that in his sado-masochistic outbursts he would beat his wife). Easy as it was for him to admit his genital masturbation, it was, however, difficult to admit other equivalent manifestations. Anal masturbation was concretedized in evacuation (retaining–expelling violently) and in the minute cleansing of the perianal zone. Another mode of masturbation observed in this patient consisted of his vomiting, which for him had become equivalent to "I didn't masturbate but I vomited"; after provoking the vomit with his fingers, his state of mind would change, and he would relax and be able to go to sleep. Through masturbation, in its different forms, he changed the scene in which he was living: from living in the external world he would enter to live in the internal world, where he would go to sleep like the inhabitants of the cavern.

Jordi could not tolerate waiting for the analyst to feed him mentally, because he feared the analyst–mummy's other baby-rivals; his desire was to eliminate them and later get into the "sensory apparatus and mental equipment of its internal object" in order to seek "the immediate emotional satisfaction of omniscience" (Meltzer, 1992a, p. 76). I recall one day on which he felt very much gratified because a local leader referred to him as "a learned man". This was a satisfaction coherent with the desire he expressed to be with me "in the session in order to learn without realizing it". His longing to be inside the analyst was defended tenaciously to the point of exploding violently against me if he did not feel that I was willing to let myself be colonized; he would attack my communications, breaking the link of melody–meaning—while he would gloat over the melody of my voice, he would reject the meaning of my words.

Jordi was so *far away from the world of human relationships* and from the developed feelings of jealousy that the only thing he could understand was the concrete behaviour of the analytic separations; for him, the analyst was either there or was not there, and if he was not there,"You are no longer a person but you have become a place", *thus eliminating my reality, just as he slips towards irreality.* He denies reality; he gets inside the object and constructs a defenceless world in which he mocks temporality and pain.

A dream allows us to understand *Jordi's relationship with objects*:

"I am with Joaquín, who tells me he is going abroad and draws up a long list of people who could occupy his flat. I am suffering because I don't see my name; he realizes this and writes down my name. I am worried because no one will know that Jordi is ___, then he writes my surname. Joaquín comments that the flat on Olano Street is good because, from there, you can see when the police are coming, as if the flat could be used to hide from police persecution. The scene in the dream changes. I am going on an excursion with colleagues from

work to a very pretty place, ecologically protected, with green hills,
beautiful and well-painted houses. I stay alone with a very beautiful
girl that I have met; she speaks to me half-affectionately and half-
pained because I have not taken any notice of her. I don't attach much
importance to this. She then asks me whether I don't remember what
she had told me, to which I answer in the negative. She says: I loved
you. I answer: you women think that we are inside your head know-
ing what you think. She feels pained and frustrated and then I say to
her: I also love you. In that spot the village was celebrating a feast;
from a balcony they were pouring milk from 'porrones'[10] *instead of*
wine. I say to them: let's get away from here before they pour some
milk on us. He associated that the dream was curious because
that same night he had gone to sleep angry because no one had
taken any notice of him. When in the dream a separation is
announced (Joaquin's departure), the immediate response is
that of occupation,[11] occupation that is carried out through the
eyes (on account of the voyeuristic overestimation of the look)
and the anus (Ol-*ano*),[12] thus managing to get into the other's
list–mind, but in which a mental state of persecution is established (the attractive object, upon being penetrated, becomes a
dangerous trap). The need to clarify his name and then his
surname arises on account of the *loss of his identity* correlative to
the invasion, which would be similar to the loss of the recollection of himself that Fabian experienced in Julian Green's novel
Si j'étais vous (1947).[13]

With the verbal ability of the ambiguous politician, who
changes his stand in the face of a committing situation, Jordi
slips into another scene: from the back part of the object to the
front side (the beautiful hills). Here, the presence of colleagues–
siblings is admitted, but only in order to stress his triumph: he
is the one chosen by the woman, but to whom he does not
really pay much attention (he neither remembers nor attaches

---

[10] A kind of jar with a spout, which is used for drinking wine without a
glass.

[11] As a child, he would always "see" his mother pregnant.

[12] The name Olano in Spanish sounds like a vocative: "Oh anus!"

[13] This was used as an example by Klein (1955) in order to illustrate the
fantasy of projective identification in the external object.

great importance to what she says). *His desire is to get inside the woman's head both to know what she is thinking, in order to attain omniscience and in order to have some sort of criterion (given his basic incapacity to obtain meaning from the observation of the external world), as well as to control that intercourse which gets mummy pregnant, and to take possession of daddy's penis.* Given his extreme dependence on the object, Jordi perceives the pain inflicted on the woman in the dream and placates it with pseudo-loving declarations ("I also love you") which lead to a manic relationship that ruins the object and renders the "porrones"–breasts (pouring out confusion) incompetent, thus returning to the persecutory situation. In this case, it can clearly be seen that the main internal object of intrusion is the maternal object, through the direct penetration of the orifices, or through the intrusion in the father's penis, as in the other dream; in Jordi there is no concern for the object but, rather, only the desire to dominate it and take possession of its qualities with the purpose of *being the object*. However, fortunately, as can be observed in the dream, persecutory anxiety prevents him from settling in the grandiosity of confusion.

Jordi, like the majority of the inhabitants of the claustrum who approach analysis, does not reside exclusively in the claustrum, but oscillates between going in and coming out of projective identification, and as a result has a greater or lesser awareness of the external world, like Hamm, who knows of the existence of the sea through the windows and through Clov. However, when from the loneliness of the claustrum they approach the threshold of the external world (with the fragility of a newborn?), they suffer enormous anxiety upon being invaded (correlative to their intrusive desires), as is reflected in Jordi's dream: "*I was alone in a room with thin glass walls*[14] *and people were looking at me, laughing around me, and I felt exposed.*" He is exposed to violent reintrojection, and, besides, his disinhabited mind is an easy target for the projective identifications of those looking at him. In order to go outside, he needs a mediator who

---

[14] This is reminiscent of the glass compartments in Meltzer's Jana case, mentioned earlier.

may tolerate a certain colonization and who may urge him to take a look at the world, as my patient expressed: "It's as if I were coming out of the cave and saw that it was not so danger-ous and that life is pretty, but I see this through Susana's[15] eyes, not through my own eyes, and then I can't enjoy it." Although it comes from another, he discovers the other. And he admits his difficulty: " It is difficult for me to desire her physically and spontaneously; she attracts me and I desire her but in a flat way", which means without emotional depth and without hav-ing achieved introjective identification with the father as a male.

Jordi is a *borderline* who oscillates between the external world of meanings and values and the internal world of objects into which he penetrates intrusively by different orifices. He can manifest an omniscient appearance enhanced by a great devel-opment of verbal expression in the service of seduction, but he lacks authentic interests. On account of his feeling of inconsist-ency, he mistrusts opening himself to the world, thus remain-ing totally dependent on the external objects and fearing being discovered in his true entity. So we see the instability and im-maturity of his sexual identity, his proclivity to being trapped in the voyeuristic–sado-masochistic perversion, and the para-noid undertone distance from intimate relationships.

Conclusion

When the intrusive part of the *self* "falls into the sensitive reality" of the cavern, it converts the objects into a "cradle and tomb" and then experiences feelings of strangeness for not having main-tained contact with the world. A thin "glass wall" prevents the intruder from establishing contact with objects that he feels to be more unattainable every time, thus increasing his loneliness and his feeling of not belonging to this community of objects, remain-ing excluded from all rights (to intimacy, to being recognized and

---

[15] A budding relationship.

remembered, to not being feared, and, on the other hand, to being loved). The trespasser wanders through the world without being in the world, and, as a result, while he remains enclosed in the object he escapes death but also loses life. In intrusive identification, one does not live, one only subsists; one only has a life which is the "pale reflection of what things really are", and one is exiled from beauty or only looks at it through the eyes of the parasitized object.

CHAPTER THIRTEEN

Reading Donald Meltzer: identification and intercourse as modes of reading and relating

James Fisher

"If a lion could talk, we would not understand him" (Wittgenstein, 1953, p. 223). Ludwig Wittgenstein's intriguing remark invites us to wonder at the mystery of communication. One response, of course, would be to think that if a lion could talk, he would be *like us*. And if he is like us, would we not, more or less, understand him? But would he be like us—or should I say, would *it* be like us? What sort of social intercourse could we have with a lion? What would we talk about? For some people, the more they think about such questions, the less sure but more intrigued they become. For others, there is nothing to puzzle over. Either the lion could make itself understood or it couldn't. Stanley Cavell suggests that Wittgenstein's remark indicates a *sensibility* rather than an assertion to be debated (Cavell, 1969b, p. 71). In this chapter, I want to explore the sensibility to reading as a form of relating that resists a premature wish for sameness, that understanding the other involves an openness to intercourse as well as a capacity for identification.

In fact, I want to emphasize how strange the other is, whether we have in mind the encounter with an author as we read, or the encounter with a patient in our consulting-*room*. And I want to invite the reader to reflect on the difference, in the encounter with the other, between a state of mind related to unconscious identification and one related to unconscious intercourse. In particular, it is a sensibility that I want to explore in reference to some questions that arise for many when reading Donald Meltzer. Surely we mean to understand *him*, although I have encountered reactions to some of Meltzer's writing which invite the thought that indeed this lion cannot be understood! Now does that mean "we cannot identify" or "we cannot have intercourse" with him?

This question has an intimate relationship, I am suggesting, with the question of the impact of an encounter on us. Consider, for example, Wilfred Bion's observation that ". . . certain books, like certain works of art, rouse powerful feelings and *stimulate growth* willy-nilly" (Bion, 1967b, p. 156, emphasis added). Bion seems to be suggesting that reading, reading certain books, or reading in a certain way can be a *developmental* experience, perhaps even running the risk of *catastrophic change*. We are prepared to entertain this idea—indeed, it might be said that we come to expect it—in our encounter with great art, in our reading of the best novels or the best poetry. Perhaps it comes as more of a surprise to consider such an experience in our reading of a psychoanalytic paper or book. Nevertheless, this is just what Bion says in *Second Thoughts* in his remarks on reading.

Linking the experience of reading with what he had been saying about the psychoanalytic session—that is, that there is no place for desire or for memory—he goes on to this somewhat paradoxical conclusion in which *development* is dependent on "letting go" as much as "taking in" (here he refers to Freud's paper "Formulations on the Two Principles of Mental Functioning": 1911b) as an example of the kind of psychoanalytic paper he had in mind):

> Freud's paper should be read—and "forgotten". Only in this way is it possible to produce the conditions in which, when it is next read, it can *stimulate the evolution of further development*. [Bion, 1967b, p. 156; emphasis added]

Acknowledging our human limitations, Bion goes on to concede:

> There is time to do this only with the best papers; but only the best papers have the power to stimulate a *defensive* reading (of

what the paper is about) as a substitute for experiencing the paper itself—what I have elsewhere called Transformation under K as contrasted with Transformation under O.

Bion's view of reading as a developmental experience entails giving the text its freedom, reading and forgetting instead of seeking to hold on tightly to what the text says, and this in turn allows the possibility of an experience of the text which leads to *becoming* rather than merely knowing, "knowing about". It calls to mind Meltzer's description of "taking in" or introjection: "When an object can be given its freedom to come and go as it will, the moment of experience of relationship with the object can be introjected" (Meltzer, 1978b, p. 468). Here I think we have a picture of a state of mind or a sensibility more closely linked with unconscious intercourse than with unconscious identification.

I should also make clear, if it is not already obvious, that I want to use this experience of reading which I have characterized as *developmental* to shed light on the developmental experience in the consulting-room in the analytic relationship. Conversely, I want to use the analytic experience of what we might describe as the "reading" of the other—whether analyst reading the analysand or the analysand's reading of the analyst—to shed light on the developmental experience in reading a text.

One place to begin this exploration is to ask what it might be, both about the text and about the clinical experience, that contributes to the potential for such a remarkable impact on us. We might think of this as a question of authority—*authority* being the question of who, or what, is the *author*. Out of what does the author speak?

The authority of the author

To explore this question of authority, or should we say "authorship", I want to turn briefly to Kierkegaard's remarkable study of the difference between real and fake authors, or what he calls "premise-authors" and "essential authors" in his little-known *On Authority and Revelations: The Book on Adler*, which remained unpublished in his lifetime (Kierkegaard, 1848). My attention to Kierkegaard's provocative book was drawn by Stanley Cavell, a contemporary American philosopher, whose title of his first book—*Must We Mean What We Say?* (1969b)—indicates the nature of his interests: how is it that we can mean what we say and say what we mean. Magister Adler was a Danish cleric who claimed to have had a revelation and was condemned by the established church as mentally deranged. For Kierkegaard, this confused, prolific author raised the question of authority, not just for the Established Church, but for our modern age. Writing himself on the basis of no authority but his own work, Kierkegaard suggests that Adler's confusion was symptomatic of "the fact that the concept of authority has been entirely forgotten in our confused age".

Kierkegaard's aim was to regain clarity in the face of what he suggests in contemporary culture is an amnesia in reference to genuine writing and reading, a corollary of our loss of the meaning of the concept of authority—and a corollary, I think, of the encounter in the consulting-room where there is an absence or a loss of something genuine. In this chapter I shall assume rather than develop this critique of the dilemma of the modern era with its psychopathology which in psychoanalytic language we might describe as narcissism. Philosophers discuss this dilemma under the heading of "scepticism".

But why link this question of the author and authority with the concept of narcissism? Consider a patient I will call Miss A, who commented at the beginning of therapy that she could identify with K in Kafka's *The Trial*.

Miss A had read *The Trial* as a 13-year-old and took it not as she later understood as a metaphor for our time, but as a literal description of what happens at a trial, where no one listens to you and people keep forgetting things and losing things, when not even the judge is listening. That is how she felt with her parents' inconsistencies, never knowing what to expect or what she was supposed to do except to try to appease them so that they wouldn't hit her—or rather to provoke the hitting by some outrageous behaviour in order to get it over. She surprised me by linking this with the observation that she never understood why people said that, since God was dead, anything was possible. If God is dead, she exclaimed with some passion, then nothing is possible. There is no one to appeal to!

Miss A went on to talk about Plato and the ancients and the idea of a "real" dog, real essences, an ultimately real world beyond the apparent "realities" which cannot be trusted. They were "building pyramids", she thought, to prove to themselves that something was real and really existed. She thought Plato must have been "really stressed," building these foolish pyramids, but she could understand how he felt. It would be wonderful to be able to believe that something was indeed real. She then startled me by going on to the Holocaust, having told me earlier in the session about a film shown to her at primary school which was trying to teach children never to accept sweets from strangers, portraying a frightening man towering over the child, but not making explicit what the danger was.

The point, she said, was that not only was she a victim, or a potential victim, but that she was aware she could just as easily have been one of the Holocaust persecutors—the peace, she said, of having orders that she would mindlessly carry out. She could as easily be the threatening man towering over the child as the child itself. She described the whole thing being eroticized, like a drug to which she could become addicted.

But just as I was taking in this insight in a young woman who was barely settled into the analytic process, she was suddenly puzzling with herself whether any of this meant anything. Was it all just words? Then she started talking about a gay male friend, someone she had lived with, and slept with, although not sexually. She had talked previously about him as a "scumbag" who supplied cocaine. She felt safe with him, since he was so awful, and they could be clever together, laughing uproariously, and then curling up in bed with him "like a child". She felt safe in the addiction to something so destructive that it could not get worse. In this perverse way, she could at last be at peace from the sense of unreality that pervaded her confused world.

How do people know how to walk upright, or do anything, Miss A continued. She observes people, but she can only imitate what they do. She has no idea how or why they do what they do or say what they say. Although she seems to function adequately, even effectively, she cannot believe in any of it. Ironically, she has aspirations to creative writing but she cannot become an author. There is no authority, either in her existence, or in her world. "Authority" has been made into a tyrannical "scum-bag". After the "death of God", or the perversion of the internal parental couple, nothing is possible. There is no one to whom she can appeal, no source of authority.

In Kierkegaard's terms, what is a "premise-author" and how do we distinguish him or her from the "essential author"? The premise-author, unlike the essential or genuine author, Kierkegaard says, feels no need to communicate himself because essentially he has nothing to communicate. He *is* a needy person. His cry is "support me" in his need for praise, to be in demand, to be told whether he means anything or not. "Instead of being *nourishing*, as every essential author is, ... every premise-author is devouring" (Kierkegaard, 1848, p. 118). Cavell links this with the dilemma of authority in modern art, the question of what is genuine and what is fraudulent:

> It is characteristic of our artistic confusion today that we no longer know, and cannot find or trust ourselves to find the occasion to know, which is which, whether it is the art or its audience which is on trial. [Cavell, 1969b, p. 139]

Popular opinion gives us no more sense of the author's authority than it does for my patient Miss A. It leaves her, as it leaves us, with only the possibility of imitation, at the mercy of the swings of popular opinion.

There is a parallel dilemma for us when we approach either an author or the author's text, and, similarly, when we approach either the patient or the patient's story. At our desks or in our consulting-rooms, if we are to trust only in our *authority* as readers without aid of "popular opinion", what is our approach? What sensibility is called for if we are genuinely to encounter the text or the patient, and thus to judge the authority of, what is genuine in, the other? Here, again, I want to turn to Stanley Cavell and his characterization of Ralph Waldo Emerson's theory of reading in his essay "Self-Reliance"—or what Cavell calls his *aesthetics* of reading:

> The test of following [Emerson's aesthetics of reading an author's words] is .. that you will find yourself known by them, that you will *take yourself on* in them. It is what Thoreau calls conviction, calls being convicted by his words, read by them, sentenced. To acknowledge that I am known by what this text knows *does not amount to agreeing with it*, in the sense of believing it, as if it were a bunch of assertions or as if it contained a doctrine. To be known by it is to find thinking in it that confronts you. [Cavell, 1986, p. 308]

This being confronted takes us into a different arena, one in which the encounter with an author, or patient, means that we "take ourselves on".

To imagine a language is to imagine a form of life

When Wittgenstein remarks that "to imagine a language is to imagine a form of life", the emphasis to my ears is on the use of the imagination. It finds an echo in Meltzer's insistence on the difference between the conception of the inside of the internal mother constructed by imagination and the product of "discovery" through omnipotent intrusion (Meltzer, 1992a, p. 62). There is also an echo with Kierkegaard's insistence that understanding a religious utterance *religiously* requires being able to share its perspective. In that, Cavell suggests, "speaking religiously is like telling a dream" (Cavell, 1969, p. 135). Understanding in the sense of "taking on ourselves" requires the capacity to imaginatively entertain—or, should we say, enter—a "form of life".

In keeping with Bion's insistence on "resisting memory and desire", Meltzer describes the process of "reading" dreams in the analytic setting in a way that illustrates dramatically what we might think of as an extension of Emerson's aesthetics of reading or Wittgenstein's encounter with the enigma of the stranger:

What seems to happen is that the analyst listens to the patient and watches the image that appears in his imagination. It might be cogently asserted that he allows the patient to evoke a dream in himself. ... From this point of view one might imagine that every attempt to formulate an interpretation of a patient's dream could imply the tacit preamble, "While listening to your dream I had a dream which in my emotional life would mean the following, which I will impart to you in the hope that it will throw some light on the meaning that your dream has for you." [Meltzer, 1983, p. 90]

One can hardly imagine a more intense intimacy than this view of the analytic encounter as one in which the patient's (implicit) invitation into the most private chamber of his or her internal world is met by an acceptance of the invitation which brings with it something of the analyst's most private chamber. It is ironic that patients will sometimes complain that they "know nothing about us" when what they are invited into is (some of) the most private, spontaneous working of our minds. Perhaps those patients are pleading for "facts", the cocktail-party kind of chatter about "what do you do", so that they can avoid having to have an encounter in which they "take on themselves" in taking us on.

This view of the analytic encounter follows the tradition of Melanie Klein in the way she listened to children. Meltzer describes her as listening "naïvely" to young children talking about the inside of their own and their mothers' bodies. He suggests that Freud could not, or at least did not, listen in a similar naïve way to the report of Little Hans talking about how he and his sister had ridden in the storkbox together. "Naïve" is not really adequate here to describe the state of mind, the sensibility. It involves the courage to enter through one's imagination *into that world*. It is striking, as Meltzer points out, that Melanie Klein's capacity to enter into the world of her child patients made possible what he calls a "revolutionary addition to the model of the mind".

My first experiences of trying to make sense of the notions of *internal objects* and *the internal world,* struggling to make a place in *my* world-view for such peculiar, disturbing "realities", was doomed to frustration and misunderstanding. In this struggle I recognized a "fellow-traveller" in Meir Perlow's review of psychoanalytic theories of the concept of mental objects (1995). Seeking clarity, he simply failed to enter into a world that was so foreign to him—the Kleinian and post-Kleinian insistence on the concreteness of the internal world and internal objects. What is required is not explanations but the capacity imaginatively to entertain a world to which only our creative artists and our children seem to find ready access.

To read Meltzer, at least to read him as Emerson and Wittgenstein suggest, one is obliged to enter into a world where the mind is structured in a way, as he puts it, ". . . so contrary to common sense, that the most evolved aspect of an individual's mind lies beyond the experience of self and is apprehended as object" (Meltzer, 1973, p. 78). Even more boldly, he suggests that in his view of the transference, "the analyst offers a share of his internal objects to his patients, and the transference is to his internal objects" (1995, p. 144).

He extends this beyond the analytic setting proper when he considers the possibility that, under some circumstances, it is possible "to meet other people on an adult level" through what he suggests is a "communal phantasy, a kind of congruence of internal objects". This "meeting", I am suggesting, is the kind of encounter possible between the reader and the author. Meltzer goes on to suggest that "it is this congruence of internal objects that brings people together and it is living in different worlds that drives them apart so that they cannot communicate with one another" (1983, p. 46). The kind of "reading" that Emerson describes as being *confronted* in a way that we *take ourselves on*, or Wittgenstein's suggestion that we can *find our feet* (or *find ourselves*) with someone, is in Meltzer's psychoanalytic mythology a *congruence of internal objects*. Might we then imagine a conversation between the author's, or the other's, internal objects and our internal objects?

This way of thinking about the encounter between the reader and the author, or between the analyst and the analysand, may give us a way of understanding what Bion describes as transformation under O. It is an intense emotional intimacy which is (potentially) transformative, developmental, since development is a consequence, or a marker, of our relationship with our internal objects as they themselves develop (or fail to) in intimate conversations with the internal objects of the other.

To return to the question with which I began—that of the attitude or sensibility with which we approach a text or a patient—and to Bion's suggestion that "certain books, like certain works of art, rouse powerful feelings and stimulate growth willy-nilly", I think he would want to add, "depending on our state of mind". The rhetorical "willy-nilly"—will he, nil he—should not blind us to Bion's frequent emphasis on our capacity for defensive manoeuvres to "protect" ourselves from any threat of *catastrophic change*.

I want to suggest in the final section of this chapter that a state of mind linked with *identification* can function as such a defensive manoeuvre, and that a state of mind linked with *intercourse* can facilitate the kind of encounter I have been trying to describe.

Identification vs. intercourse

I want to try to distinguish between a sensibility shaped by a process of unconscious identification and a sensibility shaped by a process of unconscious intercourse. We need to consider briefly the term *identification*, a term so central to our psychoanalytic vocabulary that we hardly pause to reflect on its implications outside our many discussions about forms of identification such as "projective identification", "adhesive identification", or "introjective identification". The first two are forms of narcissistic identification, with their insistence on sameness. It is with the third term that I am concerned, especially in its resistance to any claims to sameness.

There is a sense in which we can make sense of some notion of identification in reference to introjection, at least in so far as it leads to what Meltzer describes as the development of a sense-of-identity in the "adult part of the self". It is important to note that he is talking about a very specific kind of introjective identification, or better, we should say, identification with a very particular kind of object. The introjection here is not related to just any object, but is rather the introjective identification with the internal combined object, the internal parental couple, initially in part-object terms but ultimately in a whole-object relationship of intercourse. If there is a process of *identification* involved, it is an identification with the parental intercourse itself.

When Meltzer describes the state of mind that characterizes introjective identification, I think it is clear he is describing what he calls *aspiration* rather than identification:

> Commitment to this identification rests upon the emotions of the depressive position, especially gratitude and the desire for worthiness. For this reason elements of the experience of sense-of-identity that relate to introjective identification have a prospective quality, an aspirational tone that is quite different from the immediate and delusional self-feeling produced by projective identification. Tentativeness, humility, self-doubt, and like nuances of emotion therefore attach to these aspects of the sense-of-identity and make up the shadings of a person's character that most impress us as sincere. [Meltzer, 1971, p. 205]

In the state of mind appropriate to the intimacy of intercourse, one seeks to be worthy of the other, the beloved, not to *be* the other. When Meltzer describes introjective identification as "the most important and most mysterious concept in psychoanalysis" he is alluding to that most important and most mysterious relationship in human experience, the mystery of intercourse (Meltzer, 1978a, p. 459). The emphasis here must be on the notion of *invitation* as a correlate to the centrality of imagination. We can no more define for someone else the qualities that together constitute the state of mind creative of and created by the mystery of human intercourse than we can impose the experience of intercourse on the other.

I am thinking here of that marvellous scene in the film version of Michael Ondaatje's *The English Patient* (1992) when the nurse Hana, who has been tenderly nursing the English patient for whom she feels something indefinably like love, steps out into the night. There she finds a candle, then another at some distance, and another, and another, innumerable lights in the dark of the garden, following them, almost dancing in rising expectation until she comes to where Kip, the Sikh sapper waits. On his motor bike he takes her to the church in town, where in the dark shadows of the cavernous space he hoists her on a sling at the end of a rope coming from the distant dark ceiling. Then, torch in her hand, she is swung from wall to wall, each approach illuminating a medieval mural, then swinging away to the opposite wall.

That was an invitation. It is so engaging we can forget the intensity of the experience of Kip as he anticipates, but cannot know, how Hana will respond. The intercourse is a constant back and forth in the reciprocity of giver and receiver. There are, no doubt, moments in which each can identify with the other, an acceptance of the invitation to visit in imagination the mind of the other. But it is *in imagination*, not in the certainty of identification, and the underlying mood is freedom, the freedom of coming together and moving apart.

It is reminiscent of the picture that Meltzer has painted of the analyst responding to a patient's dream: here is the dream I have had listening to your dream. The hope is that the meaning of the dream in the analyst's emotional life will throw some light on the meaning that the patient's dream might have in the patient's emotional life. Like discovering Kip's candle, and another, and another—but will she follow, will the invitation be accepted? It also reminds me of Meltzer's image of the analyst shining a torch on a bit of what the patient offers in the hope that in that circle of light the patient might see something more clearly, or indeed notice something for the first time.

In contrast, the state of mind that is preoccupied with identification demands to know whether one thing is the same as another. I have one patient who is so locked into that state of mind that he invariably meets each link I make with a rejection, "no, it's entirely different". For him, any difference means "entirely different". Links are not understood to be complementary, differences that make coming together possible, but are fiercely rejected if they are not identical. "You do not understand me" means that you have a different view, your experience is not the same, identically the same, as mine.

I shall end with a dream that a young man had, who, after a year and a half of enthusiasm for what he took to be his role as a psychoanalytic patient, was just beginning to confront a growing sense that the analytic process was different in many ways from the picture with which he felt safely identified. Suddenly the relationship with me felt unpredictable and unsafe. He was meeting something that challenged both his imitation of "the good patient" and the security that he had nothing to learn that he did not already know by virtue of his identification with me and psychoanalysis:

Mr B was about to have a session, but it was in my house and other people were there as well. All of them knew him and he knew them, but they didn't know that he had sessions with me or that I was a therapist. It was time for his session, and he had just noticed a painting on the wall. He stepped back to look at it and got a splinter in his foot. The pain of the splinter was so intense he couldn't remember the painting.

When he went in there was a massive leather couch. While lying on it he saw a face appear around the door, a beautiful young woman. She ran off and he got up and ran after her, catching a glimpse of her as she disappeared, or rather catching sight of something she was carrying disappearing after her. She seemed to be carrying a huge musical instrument, which from the characteristic curved shape of the case must have been a double-bass. He thought that she must be another patient who comes to see me and had got her times mixed up. When he came back into the room, there was another man there, an older man, who seemed to be observing, like the therapy equivalent of Offsted [a British government educational inspection agency]. As he lay down again he noticed that on the wall of the room there were two huge silver disks. The older man, who seemed very wise and seemed to know him well, called them CD Max—something he'd never heard of, but it made sense since they were large CDs—and the old man suggested he should play one, he should listen to the music.

As he woke, he thought that the atmosphere was unpredictable, and he didn't know what was going to happen next—that it was not a safe atmosphere for a session.

Mr B suffers a sudden sharp pain in the dream, not at all what he expected, as he tries to stand back to admire what he believes he is there to admire, the picture of the analytic process. The atmosphere is not predictable, not what he was so sure of in his omnipotent knowledge of me and the process, and the role he believed he was meant to adopt. The state of mind, I suggest, is of an unconscious identification with this picture.

And the pangs of separation, a *splinter* in the language of his dream, are just beginning to penetrate—his omnipotent "link" with me is suddenly splintered. Nevertheless, somehow he can also be aware of an invitation, an invitation to listen to music. Perhaps the music of this couple, this wise older man and this beautiful young woman whose "double-bass"-curved shape he just caught sight of as she disappeared—the music perhaps of the parental intercourse?

The dream became a point of reference for his struggle to give up his omnipotent control of his internal objects. He has known for some time that he cannot tolerate even the hint that his partner has a different view from his, or wants and needs some space in their relationship. But when in the two sessions prior to the dream he had discovered what he perceived as fundamental differences between us, and, worse, that those differences led him to feel critical of me, suddenly everything had fallen apart, and he was overcome by a sense of chaos. His world literally began to fall apart, and in one of those sessions he had sat up on the couch in panic. And yet he and I were also able to hold on to a glimpse of something somewhere in the recesses of his mind, a picture of the beautiful disappearing musician and her wise old partner, of the two shining CDs which contained for him the potential of intercourse and reproduction. It is a music that he can still only dream of. Returning to it often, my patient and I refer to it as the *reproduction* dream.

For this young man it is a constant struggle to see distance, separation, and leaving as having any connection with intimacy. Certainly he cannot see them as a necessary condition for intimacy, although he can understand the necessity of separation intellectually; however, when he encounters it as an emotional reality it comes as a threat that is destructive to the very possibility of intercourse. How different for Kip and Hana:

> How much she is in love with him or he with her we don't know. Or how much it is a game of secrets. As they grow intimate the space between them during the day grows larger. She likes the distance he leaves her, the space he assumes is

her right. It gives each of them a private energy, a code of air between them when he passes below her window without a word . . . [Ondaatje, 1992, p. 127]

Of all of Meltzer's many lovely papers—those candles whose light entices us on—I think one of the most delightful is that little paper "A Note on Introjective Processes" (Meltzer, 1978b). In it he describes the dream of the broomstick woman, "an apparition moving at speed, a broomstick with a skirt and a white kerchief" (p. 461). He suggests that "the coming and going of the mother's breast, which stays only a moment to fill the baby and must be allowed to go its way, is also the prototype of the emotional experience, which satisfies only insofar as the object can be allowed its freedom" (p. 465). He concludes: "When an object can be given its freedom to come and go as it will, the moment of experience of relationship with the object can be introjected" (p. 468).

Can you imagine a more apt, indeed a more beautiful, characterization of the state of mind, the sensibility, creative of and created by the mystery of intercourse? Or any state of mind further from that of identification? If I read the text—or my patient—in the state of mind of unconscious identification, or with the sensibility shaped by identification, there is no "taking myself on" just as there is no *other* whom I can "take on". The sensibility shaped by unconscious intercourse, on the other hand, entails the awareness of the freedom of the other, the freedom to come or go, to take the risk of responding to my lighted candle or not. In this there is a reciprocity between reader and author. The *authority* of the author is, I am suggesting, in Meltzer's (1965) language, "a function of the relation to the primal good object" (p. 145). The candle I light is a consequence of that intercourse with my internal objects, and the offer of myself to the other is an offer of a share of my internal objects.

CHAPTER FOURTEEN

A learning experience in psychoanalysis

Psychoanalytic Group of Barcelona

This chapter is in fact part of a more extensive work, the gestation of which commenced in 1991 when our first contract with Donald Meltzer came to an end. We had the prospect before us of publishing a book that would expound some of the teachings that he had transmitted to us through clinical work. We held a meeting during which Meltzer showed little interest in this book; he did, however, show interest in a book that would give an account of our experience of working together as a group in psychoanalytic training. He put forward his idea of training based on the model of an *atelier* (*Sincerity* had not yet been published) and encouraged us to describe and define our experience.

This surprised us. We were not very convinced. We feared that it exceeded our abilities. We therefore went on with the tasks we had previously planned (the "case" book, as we called it within the group, was published: Meltzer & GPB, 1995). In spite of our perplexity, astonishment, and doubts, the idea was not abandoned; it was put off and at times forgotten, but it kept on reappearing with increasing force throughout the years. From 1991 on we held a series of meetings designed to elaborate our ideas around our experience as a training group. We felt that we did not meet the necessary requirements for observing ourselves—and even today we still have similar doubts. We do not feel that we can answer the question about the group's particularity; this query remains.

Perhaps some historical background can help us. Approximately twelve years ago, a group of people who wanted to study together approached Meltzer with the aim of achieving deeper knowledge and understanding of his work. That group already had a history of its own: it had started seven years before, with a qualified teacher, in order to study Bion's work, and it had continued during the following five years with another qualified teacher. This period of joint work had provided the group, which was composed of professionals who were working in the field of mental health in private practice as well as in institutional practice, with a certain homogeneity (despite the different levels of the participants' psychoanalytic training).

Meltzer's response was to offer a five-year psychoanalytic training plan, centred on work with clinical material, at a rhythm of three weekends a year. The only thing he wanted to know was whether the participants had been through a personal analysis and whether they belonged to any institution.

This proposal contained something entirely new. We had not expected anything of this kind. Perhaps some of us thought that we had had enough training and that all we needed was deeper knowledge and understanding. We were, of course, surprised; we felt enthusiastic, but also confused. We were persuaded by the enthusiasm, but we then encountered the first drawbacks: a good many of our colleagues decided not to go through with the experience, due to external pressure. The group was reduced from sixteen members to ten. We then decided to invite other colleagues: some accepted enthusiastically, some accepted driven by a certain curiosity; others, in the end, declined the invitation. However, we completed the required number. The composition of the group had also changed, and now it consisted of four Catalans, three Castilians who had lived in Barcelona for many years, and nine South Americans, of whom five had emigrated for political reasons. All were past middle age; all were professionals with a certain experience, having undergone a personal analysis and tangential training if one looks at it from institutional criteria; all had a professional situation in accord with the ups and downs of the country's economy, but which was on the whole stable. Could it have been the internal and external immigration, with its burden of marginality, that united us and allowed us to reach some degree of integration? Or was it age, a time in life when one's projects are considered seriously and an age at which it is crucial to take the greatest advantage of time? Or was it the fact that our basic needs were covered and we therefore did not harbour excessive expectations that patients would be referred within the group? Did all of this allow the formation of an environment that was not excessively rigid and could preserve the group from those desires that lay outside the realm of learning? As a matter of fact, we had gained a certain heterogeneity, and our fantasy was that this would probably be resolved through our joint study.

Let us go back to the situation produced by Meltzer's response. We set out to organize the confusion: we collected many works of his in Castilian—perhaps all that had been published so far, in general mimeographed—which, together with the publications in Italian, English, and French, as well as the books that had already been translated, amounted to quite a lot of material. In the time we had left before our first encounter, we dedicated ourselves to the study of his work published in books.

Our seminar previous to this encounter with Meltzer had followed the classical patterns: a theoretical exposition, exchange of opinions, queries. Given several particular characteristics, the formulation of queries had acquired great importance, as they were a product of previous discussions, and through them we attempted to centre our attention on certain themes that seemed relevant to us. It goes without saying that we also attempted to present these queries to Meltzer and through them we probably wished to manifest our knowledge of his work. In order to study more efficiently, we had already subdivided quite some years before into two subgroups, which had been formed according to some of the predominant interests (e.g. psychosis).

After working on this task for several months, the moment of our first encounter with our master took place. One of our colleagues who had recently joined the group made it possible for us to meet in a glorious art-nouveau house on the outskirts of Barcelona. With our knowledge of Meltzer's work and the consequent queries that arose from our study, together with the physical atmosphere of the venue, it is not difficult to deduce that we thought we would create an impression. Meltzer had requested that we present the material of four cases, with very little previous history, together with the transcription of two sessions of the treatment. The English translation would be handed to him at the beginning of the reading of each case because, as he said, he did not want previous knowledge to influence his perception while listening to the reading aloud of the material. (We soon discovered that the translation was not an obstacle.) The programme for each meeting of the seminar consisted of twelve hours of work divided into three encounters, two mornings and one afternoon. Those who presented the material for the first time probably had a varying range of fantasies: that of carrying out the request he had made, bringing cases that we could relate to aspects of his work that we had read; they were indeed cases that raised numerous doubts. Apart from this, of course, there were the famous queries. One colleague incorporated an element that we had never used before: he brought a tape-recorder and recorded the meetings in full; the subsequent transcription of this material proved to be an element of fundamental importance for the cohesion of the group as well as in our study and learning process.

All of us had experience—ample for some of us—of having our case material supervised. The general style of these supervisions did not differ greatly: it was only the quality of the supervisors that varied. But here we came across something entirely different: this was a different way of organizing the material; isolated details now appeared to be linked. Following a concept that comes from medicine, we could say that the "case" stayed in the background and we were able to see the patient, the person emerging. Not only did we see the psychopathology, or what the patients could be telling us, but also the possibilities of the analysands' evolution. This was a wider perspective, which contained a change of attitude towards the patient: it implied seeing the child or adolescent in the adult, and also a way of seeing children play in a different way. Plenty of new aspects were pointed out: such and such a patient had not yet entered the analytic situation; the difficulties that some patients had with symbolization appeared more clearly defined; we saw the characteristics of the transference–countertransference relation in greater perspective; we learnt what preformed transference was. We were introduced to the concept of the structure of the mind and the geography of fantasy. These were, on the whole, concepts intended to "make us think" our patients, to feel them inside us and also to dream them. This represented opening up our field of work, somewhat oriented towards the incorruptible search for the truth of the mind, which was distinct and opposed to all that could come into Column 2 of Bion's Grid. It was, we believe with good reason, catching a glimpse of the beauty of the psychoanalytic method. And there was one concept that re-echoed in us for a long time: "living in projective identification".

This had, for all or nearly all of us, a huge impact. In retrospect, and using the concepts that are now at our disposal, we can state that it was a true aesthetic impact. We were left fluctuating between admiration, enthusiasm, surprise, and confusion. And we felt the need to get together again soon so as to speak together, share those moments once more, and start thinking about them. We therefore altered the programme of our meetings in subgroups and during that same week called a meeting of the whole group. From then on, each encounter with Meltzer has been followed by a meeting of the same characteristics. We decided to try to comprehend what living in projective identification really meant.

We know that, *grosso modo*, there are two essential ways of learning: projective and introjective. The former, as its name indicates, is based on the appropriation of the knowledge that the teacher possesses by means of diverse intrusive techniques, which at times entail imitation, submission to the doctrine imparted, renunciation of the exercise of criticism and elaboration, and so on; this merely leads to getting to know something "about", as Bion says. The latter implies accepting the nourishing breast and dependence, with all that this signifies: the long road of assimilating what is new and accepting that we ourselves can change in the process. Reflecting on the different moments of our experience, we think that we have often been in the former of the two situations, and we would like to believe that we have also covered some distance along the road of introjective identification with the combined object. However, in order to be able to transmit this we had better return to our history.

During the first stage, both subgroups maintained their weekly meetings separately, and periodically there was a meeting with all the members of the "large" group, as we started to call it. We proceeded with our theoretical study: reading and discussing works that could guide us towards finding out what was meant by living in projective identification. In the course of all this, we recovered the internal publication of the first seminars, which we eagerly started to reread—as well as, of course, the paper on anal masturbation (Meltzer, 1966). It was necessary to organize within the group some meetings centred on these themes, at which we presented our own papers to serve as a guide for discussion. Had we not understood properly? Were we just repeating without knowing clearly what we were saying? What connection did this have with the preformed transference? These are but a few of the many other questions of this kind.

There were plenty of conflicts. Two colleagues—who, to be honest, had no great interest in Kleinian thought—sparked off a crisis in one of the subgroups, which ended up with their withdrawal; the effect of this was the dissolution of this subgroup. We believe that the meetings in family homes—which seems to be a specifically South American contribution—facilitated the resolution of these crises as it favoured a closer atmosphere of intimacy in our work and in the exchange of ideas. In addition, the existence of two subgroups avoided a generalization of the crisis, and rather alleviated it. The subgroup that went on functioning emerged as a model, and perhaps this is something that allowed us to preserve the idea that our work would not be interrupted. And this was probably true: at no time was the task abandoned. We went on studying, meeting, and presenting at each encounter with Meltzer the four cases that we had agreed upon when we formulated the contract. And, of course, we went on wishing to organize the confusion, the turbulence, generated by each encounter with Meltzer and to proceed with our theoretical study.

As the number of seminars gradually accumulated and were published, we decided to establish a record and detailed classification, separating the themes dealt with at each encounter, grouping together those that appeared in several, in an attempt to come to conclusions. In retrospect, we believe that this near-obsession corresponded to a particular moment of the group, which we could call a latency period. In order to carry out this task, we formed four special subgroups, composed of some of the colleagues who were in the subgroup that was still functioning and others who had proceeded with their work individually. But at this point we were able to allow ourselves a playful element reflected in the names adopted by the various subgroups. This new grouping together of the participants was probably one of the elements that channelled the development of the feeling of group membership, which had existed neither *a priori* nor in the first stages of our venture. In the beginning we felt no need of group membership; this is something that was gradually created and that developed through the contact with Meltzer. At times, the idea of institutionalizing our group or of endowing it with a stable and detailed structure has emerged; this has been discussed at length and we have come to the conclusion that it would not add anything positive to our basic task. We could say that we have learnt the benefits of working with the minimal organization.

Internal problems arose as a result of our contacts with those outside the group, such as meetings in the presence of invited guests or during the last phase of the preparation of *Clinical Psychoanalysis of Children and Adults* (Meltzer & GPB, 1995). We cannot offer a more or less finished interpretation on this matter. Respect for individual differences has been one of our most arduous tasks, as has been the protection of personal freedom and interests, while at the same time a certain unity that has allowed us to grow as a group has been preserved. Jealousy, envy, competitiveness, the feeling of lack of recognition, and so on operate in what we call the "corridors": this is something that we occasionally discuss at the meetings of the group as a whole, but it tends to emerge in the kind of gossip that goes on between two or three members. However, so far, it has not proved to be truly threatening; on the contrary, it has seemed more wholesome: these are our horror tales, of persecution, of witches, ogres, and bad children. The effect is that cordiality prevails at our meetings, and although there are moments of crisis, the right word always arises to temper and tone down the atmosphere.

We have been through phases that have ranged from the execution—even to an exaggerated extent—of the tasks, the continuous effort to understand concepts intellectually, and obsessive doubts about publication in the broad sense, to the intense learning experience entailed in agreeing as a group, the wish to structure our lives—and not only our professional lives—in a responsible way with the possibility of forgiving each other and forgiving mistakes. Perhaps now is a time when we are initiating a moment of individual production, and this has stirred up storms and provoked waves of unrest.

We believe that our development has also allowed us to work, either occasionally or systematically, with other analysts, both from the United Kingdom and South America, whom we have approached because of their characteristics or orientation. Our present group activity is centred around: (1) monthly clinical meetings, at which we can see how we have overcome our fear of showing our colleagues our work, an attitude that persisted for some time after we had got over doing so in front of Meltzer; and (2) meetings, also on a monthly basis, at which we discuss papers produced by the members of the group, either designed for internal circulation or to be read at other scientific meetings. We also hold "administrative" meetings at which we sort out matters such as conferences, the distribution of tasks, and so on. It is our belief that the group leaderships have been rotatory and never long-lasting. Specific small or large roles are performed by certain colleagues well qualified to carry them out—those who take notes of our resolutions or who remind us of the themes to be discussed, for example—which have been adopted spontaneously and not necessarily dictated by appointment. Some tasks are not at all pleasant—the accounts being one of these—and are performed in turns. Our impression is that things have been rolling: someone has always come up with an idea that has seemed beneficial or facilitating, and the group has undertaken it. While we are somewhat agile in distributing the tasks, we are slow in reaching agreement on themes about which there are strong differences of opinion. We believe that there has been a progressive increase in the trust we have in the group work. We would like to say, in Bion's terms, that there is a predominance of *social-ism* as opposed to narcissism.

When we ask ourselves about the conditions that have made it possible to carry out an experience of this kind, we must necessarily think not only about the group but also about its master. In our quest for explanations we have always ended up revolving around Meltzer, as a nuclear, containing, and regulating figure. We all agree that such an experience would have been difficult with someone else. When we look at the group, we always bear in mind the question of its duration: we are frightened of disappearing. However, we trust that, if some slacken, others will strive to keep it alive: responsibility for the group's life is an unspoken anxiety that never leaves us.

At this point we shall not go into what Meltzer's fantasies may have been prior to his encounter with us. (Ours were simply to study, and we ended up—at least we wish to believe this is so—forming a group and learning from our experience, our experience with the teacher.) We shall only mention in passing his extraordinary clinical penetration, his psychoanalytic rigour, as well as other qualities recognized in him, to stress elements that, in our view, are basic to the learning process, in the relationship between master and students. From our first encounter we were impressed by his sensitivity towards the patient that emerged from the material and his delicate treatment of the analysands and ourselves; besides this, his love for the psychoanalytic method, the beauty of which he has tried to transmit to us; his insistence on the possibility of discovering before placing oneself in a position of explaining; his feeling free to get bored or to show interest; and his struggle for the patient's development and growth—as well as ours as a group. We believe that from the very first moment we became an object of interest for Meltzer, and that this interest increased—we have the impression that he has even learnt some Castilian—to the point of converting us into an object of his care. This has led us to speak of a maternal quality in him. And it is also true that he has exerted a paternal function when, for example, he has warned us of the hazards of exposing our intimacy. It is true that, apart from studying and trying to comply with the set tasks, we also eagerly saw to his stays in Barcelona, experiencing with him not only the seminars but also other moments, such as entertainment, meals, and so on. When in 1991 we formulated this new contract with Meltzer, the number of encounters, as a group, were reduced to two a year: one in Barcelona and another in Oxford. When we went there, he arranged our lodgings and welcomed us into his home. At the beginning of this chapter, we pointed out that we received a true aesthetic impact. We also believe that there has been aesthetic reciprocity in our relationship with him. We have felt, collectively and individually, stimulated by the master in our learning and in the progress we could go on making, in the trust that has developed among ourselves, and in the work on themes that have been arduous for us.

Simultaneously a greater affective bond has been created within the group: we share joys—special birthdays, doctorates, weddings—and suffering—illnesses, at times serious. And we also share ideas: for example, we wish to avoid a hierarchical organization and external interferences or motivations alien to what unites us. This whole process has generated a climate of intimacy and trust, a solidarity that is not that of intimate friends, but rather that which can be created among people who share the same task to which they are deeply committed. Catharine Mack Smith has been in on this process and participated from the very beginning, and she has conducted some work with several members of the group. Besides this, she holds a special place for us: from first looking at her with shyness and surprise we have ended up converting her, in our fantasy, into a fervent ally, a special messenger, the guarantor of the master's good mood.

We are under the impression that in the course of this process we have learnt things that go beyond the merely instrumental. Without listing everything, we would first of all point out a greater commitment to the psychoanalytic method, which entailed having to come to terms with the realization that previously we had been carrying out more ego-reinforcing treatments than we were willing to admit; this implied that in order to learn these new things we had to un-learn the old ones. We also learnt that the psychoanalytic method consisted in accompanying the patient in a process of development before considering ourselves the privileged guides who know everything beforehand. This involves greater respect towards our patients, which seems to be connected with the respect that Meltzer showed for our work and for ourselves as people. We believe that we are freer to think and to speak to our analysands, which makes our dialogue with them more alive and not associations to which we respond *ex cathedra*. This allows us to be surprised by our patients, with whom we wish to share the process of discovery. We have the impression that we have learnt to tolerate "reasonably enough" all kinds of feelings in ourselves, which has allowed us to explore our countertransference more deeply. From a theoretical point of view, we place ourselves in a more "open" Kleinianism, more centred on what is developmental and on the relationship of the *self* with the internal objects. And, *last but not least*, we have learnt to enjoy our work more: it undoubtedly tires us much less.

We have attempted to reflect on our experience by focusing on the aesthetic conflict, which is one of the elements that our contact with Meltzer has provided us with. And we also find that we are at all times making use of Bion's concepts, which should not surprise us. Each encounter with Meltzer has been turbulent. On occasions, at internal clinical meetings we have revised the material that we would subsequently present and have advanced conjectures about what the patient has suggested to us, and we have always ended the meeting jokingly remarking that everything we have said may be valid but that Meltzer would surely give us another different, new view, one that would open up new ways of understanding the analysand. And so it has been, invariably, from the very first time we presented a patient as well as at subsequent supervisions. We have always found ourselves filled with anxiety in the face of something new—a concept very dear to Pichon-Rivière—immersed in that confusion which is qualitatively different from that which is attributed to a failure in splitting. And we have oscillated, logically, between PS and D, going through periods of dispersion and integration; in all of this, we believe that the group has operated as a container for the individual and group anxieties.

The internal publication of the seminar meetings has proved to be of fundamental importance when having to reconnect with Meltzer; it consists of recollections that were transformed into memory and have become, in our view, an initial element in the development of alpha function—because in the beginning, on the surface, our problem was the time that elapsed (which seemed interminable) between the meetings; most probably the absence of the object was, as Freud and Bion point out, a basic element in the beginning and development of the process of thinking.

We suppose that there are elements of passive and active dependence in the learning process, which leads us to identify different moments according to whether one or the other predominates. However, in order for there to be a learning experience that implies what we understand as a necessary modification in the one or ones who carry it out, one has to pass from projective to introjective processes. We learn—we receive—from the internal combined object—as well as from the external one. With the latter, we also establish a love relationship, similar to that pointed out by Freud (1916–17) for the analytic relationship when he referred to the "simmering heat [*Siedehitze*] of the transference"; Racker (1985) states clearly: "The analytic transformative process depends, then, to a large extent, on the quantity and quality of *eros* the analyst is able to put into action for his patient" (p. 32). All of this necessarily leads us to the aesthetic conflict.

In our case, we prefer to speak of a sustained aesthetic encounter. We have the impression that the expression *conflict* places a greater emphasis on the first moment, that of being dazzled, and what this moment causes as an impact. Perhaps a good working expression would be an *aesthetic process*, a process that allows us to understand the projective regressions and the introjective advances and also the factors that have sustained—as is the case of our internal publication of the seminars—aesthetic curiosity, which gives rise to the continuing relationship with the aesthetic object. Aesthetic reciprocity occupies a choice position in this process, equivalent to the analyst's *eros* according to Racker's quotation. It is our impression that there is no advance if these conditions are not fulfilled. For us, the idea of the evolution of the group is bound to this specific learning process. We understand that it is a process and not a result.

Bion speaks about the difference that exists between the intimacy of analysis and its publication, which he terms the *public-a(c)tion*. We are showing a part of our intimacy in this chapter. It has not been easy to do so, and we do not know what it will result in. We hope that our relationship with the combined object can help us.

REFERENCES

Alvarez, A. (1968). *Beyond All This Fiddle*. Harmondsworth: Penguin.

Alvarez, A. (1973). *Beckett*. London: Fontana.

Beckett, S. (1931). *Proust*. London: Chatto & Windus.

Beckett, S. (1957). *Fin de Partie*. Paris: Les Éditions de Minuit, 1993. [*Endgame*, trans. by S. Beckett. London/Boston, MA: Faber & Faber, 1988.]

Beckett, S. (1986). *The Complete Dramatic Works*. London: Faber.

Beckett, S. (1988). *Endgame*. London/Boston, MA: Faber & Faber.

Bick, E. (1961). Child analysis today. In: M. Harris & E. Bick, *Collected Papers of Martha Harris and Esther Bick*, ed. by M. Harris Williams. Perthshire: Clunie Press, 1987.

Bick, E. (1964). Notes on infant observation in psychoanalytical training. In: M. Harris & E. Bick, *Collected Papers of Martha Harris and Esther Bick*, ed. by M. Harris Williams. Perthshire: Clunie Press, 1987.

Bick, E. (1967). The experience of the skin in early object relations. In: M. Harris & E. Bick, *Collected Papers of Martha Harris and Esther Bick*, ed. by M. Harris Williams. Perthshire: Clunie Press, 1987.

Bion, W. R. (1959). Attacks on linking. In: *Second Thoughts* (pp. 110-

119). London: Heinemann, 1967. [Reprinted London: Karnac Books, 1984.]

Bion, W. R. (1961). *Experiences in Groups and Other Papers*. London: Tavistock.

Bion, W. R. (1962). *Learning from Experience*. London: Heinemann. [Reprinted London: Karnac Books, 1984.]

Bion, W. R. (1965). *Transformations*. London: Heinemann. [Reprinted London: Karnac Books, 1984.]

Bion, W. R. (1967a). Commentary. In: *Second Thoughts*. London: Heinemann. [Reprinted London: Karnac Books, 1984.]

Bion, W. R. (1967b). *Second Thoughts*. London: Heinemann. [Reprinted London: Karnac Books, 1984.]

Bion, W. R. (1970). *Attention and Interpretation*. London: Tavistock. [Reprinted London: Karnac Books, 1984.]

Bion, W. R. (1975). *A Memoir of the Future*. Rio de Janeiro: Imago. Combined edition, London: Karnac Books, 1991.

Bion, W. R. (1977). Caesura. In: *Two Papers: The Grid and Caesura* (pp. 35-56). London: Karnac Books, 1989.

Boston, M., & Szur, R. (Eds.) (1983). *Psychotherapy with Severely Deprived Children*. London: Routledge & Kegan Paul.

Cavell, S. (1969a). Kierkegaard's *On Authority and Revelation*. In: *Must We Mean What We Say?* New York: Charles Scribner's Sons. [Reprinted in *The Cavell Reader* (pp. 127–142), ed. by S. Mulhall. Oxford: Blackwell Publishers, 1996.]

Cavell, S. (1969b). *Must We Mean What We Say?* New York: Charles Scribner's Sons. [Reprinted: Cambridge: Cambridge University Press, 1976.]

Cavell, S. (1986). Being odd, getting even. In: T. C. Heller, M. Sosna, & D. W. Wellbery (Eds.), *Reconstructing Individualism*. Palo Alto, CA: Stanford University Press. [Reprinted in *The Cavell Reader* (pp. 295–320), ed. by S. Mulhall. Oxford: Blackwell, 1996.]

Chomsky, N. (1972). *Language and Mind*. New York: Harcourt Brace Jovanovich.

Cronin, A. (1996). *Samuel Beckett: The Last Modernist*. London: Harper Collins.

Duffy, R. (1995). *La riparaziona*, ed. by M. Monteleone, A. Consanza, & G. Polacco Williams. Teirrenia: Il Cerro.

Fechner, G. T. (1873). *Einige Ideen zur Schöpfungs- und Entwicklungsgeschichte der Organismen* (Part XI, Supplement, 94). Leipzig.

Ferrari, A. B. (1994). *Adolescenza. La seconda sfida*. Rome: Borla.

Freud, S. (1911b). Formulation on the two principles of mental functioning. *Standard Edition, 12.*

Freud, S. (1914c). On narcissism: an introduction. *Standard Edition, 14.*

Freud, S. (1915e). The unconscious. *Standard Edition, 14.*

Freud, S. (1916–17). *Introductory Lectures on Psycho-Analysis. Standard Edition, 15–16.*

Freud, S. (1918b [1914]). From the history of an infantile neurosis. *Standard Edition, 17.*

Freud, S. (1920g). *Beyond the Pleasure Principle. Standard Edition, 18.*

Freud, S. (1925a [1924]). A note upon the "mystic writing-pad". *Standard Edition, 19.*

Freud, S. (1940a [1938]). *An Outline of Psycho-Analysis. Standard Edition, 23.*

Freud, S. (1950 [1892–1899]). Extracts from the Fliess Papers, Draft M. *Standard Edition, 1.*

Gardiner, M. (Ed.) (1972). *The Wolf Man and Sigmund Freud.* London: Hogarth Press. [Reprinted London: Karnac Books, 1989.]

Gilman, R. (1995). *Chekhov's Plays: An Opening into Eternity.* New Haven, CT: Yale University Press.

Gittings, R. (Ed.) (1987). *Letters of John Keats.* Oxford: Oxford University Press.

Graver, L. (1989). *Waiting for Godot.* Cambridge: Cambridge University Press.

Green, J. (1947). *Si j'étais vous* . . . Paris: Seuil, 1983.

Harris, M., & Bick, E. (1987). *Collected Papers of Martha Harris and Esther Bick,* ed. by M. Harris Williams. Perthshire: Clunie Press.

Harris Williams, M. (1997). "The Aesthetic Perspective in the Work of Donald Meltzer." Paper presented at the conference "Exploring the Work of Donald Meltzer", London (January 1998).

Heimann, P. (1942). A contribution to the problem of sublimation and its relation to processes of internalization. *International Journal of Psycho-Analysis, 23:* 8–17.

Henry, G. (1969). Some aspects of projective mechanisms in the Jungian theory. *Journal of Child Psychotherapy, 2* (3): 43–56.

Hinshelwood, R. D. (1991). *A Dictionary of Kleinian Thought.* London: Free Association Books.

Honig, E. (Trans.) (1993). *Calderon de la Barca: Six Plays.* New York: Iasta Press.

Houzel, D. (1989). Precipitation anxiety and the dawn of aesthetic feelings. *Journal of Child Psychotherapy, 13* (2): 103–114.

Houzel, D. (1995). Precipitation anxiety. *Journal of Child Psychotherapy, 21* (1): 65–78.

Houzel, D. (1997). "Three levels of integration of psychic bisexuality." Lecture delivered to the Squiggle Foundation, London (28 June).

Kierkegaard, S. (1848). *On Authority and Revelation: The Book on Adler*, trans. by W. Lowrie. Princeton, NJ: Princeton University Press, 1955. [Reprinted in *Fear and Trembling* (pp. 113-302). New York: Alfred A. Knopf, Everyman's Library, 1994.]

Klein, M. (1923). Early analysis. In: *The Writings of Melanie Klein, Vol. 1: Love, Guilt and Reparation and Other Works*. London: Hogarth Press, 1975. [Reprinted London: Karnac Books, 1992.]

Klein, M. (1929). Personification in the play of children. In: *The Writings of Melanie Klein, Vol. 1: Love, Guilt and Reparation and Other Works*. London: Hogarth Press, 1975. [Reprinted London: Karnac Books, 1992.]

Klein, M. (1930). The importance of symbol-formation in the development of the ego. In: *The Writings of Melanie Klein, Vol. 1: Love, Guilt and Reparation and Other Works*. London: Hogarth Press, 1975. [Reprinted London: Karnac Books, 1992.]

Klein, M. (1946). Notes on some schizoid mechanisms. In: *The Writings of Melanie Klein, Vol. 1: Love, Guilt and Reparation and Other Works*. London: Hogarth Press, 1975. [Reprinted London: Karnac Books, 1992.]

Klein, M. (1948). The theory of anxiety and guilt. In: M. Klein, P. Heimann, S. Isaacs, & J. Riviere, *Developments in Psychoanalysis*. London: Hogarth Press, 1952. [Reprinted London: Karnac Books, 1989.]

Klein, M. (1955). On identification. In: *New Directions in Psycho-Analysis*. London: Tavistock.

Klein, M. (1957). Envy and gratitude. In: *The Writings of Melanie Klein, Vol. 3: Envy and Gratitude and Other Works*. London: Hogarth Press, 1975. [Reprinted London: Karnac Books, 1993.]

Klein, M. (1961). *Narrative of a Child Analysis. The Writings of Melanie Klein, Vol. 4*. London: Hogarth Press, 1975. [Reprinted London: Karnac Books, 1996.]

Kolakowski, L. (1995). *God Owes Us Nothing*. Chicago, IL: University of Chicago Press.

Langer, S. (1951). *Philosophy in a New Key*. Cambridge, MA: Harvard University Press.

Maiello, S. (1995). The sound object. *Journal of Child Psychotherapy*, 21: 23–41. [First published as: L'Oggetto sonoro. *Richard e Piggle, 1* (1993): 31–47.]

Maiello, S. (1997). Prenatal trauma and autism. *Primitive Mental States, Vol. 2*. New York: Jason Aronson, 1998.

Mancia, M. (1981). On the beginning of mental life in the foetus. *International Journal of Psycho-Analysis, 62*: 351–357.

Meltzer, D. (1955). Towards a structural concept of anxiety. In: *Sincerity and Other Works: Collected Papers of Donald Meltzer*, ed. by A. Hahn. London: Karnac Books, 1994.

Meltzer, D. (1959). A transient inhibition of chewing. In: *Sincerity and Other Works: Collected Papers of Donald Meltzer*, ed. by A. Hahn. London: Karnac Books, 1994.

Meltzer, D. (1960) (in collaboration with Esther Bick). Lectures and seminars in Kleinian child psychiatry. In: *Sincerity and Other Works: Collected Papers of Donald Meltzer*, ed. by A. Hahn. London: Karnac Books, 1994.

Meltzer, D. (1965). Return to the imperative: an ethical implication of psychoanalytic findings. In: *Sincerity and Other Works: Collected Papers of Donald Meltzer* (pp. 142–151), ed. by A. Hahn. London: Karnac Books, 1994.

Meltzer, D. (1966). The relation of anal masturbation to projective identification. *International Journal of Psycho-Analysis, 47*: 335.

Meltzer, D. (1967). *The Psycho-Analytical Process*. London: Heinemann Medical.

Meltzer, D. (1968). Tyranny. In: *Sexual States of Mind*. Perthshire: Clunie Press, 1973.

Meltzer, D. (1971). Sincerity: a study in the atmosphere of human relations. In: *Sincerity and Other Works: Collected Papers of Donald Meltzer* (pp. 185–284), ed. by A. Hahn. London: Karnac Books, 1994.

Meltzer, D. (1973). *Sexual States of Mind*. Perthshire: Clunie Press.

Meltzer, D. (1975). Adhesive identification. *Contemporary Psychoanalysis, 11*: 289–310. [Reprinted (without the Discussion) in: *Sincerity and Other Works: Collected Papers of Donald Meltzer*, ed. by A. Hahn. London: Karnac Books, 1994.]

Meltzer, D. (1978a). *The Kleinian Development, Parts I, II, & III*. Perthshire: Clunie Press. [Reprinted London: Karnac Books, 1999.]

Meltzer, D. (1978b). A note on introjective processes. In: *Sincerity and Other Works: Collected Papers of Donald Meltzer*, ed. by A. Hahn. London: Karnac Books, 1994.

Meltzer, D. (1981). Does Money-Kyrle's concept of misconception have any unique descriptive power? In: *Sincerity and Other Works: Collected Papers of Donald Meltzer*, ed. by A. Hahn. London: Karnac Books, 1994.

Meltzer, D. (1983). *Dream-Life—A Re-examination of the Psychoanalytical Theory and Technique*. Perthshire: Clunie Press.

220   REFERENCES

Meltzer, D. (1988). Aesthetic conflict: its place in development. In: D. Meltzer & M. Harris Williams, *The Apprehension of Beauty*. Perthshire: Clunie Press.

Meltzer, D. (1992a). *The Claustrum. An Investigation of Claustrophobic Phenomena*. Perthshire: Clunie Press.

Meltzer, D. (1992b). Life in the claustrum. In: *The Claustrum: An Investigation of Claustrophobic Phenomena*. (pp. 69–95). Perthshire: Clunie Press.

Melzer, D. (1994). *Sincerity and Other Works: Collected Papers of Donald Meltzer*, ed. by A. Hahn. London: Karnac Books.

Meltzer, D. (1995). Donald Meltzer in conversation with James Fisher. In: *Intrusiveness and Intimacy* (107–144), ed. by S. Ruszczynski & J. Fisher. London: Karnac Books.

Meltzer, D., & GPB (1995). *Clínica Psicoanalítica con Niños y Adultos* [*Clinical Psychoanalysis of Children and Adults*]. Buenos Aires: Ediciones Spatia.

Meltzer, D., Albergamo, M., Cohen, E., Greco, A., Harris, M., Maiello, S., Milana, G., Petrelli, D., Rhode, M., Sabatini Scolmati, A., & Scotti, F. (1986). *Studies in Extended Metapsychology. Clinical Applications of Bion's Ideas*. Perthshire: Clunie Press.

Meltzer, D., Bremner, J., Hoxter, S., Weddell, D., & Wittenberg, I. (1975). *Explorations in Autism: A Psycho-Analytical Study*. Perthshire: Clunie Press.

Meltzer, D., & Harris, M. (1976). A psychoanalytic model of the child-in-the-family-in-the-community. In: D. Meltzer, *Sincerity and Other Works: Collected Papers of Donald Meltzer*, ed. by A. Hahn. London: Karnac Books, 1994.

Meltzer, D., & Harris Williams, M. (1988a). *The Apprehension of Beauty*. Perthshire: Clunie Press.

Meltzer, D., & Harris Williams, M. (1988b). The undiscovered country: the shape of the aesthetic conflict in *Hamlet*. In: *The Apprehension of Beauty* (pp. 84–133). Perthshire: Clunie Press

Mendelson, A. (1997). Pervasive traumatic loss from AIDS in the life of a 4-year-old African boy. *Journal of Child Psychotherapy*, 23 (3).

Money-Kyrle, R. (1977). Postscript. In: *Collected Papers of Roger Money-Kyrle* (pp. 430–433), ed. by D. Meltzer. Perthshire: Clunie Press, 1978.

Money-Kyrle, R. (1978). *The Collected Papers of Roger Money-Kyrle*, ed. by D. Meltzer. Perthshire: Clunie Press.

Ondaatje, M. (1992). *The English Patient*. Picador: Macmillan.

Perlow, M. (1995). *Understanding Mental Objects*. London: Routledge.

Piaget, J. (1946). *Le développement de la notion de temps chez l'enfant.* Paris: P.U.F.

Pichon-Rivière, E. (1974). *Del Psicoanálisis a la Psicología social.* Buenos Aires: Nueva Visión.

Piontelli, A. (1993). Some reflections on infantile amnesia. *British Psycho-Analytical Bulletin, 29* (1): 11-19.

Porte, M. (1990). "Psychanalyse et sociologie. Études épistémologiques en dynamique qualitative et en métapsychologie." Thèse d'État, Université Denis Diderot, Paris VII.

Proust, M. (1913). *Remembrance of Things Past: Swann's Way,* transl. C. K. Scott Moncrief. London: Chatto & Windus, 1971.

Proust, M. (1990). *A la recherche du temps perdu: Le temps retrouvé.* Paris: Editions Gallimard.

Racker, H. (1961). "Psicoanálisis y ética." Unpublished, posthumous paper read on occasion of a tribute to Racker at the Argentine Psychoanalytic Association, Buenos Aires.

Racker, H. (1985). *Transference and Countertransference.* London: Karnac Books.

Rhode, M. (1982). "The Parallel Structure of Words and Objects as a Stage of Language Development." Unpublished paper presented to the New Imago Group, London (May).

Roy, A. (1997). *The God of Small Things.* London: Flamingo.

Rustin, M. (1987). Introduction: Mattie as an educator. In: M. Harris & E. Bick, *Collected Papers of Martha Harris and Esther Bick,* ed. by M. Harris Williams. Perthshire: Clunie Press, 1987.

Stokes, A. (1963). *Painting and the Inner World.* London: Tavistock.

Tustin, F. (1986). *Autistic Barriers in Neurotic Patients.* London: Karnac Books.

Verlaine, P. (1869). Clair de lune, Fêtes galantes. In: *Oeuvres poétiques complètes.* Paris: Gallimard, 1951.

Wittgenstein, L. (1953). *Philosophical Investigations,* trans. by G. E. M. Anscombe. Oxford: Basil Blackwell.

Wollheim, R. (1971). *Freud.* London: Fontana Collins.

Yoshimoto, B. (1989). *Tsugumi.* Milan: Universale Economica Feltrinelli, 1994.

INDEX

erotic, 2, 53, 54, 145, 146
    paternal, 55
gathering of, 2
interpretations, 52
preformed, 2, 8, 207, 208
relation, 105
simmering heat [*Siedehitze*] of,
    214
traumatic anxiety of autistic
    children, 121
Tustin, F., 21, 46, 76, 119, 120, 121,
    129

unconscious identification, 189,
    190, 197, 201, 202
unidirectional time, 101
unimaginable anxiety, 129

values, 27–42
Verlaine, P., 54

Weddell, D., 21, 22
Williams, G., xviii, xxi, 136–151
Winnicott, D. W., 121, 124, 129,
    137
Wittenberg, I., 21, 22
Wittgenstein, L., xxi, 7, 188, 194,
    196
"Wolf Man", Freud's case of, 29, 42,
    174, 179, 180
work group, 31, 32, 41

Yoshimoto, B., 103

Zolotnicki, V., xviii